Irish Musical Studies

In the *Irish Musical Studies* series

Irish Musical Studies

3: MUSIC AND IRISH CULTURAL HISTORY

Edited by

Gerard Gillen & Harry White

IRISH ACADEMIC PRESS

This book was typeset by
Carrigboy Typesetting Services
in 11 on 12.5 pt Times for
IRISH ACADEMIC PRESS LTD
Kill Lane, Blackrock, Co. Dublin
and in North America by
IRISH ACADEMIC PRESS LTD
c/o International Specialized Book Services,
5800 NE Hassalo Street, Portland, OR 97213

ISBN 0–7165–2536–4

A catalogue record for this book is
available from the British Library.

The Editors and Publisher gratefully acknowledge grants in aid of
publication from the Faculty of Arts Revenue Committee, University
College Dublin; the Publications Committee of St Patrick's College,
Maynooth; and the Senate of the National University of Ireland. Grateful
acknowledgement is also due to Faber and Faber Ltd (London) for
permission to quote from 'In Memoriam Sean O'Riada'
by Seamus Heaney (*Field Work*, 1979).

Printed in Ireland by ßetaprint, Dublin

Contents

Contributors

ANN BUCKLEY, a former lecturer in music at University College, Cork, is currently a research associate of Corpus Christi College, Cambridge. She specialises in historical musicology and ethnomusicology, and has published many papers on music in Ireland and eastern Europe, as well as on medieval monophony and the sociology of music. She is a contributor to volume I of the Royal Irish Academy's *A New History of Ireland* and to the *New Grove*. Dr Buckley's book on the Old French lyric *lai* is due for publication with Libreria Musicale Italiana. A book on music in Irish social history is in preparation for a north American publisher.

RAYMOND DEANE was born in the west of Ireland and graduated in music from University College, Dublin, in 1974. He has lived in Basel, Cologne, Berlin, Oldenburg and Paris, and has worked as music teacher, journalist and translator, but is best known as a composer of classical music, in which capacity he was elected to Aosdána (Ireland's academy of creative artists) in 1986. He was the Irish delegate at the 1993 ISCM World Music Days in Mexico City. His first novel, *Death of a Medium*, was published in 1991.

GERARD GILLEN is professor of music at St Patrick's College, Maynooth. Co-editor of *Irish Musical Studies*, his research interests include the history of the organ, performance practice and seventeenth-century keyboard music. His study of Irish organs in the classical tradition will be published in 1997. Professor Gillen was John Betts fellow in the University of Oxford in 1992.

FRANK HENEGHAN is director of cultural affairs at the Dublin Institute of Technology. As former director of the institute's College of Music, his interests have been concentrated on the training of performers at all levels; he has taught a significant number of the younger generation of Irish pianists. Research interests include the philosophy and aesthetics of musical interpretation, and general music education in Ireland. He is currently organising the DIT national debate on music education.

PATRICK O'DONOGHUE is a priest of the archdiocese of Dublin and diocesan director of music, and teaches music at the diocesan seminary, Clonliffe College. He studied music and liturgy at the Catholic University of

America, specialising in the history of sacred music. He has a particular interest in the encouragement of an indigenous Irish expression in liturgy and music.

RIONACH UÍ ÓGAIN has been an archivist/collector with the department of Irish folklore, University College, Dublin, since 1979. She has published numerous articles on traditional song and music and has lectured widely on the subject. Among her publications is a CD/audio-cassette entitled *Beauty an Oileáin: Music and Song of the Blasket Islands*, a paper entitled 'Music learned from the Fairies' (*Béaloideas, 60*), and a book consisting of an index of traditional songs collected in the west Galway area, *Clár Amhrán Bhaile na hInse* (Clóchomhar).

JOSEPH RYAN is an officer in the Irish defence forces where he holds the rank of commandant and is conductor of the Army No. 1 Band. He contributed chapters to *Irish Musical Studies I* and *II* and his research is concerned with music in Ireland from 1750 to the present, an area in which he obtained his doctorate in 1991 and which continues to be his primary research interest.

HARRY WHITE was appointed to the chair of music at University College, Dublin, in 1993. His research interests include the music of Johann Joseph Fux, the cultural history of music in Ireland and the history of musicology since 1945. He is currently completing a monograph on Irish music.

Preface

Music and Irish Cultural History is the third volume in the series *Irish Musical Studies*: its predecessors are *Musicology in Ireland* (1990) and *Music and the Church* (1992). All three books are respectively characterised by the exploration of a prevailing issue: the condition of Irish musical scholarship, church music in Ireland, the presence (and absence) of music in Irish cultural history.

Each of these themes is sounded in *Music and Irish Cultural History*, but it is the last of them which is of greatest account in this instance.

As with the preceding volumes in this series, this book to some extent breaks new ground. It is perhaps a commonplace to acknowledge that the fabric of Irish cultural history is layered and complex, but it is only in the recent past that the question of music within this fabric has received significant scrutiny. The sheer narrative of Irish musical history awaits comprehensive address, and whereas significant inroads have been made by scholars including Ann Buckley, Brian Boydell, Joseph Ryan and Hugh Shields (all of them contributors to the series thus far), the relationship between music and Irish political and social history is undoubtedly complicated by the *in vacuo* condition which attends much of this field of research. But the situation is incomparably more promising than it was ten years ago: the past decade has seen a phenomenal resurgence of interest in the study of music in Ireland which is symbolised in some small measure by the series to which this book belongs.

That this scholarship has been overwhelmingly positivistic in focus simply reflects the lacunae of information which for so long silently awaited investigation. The point to emphasise here is that such investigation has at last been undertaken in significant measure. Without any claim whatever to inclusiveness, one might usefully refer, for example, to the steady accumulation of dissertations, scholarly articles and monographs which since the early 1980s has borne upon the following: the ballad tradition, the ethnic corpus of vocal and instrumental music, the history of musical instruments, the musical repertory of the Ascendancy in eighteenth century Dublin, the history of music education, the impact of nationalism on Irish music since the Act of Union, the history of church music, the transmission of oral musical culture, the sources of music in early and late medieval Ireland. If much work remains to be done, it is nonetheless valid to remark in the light of these achievements that the time has never been so ripe for a significant coherence of this scholarship. A positivistic enterprise *par excellence*, the undertaking of an encyclopedia of music in Ireland, is one such coherence which has been advanced within the pages of *Irish Musical Studies*. Its realisation has now become a probability rather than a pious hope, not least because of the current condition of Irish musical scholarship.

But positivism in scholarship (musical and otherwise) cannot hope to monopolise or exhaust the truth of enquiry. Certain modes of investigation lie beyond its purview. In particular, the pursuit of cultural history enlists a critical mode which is distinct from the accumulation and appraisal of musical information. Such a rudimentary observation would not be of much moment, were it not for the fact that one prevailing lacuna in Irish musical scholarship continues to inhibit the integration of music into the history of Irish ideas. *Music and Irish Cultural History* variously identifies and addresses that lack.

It does not do so comprehensively. Lacunae, in this book as elsewhere, abound. But the essays presented here are *primarily* concerned with the relationship between music and context in Ireland. That context is various: it embraces political and social ideology, linguistic and literary symbolism, education and the proposition of original Irish music. In historical terms, it ranges from early medieval Ireland to the cultural preoccupations of the present day. It is context, in short, which determines the focus of the book, collectively and individually, rather than the disclosure of musical information *per se*. And it is this investigation of context which allows the primary question of cultural history to arise in relation to music in Ireland, namely, the extent to which that music attains extra-musical meaning or significance.

The terms in which this question is formulated differ widely throughout the book. Ann Buckley's understanding of music in pre-Christian and Early Christian Ireland, for example, strongly advances a thorough deconstruction of 'celticism' as a tenable concept for the interpretation of musical symbolism and textual allusion in this period. The interdisciplinary techniques of research which she enlists (rather than merely advocates) productively depend in part on the revisionism of Kim McCone, but in terms of cultural history her achievement is remarkably to identify a host of non-musical (textual) sources which disclose a fundamental seam of musical significance. Her account of the sociology of music which these sources provide, and her scrutiny of symbolic and allusive projections of music in the texts themselves, radically widen our perception of music in the fabric of early Irish cultural history.

At the other end of the historical continuum, Raymond Deane's bleak assessment of the composer in contemporary Ireland offers a rather different reading of the relationship between music and Irish social history. It is a dismaying account, but however gloomy Deane's perception of the current condition of Irish composition (specifically in regard to his critique of those state institutions by which music is promoted), this essay enjoys not inconsiderable authority and authenticity, both of which derive from the author's own standing as a composer. 'The Honour of Non-Existence' is almost certain to provoke commentary, and itself attains to the status of a document in Irish cultural history. The issues it raises are likely to endure for some time to come, especially as to whether Ireland has exchanged one kind of colonial servitude for another.

Between Buckley and Deane, a gamut of other cultural issues is engaged: Frank Heneghan's extensive meditation on music education in Ireland (an issue which is also representative of widespread concern in the 1990s), Rionach Uí Ógain's exposition of the traditional repertory as (in part) a phenomenon of socio-cultural transmission and Patrick O'Donoghue's contemplation of music as an expression of a notably complex socio-religious matrix variously explore ways in which music has become intelligible in the plural terms of Irish cultural history. A short but compelling essay by Joseph Ryan (whose command of art music in Ireland between 1800 and 1950 is perhaps unrivalled) addresses a central theme in the relationship between music and its cultural reception, namely, the impact of nationalist ideologies on the development of voice, style and identity in Irish music. The closing chapter of the book also adverts to this theme in its scrutiny of music in a verbally-dominated culture.

If *Music and Irish Cultural History* succeeds in stimulating debate and further research on these issues, it will have served its purpose. Other questions might well have been investigated here, including an assessment of the difficult boundary which exists between popular (commercial) music and its reception in Irish cultural discourse. It had been our hope to include research on precisely this question, but a year's prevarication did not, in the end, make the wait worthwhile. The topic itself, however, is surely of abiding interest and may yet attract the attention of a competent scholar.

The editors would like to thank Michael Adams and Martin Healy for their wise counsel and greatly valued assistance in the preparation of this volume for publication.

'and his voice swelled like a terrible thunderstorm . . . '[1]

MUSIC AS SYMBOLIC SOUND IN MEDIEVAL IRISH SOCIETY

ANN BUCKLEY[2]

1. INTRODUCTION

It has become a commonplace to introduce this topic with a litany of apologetic negatives, expressions of regret for what is lost and what may once have existed as evidence for the practice of music in medieval Ireland. Sources which survive are opaque, usually indirect in nature. Surviving notated manuscripts amount to a mere handful of liturgical codices, all of them dating from after the establishment of Hiberno-Norman ascendancy. There are no notated manuscripts of secular repertories, and because of the feudal and non-centralised structure of Irish political-administrative units, no centralised account books or rolls in which might have been preserved details on the engagement of musicians for official court ceremonies. The only such documents are the collections of annals which, though of relatively late date, incorporate information from much older sources and record obituaries of some thirty musicians associated with the most important ruling families. Invariably only players of stringed instruments were included, as of musicians these alone were entitled to hold office and thus enjoy social standing of any importance. Information about music, there as elsewhere, is usually embedded within other accounts and not therefore preserved for the purpose of communicating technical detail, with the exception of one category, as we shall see.

In spite of the unpromising state of affairs with regard to documentary accounts of individuals and actual historical events, the Brehon Law codes attest in some detail to the status and ranking of musicians, sometimes including information which considerably enhances our understanding not only of their respective social functions but also of technical matters, such as the classification of instruments. The narrative literature abounds in allusions to musicians, instruments and occasions of music-making, and reveals

13

a rich and detailed vocabulary to describe all manner of sounds. The Irish soundscape is well attested also in poetry and, not unrelatedly, the range of linguistic terminology and elaborate description in respect of 'musical' (and non-'musical') timbres, forms and instruments is considerable and varied. This is surely no surprise among social groups which evidently possessed highly-developed, sensitive awareness in matters of rhyme, alliteration and assonance – as witness medieval Irish Gaelic and Hiberno-Latin poetry.

An example is provided in a poem about a hermit,[3] from which the following stanzas are taken (the translation is Carney's, italics have been added for emphasis):

> Mét me boithe; beccnat becc,
>   baile sétae sognath;
> *canaid sian mbinn* día beinn
>   ben a lleinn co londath.

> This size my hut; the smallest thing,
> homestead amid well-trod paths;
> a woman – blackbird clothed and coloured –
> *is singing sweetly*[4] from its gable.

>   (ll. 9–12)

> *Céola* ferán mbruinne forglan
>   foram ndil,
> *dordán*[5] smálcha *caíne*[6] gnáthcha
>   úas mo thig.

> Tellinn, cíarainn, *cerdán* cruinne,
>   *crónán séim*;
> gigrainn, cadain, gair ré Samain
>   *seinm*[7] *ngairb chéir*.

> Tecat caínfhinn, corra, faílinn,
>   fos-*cain* cúan;
> ní *céol ndogra cerca odra*
>   a fráech rúad.

> *Fogur* gaíthe fri fid flescach
>   forglas néol,
> essa aba, *esnad* eala,
>   *álainn céol.*

Pigeons *cooing*, breasts are gleaming,
beloved flutter;
on my house-top *constant music*,
song of thrushes.

Bees and chafers, *gentle humming*
and *soft crooning*;
wild geese come with *rough dark music*
before All Hallows.

Then come dear white ones, herons, sea-gulls
sea-chant hearing;
no *harsh music* when grouse is *calling*
from russet heather.

The *sound* of wind in branching trees,
day grey and cloudy;
stream in torrent, swans are *singing*,
sweet the music.   (ll. 45–60)

These and similar terms are used over and over again to describe the sound of instruments, of singing, and chanting, as well as those less-than-intentional sounds produced by non-human nature (i.e., animals, the elements), often, it seems, with keener awareness of aural than of visual experience. Sometimes the analogy with the performance of music is even more direct, such as in a line from a ninth- or tenth-century Old Irish song in celebration of May Day: '*seinnid crot caille céol*' (the *crot* of the forest plays music),[8] to describe the sound of the wind in the trees, which has further implications also, as I shall discuss below. The problem for historical enquiry is the non-specificity of these terms, their cognitive codes now out of our reach. References are descriptive rather than analytical, and usually emotive, metaphorical – but rarely technical or systematic – their primary function being to counterpoint other matters: invoking a certain mood, social prestige, display of wealth, the proper ordering of society according to status, avoidance of taboos, maintenance of a Christian worldview of moral good and evil. Thus we have a variety of accounts of the ubiquity and importance of music, particularly in secular and ecclesiastical institutions; but detailed information on repertories, methods of instruction, etc. is simply not preserved, and was probably never recorded.

A related problem concerns the human voice. Terms like *canaid* (s/he sings), or the alternation of the Latin terms *cecinit* and *dixit*, for example, in interpolated lyric such arises in Acallam na Senórach,[9] are vague indicators of what may have once occurred in performance. They are used inconsistently, and so one cannot rely on them for a clear indication of the different registers of speaking, declaiming, chanting or intoning, or some kind of more melodically developed singing.[10] Irish sources are no different in this respect from other medieval literatures; though some French manuscripts containing interpolated lyric actually include notation, suggesting that this reflects a norm in performance terms. More important in the Irish sources is the context in which the performance took place, its intentionality and ritual function (for example, joyous music, a lament, a battle-cry, a praise-song). There is one specific term, *airfitid* (*oirfidech*), which refers specifically to the entertainment provided by professional musicians, but that, while providing an important insight, would be far too narrow a criterion for the topic of our interest, which is the documentation of symbolic sound in its widest sense, including humanly-organised intentional sound, and not only that which was confined to occasions of court entertainment or other leisure pursuits. A lament would not be classed as *airfitid*, nor would hymn-singing or liturgical chant. Other performance arts, such as the magic incantations of the much-despised druids, or the entertainment provided by low-class entertainers such as buffoons, also come into our sphere of concern, but again, we lack any kind of orientative description which would enable us to classify those repertories according to genre in the strict sense.

The iconographic record for sound, the bulk of which survives in the form of carvings on Irish high crosses of the ninth and tenth centuries and on metalwork of the eleventh to fourteenth, while not extensive, is of particular importance in providing insight into early Christian Irish interpretations of biblical stories, at times introducing music-making scenes which are not described in the Bible, leaving little doubt that they reflect local norms, thereby informing us as to contemporary activities and associations, particularly when complemented by references in literary sources. And so while one can only regret the loss to modern scholarship of technical information concerning so important and central an activity, which would enable us better to assess its forms, contents and symbolic functions, there are nonetheless extensive allusions in the sources to the respective rôles and status of various kinds of musicians, their repertories and instruments, and the many functions of the human voice, which have an important bearing on any understanding on the type of society they represent. Furthermore, the quantity and range of literary and iconographic materials from early medieval Ireland is greater than for any other part of Europe of this period. The fact that the sources are often classed as 'mythological' need not deter us in our quest, for myths are retained, and adapted, only in meaningful ways; if they have no meaning, they are discarded. Hence, whether we refer to actual historical events or to constructs of the mind only, the material, the way in which it is conceived and communicated, the issues, the challenges, the mores, the priorities and emotional attachments, are also 'facts' rich with insight on their creators and consumers, without whom they could not have come into being or remained in use. It is relevant to bear in mind that medieval Irish literature, while revealing of attitudes, associations and belief-systems inherited from a multiplicity of traditions, including Hindi, Persian, Hebrew, Celtic, Greek, Roman, Arabic, has a clear overlay of Christianity, Irish Christianity, created, recorded and transmitted within Irish society, thus bearing the hallmark of the scholars and scribes who committed it to writing, and for motives which have often been misunderstood. Kim McCone, in his brilliant analysis of the purpose and context of this massive scribal initiative, has demonstrated eloquently the law-giving, justificatory ideology of the material as a whole, which he sums up as the product of interrelated activities of clerics, jurists, poets whose scheme:

> daringly represented Patrick's fifth-century mission to Ireland as a small-scale reenactment of Christ's appearance in the world to bring the Old Testament law and prophets, including history, to fulfilment in the New. Historical typology could then accommodate the pagan past to the Christian present by viewing it as an Irish 'Old Testament' perfected rather than abrogated by the national apostle's Christian dispensation. In this way all Irish legal, genealogical and mytho-historical *senchus*, whether set in the pre- or post-Patrician era, could embody a broadly identical set of contemporary values and customs represented as essentially immutable but in fact adjusted to the Church's ongoing interaction with current social and political realities.[11]

Thus whether we are dealing with pseudo-etymology or myths of origin of music instruments, or with fairy musicians rather than actual historical figures, we learn terms of reference and acquire understanding of attitudes and associations, of appropriate and inappropriate behaviour, through these exemplary or cautionary tales. The challenge is to interpret them historically by drawing on comparative information and endeavouring to understand their terms, which can only derive from the known world, when not inherited, and perhaps garbled, from older sources; and if the latter, then adapted to make sense in their present(s). To unravel these distinctions is our task, and one which can yield significant fruit. Work of this nature on Irish sources is still at a relatively early stage, often held back, as it has been, by a purist, nativist view of a self-contained Celt with a vivid imagination, untouched by the wider world and innocent of any conceit. There is much revision and analysis yet to be undertaken on Irish narrative literature and related materials which in the past have all too often been viewed as 'more or less mindless

antiquarian compilations'[12] rather than acknowledged as intentional compositions representing the conceptual net or *Weltanschauung* of the intelligentsia (clerics, jurists, scholars) of early medieval Ireland, and of those
with whom they were interdependent.

But here is need for caution, on two counts in particular. First of all, there
is the risk of appearing to view the literature too starkly in a 'before and
after' kind of framework. Because of the evident absorption of existing
beliefs and practices by Christian clerics as the church became consolidated,
and the need to interpret the sources in the form in which they survive as
products of an élite, ' . . . highly trained, highly self-aware mandarin class',[13] it
is critical that we do not fall victim to any assumptions that our Noble-Savage,
Ur-ancestors were enjoying a kind of primitive communist existence in pre-
Christian Tír na n-Óg. This view has sometimes proved irresistible to writers who have found it difficult to disengage from their own prejudices and
preferences. There are examples of the problem in some recent historical
studies of so-called 'popular culture', such as the following comment by
Aron Gurevich in an otherwise exceedingly rich and insightful work:

> The culture common to all people in pre-class society becomes the cul-
> ture of the 'common people' in a class society, counterposed to the
> 'official' clerical culture; it becomes a persecuted culture driven back
> to the periphery of spiritual life. Paganism, which has permeated myth
> and epic, degenerates into 'superstition'. The traditional vision of the
> world is broken into fragments under the blows of ecclesiastical ideol-
> ogy and is only partially absorbed by the new world-view. The tri-
> umph of the new culture does not imply the total defeat of the archaic.
> In many respects popular culture retains its 'pre-medieval' features.[14]

The 'two-tiered model' of pagans and Christians, clergy and 'common folk',
though still much in evidence in medieval studies, has justly been criticised
by Peter Brown, a specialist in the religious history of Late Antiquity whose
comments on late-fourth-century Christian communities are equally applicable to the subject of our study here:

> It is time . . . to step aside from this form of explanation and to set the
> conflicts in religious practice to which the late-fourth-century debate
> on "superstition" pointed against a wider background [and rather] to
> view the Christian church in late antiquity through 'kinship coloured
> glasses'.[15]

> . . . we must remember that the Christian church had risen to promi-
> nence largely because its central ritual practices and its increasingly

centralized organization and financial administration presented the pagan world with an ideal community that had claimed to modify, to redirect, and even to delimit the bonds of kin. The church was an artificial kin group. Its members were expected to project onto the new community a fair measure of the sense of solidarity, of the loyalties, and of the obligations that had previously been directed to the physical family.[16]

Instead of a dialogue on 'superstition' conducted between the disapproving 'few' and the 'common herd,' we must begin with a conflict more plausible to late-Roman men – a conflict between rival systems of patronage.[17]

Any attempt to chip away at the clerical superstructure, or at interpretations of history which can be read from genealogies and myths of origin of Gaelic ruling families, is not only an impossible task but a naïve one. While there are undoubtedly elements of older myths and lifestyles to be brought to light with laser-beam penetration of the layers of re-interpretation and re-presentation, like geological strata, one could only hope at best to discover older figurations, earlier groups of established and outsiders, earlier recountings of history reflecting in turn the glories and triumphs of leaders of yet former times. It is one of the universals of human societies that the strong oust the weak and spend most of their resources on maintaining and defending their position of ascendancy (and their surplus energy on singing about it!). It is as true of the clerical and secular élites of medieval Ireland (and Europe generally) as of Egyptian pharaohs, Roman emperors, Norman barons, eighteenth/nineteenth-century colonial expansionists, communist dictators of the twentieth century, and indeed, leaders of western democracies – but with the difference that in the civilizing process[18] of learning to live peaceably together in ever larger groups in increasing interdependence, there is a concomitant process of increasing tolerance of criticism and self-awareness. In short, the notion of ultimate origins or of zero-points is not helpful in attempting to understand human behaviour. Any point along the continuum of time and space needs to be examined also on its terms.

A related problem in over-identification which can all-too-easily dog studies of past societies, and from which it is indeed difficult to disengage, is the notion that 'we' are investigating 'our' past, and that there is a flowing stream of consistent consciousness linking us in perpetuity with our notional forebears. At its crudest, this problem becomes one more weapon in the arsenal of latter-day nation-state or regional politics. That is indeed another topic, which far exceeds my present purpose. But to relate it specifically to our concern here, music, it is all too easy to impose our own aesthetic assumptions and to derive satisfaction from, say, the praise which Gerald of Wales felt disposed to heap on Irish harpers whom he heard performing in the late twelfth century; or, motivated by a search for pre-Norman Celtic Christianity (which in some respects is not theoretically dissimilar from the idea of trying to isolate pre-Christian Celtic paganism), to rule out the study of materials in Irish or Irish-related sources which appear more likely to have been representative of 'European' or 'generally medieval' practice as distinct from those appearing to reflect uniquely Irish norms. Similarly, we risk complete distortion by any attempt to distinguish, according to our twentieth-century lights or our subjective preferences, between notional 'art' and 'folk' music, or other any 'high-and-low', two-tiered models, as underlined in Brown's important and persuasive argument. Mutually exclusive, static categorisations are of little use in attempting to understand human behaviour, which is always dynamic and in a state of flux.

This 'uniquely Irish' or 'ancient Celtic' theme has tended to dominate study of Irish liturgical music until relatively recently, for example, in the search for *the* 'Celtic' Rite whereby differences from the Roman church were viewed as all-important; similarly, a resistance to studying Irish Sarum materials, which represent the only notated liturgical books for any Irish medieval chant, and the general reluctance to look more widely to information which demonstrates the integration of some Irish mores within the European world, as distinct from local or regional characteristics which, if taken out of context, falsely emphasise segregation and suggest isolation.

From the opposite standpoint, this marginalisation of Irish (as well as of Scottish and Welsh) materials continues to dog more general studies of medieval European musics, except in the negative sense where commentators still tend to fall back on a presumed Celtic or Irish origin for much that remains unexplained – because undocumented, or 'non-Roman' (in the case of liturgical chant) – in early medieval, north-European music history. Such a practice confirms the continuing relevance of J.R. Tolkien's perceptive remark concerning those who persist in regarding Celtic matter as 'a magic bag into which anything may be put and out of which almost anything may come'.[19]

Common examples include a tendency to associate references to harp-playing necessarily with the so-called Celtic fringe – whether directly, through some historically-connected chain of events, or indirectly through a presumption of what may have been associated memory in the minds of contemporaries.

For instance, a particular type of small harp from the High Middle Ages, well-known from Gothic (i.e., twelfth- to early fourteenth-century French, English and German) manuscripts, is still in modern writing (including scholarly writing) often referred to as an Irish harp. The sources for this appellation depend, no doubt, on the use of a particular kind of small harp as a symbol of Ireland on Henry VIII's coat of arms and on Irish coins of the period, and on references in Renaissance organological treatises (such as Michael Praetorius's *Syntagma Musicum* of 1619) reflecting of current music practices. Such an Irish harp, with its characteristically T-shaped forepillar, deep neck and thick soundbox cut from one piece of wood, dating from about the fifteenth century, has survived the ravages of time and is now preserved in the Library, Trinity College Dublin. It was further distinguished by being fitted with metal strings which were plucked with the fingernails.

But it is often overlooked there may have been different kinds of small medieval harp, or at least regional variations thereof, probably more than we shall ever know, owing to the lack of surviving examples. Nevertheless, it is salutary to be reminded that a frame harp of similar size, though slimmer in construction, is recorded as a *cithara anglica*[20] in a twelfth/thirteenth-century source, now lost but recorded in Gerbert's *De cantu et musica sacra*, where it is distinguished from a *cithara teutonica* or rounded, figure-of-eight Germanic lyre, quite a different instrument, in spite of the common Latin nomenclature.[21] The instrument depicted on *Breac Maedóic*, an Irish-made reliquary of the eleventh century (illustrated on the jacket of the present series), is in fact closer in appearance to this 'English harp' than it is to the later, sturdier, TCD version.[22] However, it helps little to attempt to reach zero-points or absolute beginnings; we achieve more by documenting the processes and dynamics of observable behaviour.

As far as concerns their longer-term history, there is a strong likelihood that harps may have been developed in Anglo-Saxon England, transmitted northwards to Pictland and thence westwards to Argyll and Ireland, as is suggested by the chronological sequence and evidence from manuscripts and stone carvings.[23] But this question must remain open in the absence of more reliable evidence.

If Celtic Studies and the study of Irish affairs generally are now hopefully on course towards wider, more integrative world-views of past events, this is not yet necessarily true of scholars outside of those fields or of how they view the place of Irish materials within their scheme of things – a problem which perhaps besets the study of music more acutely than other fields. The 'magic bag' syndrome has the added disadvantage of a continued ghettoization within, or more accurately, beyond the frontiers of European medieval studies. As long as Celtic Studies remains (or is kept) aloof, this problem is set to continue, maintaining the ascendancy of certain world views which are well-established and serve excellently the *status quo*, by not admitting challenges which would alter considerably the way in which medieval music, to name but one subject, is currently studied. For example, by an almost exclusive reliance on the notated heritage, music historians are overlooking large tracts of evidence which have an essential bearing on understanding the very *raison d'être* of repertories which can be tracked, analysed and reconstructed for performance purposes. And this of course diminishes from the very outset the valuable insights into the medieval world which are provided by literary and iconographic sources (of which Irish materials represent a significant part), and by archaeologically-excavated artefacts. Concomitantly, by dropping into this Celtic 'magic bag' much which cannot be investigated because of lack of notated sources,[24] questions which could be brought to bear about real people in real social situations are often ignored when, by recourse to a more context-sensitive approach,[25] much could be advanced, in terms of constructive theories and hypotheses, on the basis of informed argument. The wider context or the so-called 'European dimension' of Irish music study will be addressed in the final section, in an attempt at appraising the current state of knowledge and ongoing research. Meantime, I shall return to discussion of the problems of interpreting the source materials.

With the considerable advances in study of the sources of medieval Irish (Gaelic, Hiberno-Norse, Hiberno-Norman) history and archaeology in recent years, we now have a better understanding of how medieval Irish men, women and children organised their lives, built homes, related to their kith and kin; how their religious and secular leaders acquired, maintained or lost power; how their battles were waged; how they were schooled; what occupied their visual world, for example, in landscape, architecture, sculpture, metalwork, illuminated manuscripts.

Some of the interpretative issues are beginning to be addressed by at least some historians and scholars of literature and linguistics; and it is to be hoped that increasing energy will be expended on systematising the material (including much more detailed indexing of textual editions than currently obtains), thereby making it more accessible for comparative study of individual aspects of human symbolic behaviour in matters such as music, cosmology, magic, time, medicine, food, clothing, the body, manners, humour, colour, and a host of other topics. It will require a significant shift towards more sociological interpretations of the sources.

Our task here is to explore the aural world of medieval Ireland. It has to be emphasised that this essay is but a tentative approach to most of the issues involved: its conclusions, where they exist, are provisional, one of its aims being to synthesise and evaluate the current state of knowledge in preparation for further work.[26] If one may resort to McCone's own words:

> Formidable linguistic difficulties associated with the vast corpus of Old and Middle Irish texts . . . have tended to restrict the number of scholars working upon this material. . . . Because the pioneers of the

new discipline rightly concentrated their efforts upon improving the linguistic analysis indispensable for a proper understanding of the material and upon making texts, translations and synopses available to a wider scholarly audience, broader questions of interpretation were, by and large, postponed until a later and fairly recent stage. Hence the paradox that Europe's most abundantly documented early medieval culture, particularly where vernacular sources are concerned, remains among the least thoroughly researched. Rich seams of information have yet to be tapped, and these can be expected to enhance our appreciation of early medieval European literature and civilization as a whole'.[27]

Such an exercise would require teams of scholars in a truly interdisciplinary enterprise, as yet very difficult to achieve because much information remains embedded within the covers of specialist journals, or indeed, in the mental recesses of those more familiar with the primary sources. Concomitantly, teamwork in research is unfortunately almost non-existent anywhere in the human sciences – unlike the so-called 'hard' or natural sciences. Although the configurations of institutional career-structures often impede cooperation of this kind, it is clear that an excess of individualism and display of self-sufficiency mitigate against the higher motive of scholarly endeavour: countless numbers of individuals work in parallel, finding out more and more about less and less, often merely re-inventing the wheel, and thereby holding back progress on matters the equivalent of which have long stabilised in the natural sciences.

It is to be hoped that further synthetic work, such as the path-breaking exercise undertaken by McCone, will be followed in the future by integrative accounts of other aspects of the mental and social worlds, the conceptual net, of the inhabitants of medieval Ireland, comparable to, say, the broad sweep of enquiry on French, German and, increasingly, Anglo-Saxon, materials. Needless to say, the wealth of archival holdings for France, in particular, can hardly be matched for Celtic Studies. On the other hand, early medieval Irish sources are the richest for Europe of their time. By honing the right cognitive tools, many issues of social process, of broad cultural-historical concern, can indeed be fruitfully addressed, which should stimulate debate and contribute to more integrative work not only within Irish Studies but within the wider framework of Medieval European Studies with which the former is, by definition, interdependent. Hence, the purpose of the present exercise is not so much a listing of documentary sources *per se* but rather an exploration of processes, ways of hearing, thinking about and responding to sound within the social environment of medieval Ireland, and, it must be emphasised, within the limits of current research.

2. SYMBOLIC SOUND AND HUMAN FIGURATIONS

In this essay the question of music in medieval Irish society will be addressed from the point of view of its uses as a symbol of political power and status; its magico-mythical properties (which also represent symbolic power, usually perceived as from beyond the human or known world); and the status and function of musicians within this spectrum. In other words, the topic of music as revelatory of medieval Irish social structure and evolving *mentalités*. My purpose is not so much to give a blow-by-blow account of institutions, instruments and repertories as a primary focus, but rather to regard these as indices of social processes: who performs what? for which social groups? why? when? what are the associations for particular sounds? what is the symbolic function of an occasion of music-making or of a particular kind of sound? what is sound? what is music? what is the nature of the distinction?

In modern societies, where aesthetic preferences are important symbols of social status, the question of what music is tends to be regarded as self-evident – to specialists and non-specialists alike, and is usually determined by the awarenesses and habits of those involved. This needs to be understood on its terms as an index of contemporary social figurations, but it may be a weak basis for academic enquiry or scientific understanding of other times and other places, or indeed of much which is going on in our own immediate surroundings! To adapt a well-known aphorism, one person's music is another's noise. However, one is well advised to lay aesthetic preferences aside when endeavouring to make sense of social phenomena; otherwise, there is no science. But to put it more positively, more constructively, we cannot begin to understand and explain music processes without exploring the wider world of sound as it is perceived by human beings – particular human groups in particular times and places. Music is an aspect of civilization, a result of ordering and refinement of our own nature and that of the world around us, a process which is not entirely invented, or entirely natural in the sense of being instinctive, but represents a combination of the two. And so, before proceeding, it is necessary to explore the implications of the sound–music spectrum.

Many of us who live in the late-twentieth-century Western world enjoy a relatively secure existence, armed with many kinds of protection and defence against non-human nature (and with a firm control over most aspects of human nature also), in a world which relies more on attenuative planning, knowledge and foresight than any society in the past. It is therefore difficult, from our perspective, to appreciate the importance, proximity and fear presented by the non-human world in other times and other places. For example, in a society where a thunderclap or a flash of lightning is interpreted as a sign of imminent threat from an angry god, perhaps vengeance for lack of due sacrifice and homage, or for some past crime, the sounds of nature take on a vivid presence and are assigned a much more dominant, even primary, role in human affairs. Thus dance, music and attendant religious rituals take the form of active communion with non-human nature, whether with the heavens, the forest, rivers or mountains. These rituals may be used for purposes of appeasement, or for intercession directed towards a particular cause, such as rain to make the crops grow, or sunshine for the harvest, or more indirectly, protection in battle, cure from illness, a curse upon an enemy, etc.

The uniquely human civilizing process can be explained as a gradual movement away from such belief systems towards a more ordered, planned society in which increasing understanding, and therefore self-control, is accompanied by a shift away from belief in gods, autonomous 'powers' or 'forces' which interpose in human affairs from beyond the known world. This does not mean to suggest that we are nowadays emotionally or psychologically unaffected by the non-human environment: just because we know that a thunderstorm is a consequence of electricity produced by high pressure in the atmosphere does not mean that we may not be alarmed by the experience. Or if we have a run of bad luck, it is not always easy to remain confidently distant from the thought that we are being punished by some outside force. Similarly, with sounds, there is little use in explaining the effects on our emotions of the slow movement of a Mahler symphony, liturgical chant, *sean nós* singing, the timbre of uilleann pipes, or the jubilant anthems of the crowd at a football match, in terms of analysis of the physics of sound production. Nor indeed is it sufficient to analyse an art object (whether it be music, painting, sculpture, or whatever) only in terms of its surface structure in order to explain its emotional-aesthetic appeal – or, for that matter, lack of appeal. People's uses of, and responses to, artistic products cannot be separated from the very complex accumulation of attitudes, memories and associations which are the engine of human conduct or self-steering. And thus when philosophical and other so-called 'rational' avenues are explored (such as formal and structural analysis), there are certain aspects of the experience of music (and indeed of all other human experiences) which are completely overlooked. While they may not easily be fully explained, much can be understood through attempting to consider empirical aspects as integratively as possible. Music, being the most abstract, least 'tangible' of the arts tends to be regarded as somewhat separate from the physical world of people, but without understanding its *raison d'être*, the fact that it is produced by people for people in social figurations in specific times and places, we cannot really begin to understand music: who is performing what? for whom? why? in what circumstances? remain fundamental to any exploration of the uses and meanings of humanly-organised symbolic sound, as well as of its formal structures.

In accounting for music in any society, but particularly one different from one's own, in space or time (the past is also an 'Other'), it is essential first of all to identify what is understood by the term, or its equivalents, and how they are (or were) used. All too easily, one may overlook important aspects of sound which, from a twentieth-century Western standpoint, do not conform to the usual definition of music, and yet perform an important symbolic function in the society concerned. We ignore such information to our considerable disadvantage, just as we often ignore symbolic sounds in our own environment which may be highly revealing and explanatory of 'musical' behaviour, simply because they are not the product of a particular kind of schooling.

Reinhold Hammerstein[28] has brought important and rich information to light which has been marginalised, if not ignored, in music scholarship. His concern is with automatic sound-producers, mechanical instruments, hydraulic and wind-driven (e.g., organs), as well as instruments made to vibrate by unharnessed natural forces as in the case of sounds produced by the wind blowing through an Aeolian 'harp'. But his keen perception of their relevance to music history applies equally to other kinds of sound. While 'automatic' in the sense that such instruments are not made to sound necessarily by the operation of a musician, or that they are not necessarily tuned or used to produce regulated melodic compositions, they are artefacts, made and used by humans in a symbolically meaningful way, in order to serve a human-social purpose. Thus they may be viewed as instruments of 'paramusical' sound, being different from 'natural', non-humanly-controlled sounds such as birdsong, rain, wind, thunder and lightning, and so further along the scale in the direction of what is generally recognised as 'music' in the approved Western scholastic sense, that is, fully regulated, complexly organised composition. All of these rightly come under the scrutiny of musicological study to the extent that they form part of the human environment, are perceived by human beings, and are loaded with meanings attributed to them by those human beings. At a theoretical or experiential level we cannot usefully separate 'music' from the overall experience of sound, since at fundament is the human capacity to perceive and produce sound, a 'natural' quality.

Nature and nurture are equally present in all human behaviour; to exclude either is to ignore an important part of the evidence. The body is the primary sound-producer, a response to nature within and nature without. From this was produced sound, including vocal emissions, body-slapping, foot-stamping, and their extensions in the form of various kinds of sound 'tools' such as sticks and stones, gourds, reeds, stretched membrane and animal gut; from these were developed other, more technologically-advanced instruments, up to and including those of modern times. In Hammerstein's words (and to extend, by implication, their applicability to all humanly-organised sound):

Musicology has hardly, or only marginally, been concerned with the question of automatic sound producers because it is assumed that these have nothing to do with 'real' instruments of music. . . . Such a distinction . . . between real and non-real instruments is of course not entirely incorrect, but consequently characterises a narrow conception of an instrument, and in particular, of music for which only those sound phenomena and those instruments are regarded as worthy of attention which operate on the basis of a regulated tonal system and which can produce entire pieces, melodies or even polyphonic music, whether as improvisation or as composition.

The rationalisation of music and its connection with the rise and increasing consolidation of regulated, written, polyphonic composition – a process which includes firstly vocal but increasingly also instrumental music – is indeed one of the most important facts in the history of music of the Middle Ages. But that in no way signifies the end of previously existing or other, pre-compositional, preliterate, pre-regulated practices, not least that of automatic sound producers. On the contrary, they continue to exist alongside or within artificial music. Moreover, their place is, after as before, on the margins and in the forefront of music, and the borderline with regulated music remains absolutely fluid.[29]

These would have been of profound spiritual significance in pre-Christian (and most likely also Christian) times, representing communion with gods and ancestors of the Otherworld. Thunder, rainstorms, lightning, birdsong, wind in the trees, or a flock of birds may all be accorded supernatural meanings in pre-scientific societies. By extension, the striking of a particular stone or performing on an instrument made from the wood of a particular tree may take on profound symbolic meaning. The importance of these physical symbols needs to be understood in a pre-Christian context, where Nature in the form of trees, water, stones, was perceived as animate and needed to be attended upon.[30]

Sounds similar to those of natural forces, or sounds with such associations, may also form the material of composed, regulated sound structures which are then, in mimetic presentation, referred to as 'music'. The same symbolism is common to both; even if affects and understanding of them may be different. This does not apply only to what is specifically termed 'programme music' where the connection between sound and visual imagery is deliberately outlined through the medium of explanatory words (programme notes) or dance (as in ballet). All music evokes reponses that are developed through association and memory. To put it at its most fundamental level, the history of music is the history of human harnessing and manipulation of the sounds of nature, extending from use of the voice and natural sound tools through to the development of technologically simple artefacts and artificial imitations in the form of more complex and elaborate designs. All of these humanly organised sound producers, inclusively, whether the human voice, a reed cut from the marsh, a conch shell or a rock, or whether a worked wooden flute, a skin drum, a violin, an oboe or an electronic organ, are called music instruments. They are vehicles for communicative, orientative, symbolic sound, and all of them, without exception, rightly come within the purview of understanding of human music-behaviour, as distinct from the less intentional, more instinctive sounds of non-human nature, for example, in the animal world.[31]

At a deeper level, the 'spine-tingling' effects of certain timbres, harmonies, melodic contours, and the emotional responses to sounds which may be regarded by particular groups as 'sunny', 'bright', 'sad', tragic', 'humorous', are not totally unrelated to the experience of association of different moods with the weather, the seasons, or weekend leisure time as opposed to weekday work time. When an Irish court musician is described as playing in turn weeping music, laughing music and sleeping music, we can still understand the concepts – we know about those affects of emotion arousal, we also know that they can be achieved through use of mimetic arts – even if we do not believe that there are supernatural powers at work, or being invoked, which may completely control us so that we no longer can resist the will of others to manipulate us as they please. On the other hand, there are instances where these affects can also be achieved, through drugs, trance, group hysteria, but these are the exceptions rather than the rule in Western societies.[32] In order to understand mimetic expression, therefore, we must also understand its associations and the memories invoked: all form part of the conceptual world of the human groups involved.

In medieval Irish literature one is very aware of the power of sound as a weapon to inspire fear, to control or otherwise manipulate the emotions, for example, the quotation at the beginning of this essay which refers to St Colm Cille and his companions who wished to hold Vespers near the fort of the Pictish King Brude, son of Maelchon, as was their custom. The king's druids tried to prevent them, but the saint began to sing the forty-fourth psalm in a voice which at that moment 'rose in the air like a terrible thunderstorm', terrifying both king and people.[33]

This use of the voice to instil awe and ultimately control over opposition is well-attested as a weapon of warfare in tales of Find MacCumhall and his warrior band, the Fianna. Their battle-sound, the *dord-fhian* (presumably some kind of deep-throated growl or drone), was said to scatter the enemy as effectively as any other form of assault. Such accounts are attested also by Latin writers such as Polybius concerning the Continental Celts (to be discussed more fully below).

It would be rash to overlook these ritualised vocal utterances as being completely outwith the realm of musicological enquiry while, for example, including war horns because they more closely resemble our notion of a music instrument. This point becomes clarified when it is understood that such instruments were not intended for playing melodies in the conventional sense (any more than were the Bronze Age horns from prehistoric Ireland). They were intended to communicate certain kinds of signals; but the difference between a sound produced by the human voice and one produced by means of an aerophone cannot be one of fundamental difference in symbolic function, only in degree; similarly, to ignore both, or either, and limit ourselves to some modern Western notion of melodically or harmonically developed sound structures is to ignore many of the feature that identify the nature and processes of music behaviour itself. Hence we must be inclusive and integrationist, not exclusive and isolationist, if we are to attempt to understand the scope and associations of humanly-organised sound.

With respect to symbolic meanings attributed to the non-human world, Francis J. Byrne has referred to the importance of a sacred tree or grove as an inauguration site of kings and the essential use of a slab or flagstone in the ritual.[34] Relatedly, McCone describes the role of Cormac Mac Airt in Irish literature as that of one whose own conversion prepared the way for the Patrician conversion of the island: 'For Cormac had faith in one God according to law. For he had said that he would not worship stones or trees but would worship the one who had made them and was lord behind every creature'.[35] Connolly refers to pilgrims paying their respects to a stone believed to have transported St Declan's bell across the sea from Rome – a possible indication of christianisation of a pagan ritual object.[36] We also need to be mindful of the possible range of symbolic meanings attached in medieval Ireland to the prehistoric megalithics which dot the countryside. Regarding the animation of non-human nature in an Irish context, one has only to consider the belief in fairies up to modern times, for example, in the fear of a *lios* or 'fairy dwelling', in the practice of dressing small boys to look like girls in case they would be stolen by the *síde*, or in being unlucky enough to experience the wailing of the *banside*.[37]

A reference in the Annals of Ulster describes the custom of clapping of hands on St Michael's feastday, to simulate the sounds of thunder associated with the Last Judgement. According to the entry, St Michael's Day was celebrated at the 'fair of the clapping of hands [*oenach inna lam-comarthae*] in which was fire and thunder like the day of judgement' with the interpolation 'The clapping of hands on the feast of Michael, of which was said the fire from heaven' (from Annals of Ulster for the year 772).[38] One wonders what purpose such a ritual might have served in a pre-Christian context, to which it is likely to have been previously linked.

For court ceremonial, certain types of shout or acclamation were evidently customary. An Irish *Speculum Principis* ('Advice to a Prince') is informative about different types of acclamation. For example, in praise:

> Three shouts of victory [*gáire buada*] for a king, because of the excellence of warriorship in his land: a shout of triumph [*gáir ilaig*] after a stiff victory, a shout of high commendation [*gáir molta muaid*], a shout at a feast [*gáir im fhleid*].[39]

These rituals were undoubtedly an Irish equivalent of the *Laudes Regiae* known from the Carolingian period which were later associated particularly with liturgical practice (and for which some notations survive). A broader, historical study of this topic would undoubtedly enrich our understanding of a widespread practice, for example, by including information on litanies and other forms of devotional prayer for which there is Irish and other Insular evidence from the eighth century. But of course such public honouring of potentates is traceable also to Byzantine and Roman emperors. Other sounds, perhaps not all representing ritualised cries, nonetheless underline the importance of the aural world in maintenance of reputation, and ultimately, political power. The ensuing paragraph of 'Advice to a Prince' contrasts the good and successful ruler with the failure:

> Three shouts of discomfiture [*gáire dimbuaid*] for a prince are the shout of satires [*gáire glám*] to wound him, be it far off or near, the cry of his womenfolk [*gáir a ban*] in the grasp of enemies, the cry of his household [*gáir a muintire*] when he has been defeated in battle.[40]

Relatedly, we note a passage in the tale of Donn Bó, royal entertainer, who declined to perform on eve of the Battle of Allen (718 A.D.) because he had a premonition of disaster. The king's buffoon, Hua Maighléni, was brought in and he regaled the company with vivid accounts of the brave deeds of the Leinstermen, so that fear and dread (as well as the winter storm) prevented Fergal and his men from sleeping well that night.[41] During the slaughter on the following day, he was captured and beheaded along with Fergal Mac Maeldúin, king of Ireland, and his entire army by the men of Leinster. Among the dead were the royal buffoon (*rigdruth* or 'king's druid'), Hua Maighléni who, when taken prisoner during battle, was commanded to let out the 'buffoon's roar' (*géim drúith*) which, the story emphasises, was loud and sweet. But when his head was cut off, ('according to some scholars') the roar lasted for three days and nights and it remained thereafter with the buffoons of Ireland.[42] Also laying dead in the battlefield were the professional men (*aosdána*) of Fergal's court, such as the players of *corn, cuisleann*, and *cruit*. And the wail or *dordfhiansa* emanated from Donn Bó's severed head.[43] It was brought back to the camp of the victorious Leinstermen and placed upon a post, and Donn Bó was asked to provide amusement, where-upon he turned his face away towards the wall (in order to be in the dark) and let out the *dordfhiansa*[44] which in its plaintive sweetness moved even his enemies to tears and lamenting.[45]

There are other terms which appear to have definite contexts, but which it is equally impossible to understand with the distance in time, for example, *aidbse, cepóc* and *certán*, all of which refer to ritualised vocal sounds. The first of these may refer to recitation or to choral music; it is used to describe the praising of Colm Cille by the gathered company of the poets of Ireland on the occasion of the Synod of Droim Cet.[46] *Certán* refers to humming, or to 'little' music; *crónán* to humming – *crónánaigh* are included as a partic-ular class of entertainers, grouped with *fedánaig*, in late glosses concerned with the classification of royal retinue.[47] *Dord* seems to refer to a drone, a low humming sound used in a variety of contexts. For example, the low murmuring of the great brown bull of the *Táin*, the *Dond Chuailgne*:

> It was one of the gifts of the Dond Chuailgne that the *cranndord* which he performed every evening at coming home to his fastness and his cow-house and his cow-stand, was music (*ceoil*) and entertainment (*airfiti*) sufficient for the persons who were at the northern extremity, the south-ern extremity, and in the centre of the entire cantred of Cuailgne.[48]

This represents a most interesting example of the symbolic power of sound: the use of quasi-technical terms emphasises the importance attached to the ownership of this magnificent beast, and to the high, even supernatural, status attached to bulls and to cattle in general in medieval Ireland. Considering that the honour-price or legal status of members of human society was eval-uated in terms of cattle, and wealth and social status depended to a large extent on the size of one's herd, the low murmuring of an almost god-like creature like the Bull of the Táin must have been an awe-inspiring, emotion-arousing experience.

The term *dord* occurs most frequently in association with the Ulster Cycle tales of the Fianna, in forms such as *dordán, andord*, and *dordfhiansa*. There is insufficient detail in the sources to formulate any clear technical distinction between these, but they all appear to occur in the context of male group-bonding. In a tale from Acallam na Senórach, there is an account of a band of herdsmen who sang sweet music for Cailte, one of Fionn Mac Cumhaill leading associates, when he encountered them while travelling in what is now Co. Kerry. This reminded Cailte of the singing of the Fian warriors when they were young men. Their repertory included *dordán, dord, dord-fhiansa, cronán*, in addition to *fead* (a whistle); they sang the *dord* when on the march, and also when visiting the fair of Cruachan. The term *andord* (literally, 'non-*dord*') occurs in the Lament of Deirdre for the Sons of Uisnech:

> The heavy wave-voice of Nois
> It was sweet music for ear to be ever hearing;
> Ardan's *cobhlach* was good;
> and Ainle's *andord* towards his wild hut.[49]

O'Curry interpreted this passage as referring to four-part, concerted singing because the description, taken from *cruit*-string terminology, refers to four registers, low, medium, high and very high. However, there is every justification for scepticism and it is equally likely that it represents a more general account of the vocal range of the warriors concerned, in other words, their personal characteristics. It may perhaps have a further symbolic implication of a balanced, integrated group, forming a single 'instrument' in the same way as a *cruit* has four tonal registers to produce a vibrant, melodious whole.

There is somewhat more ground to be gained in investigating the function of the *dordfhiansa*, exclusively associated with the Fianna warriors, and sometimes described as being performed to the clashing of the wooden handles of their gold-socketed spears – possibly a sword dance accompanied by singing. It is referred to in the context of a display of prowess when members of the Fianna arrived on formal visitations, for example, in a story from the Acallam where Find Mac Cumhaill arrives at the gates of Emania and the entire group perform the *dordfhiansa* outside of the palace before seeking the hand of the king of Ulster's daughter. A similar tale is told in the story of the Battle of Ventry (*Caith Finntraigh*) of a visitation to the princess of Munster when Coel set out to woo her.[50]

It may be significant in that the association of spear-dancing with the Fianna corresponds with what is known also of early medieval Germanic warrior activities. *Männerbünde*, or brotherhoods of landless warriors, young men between childhood and full adulthood, awaiting their inheritance, formed themselves into warrior bands and roamed the countryside in search of fortune and adventure.[51] The particular songs and sword-dances (or in the Irish case, spear-dances) which they performed reinforced their sense of group identity and were used as a display of physical prowess. These practices form part of the long-term history of morris dancing, recruitment dances etc. which still survive in living memory in Central and Eastern Europe.[52] We do not have a very clear picture of their use in Ireland, but references do exist to sword- and withy-dancing in a report from Fynes Moryson *c*1600.[53] Such a dance is depicted on a bone book-cover found in a private house in Donabate, Co. Dublin in 1850. It is thought to date to the fifteenth/sixteenth centuries[54] and seems to have originated in Munster, since it bears the arms of one of the Desmond Fitzgeralds. Whether the dancing group represent an actual recruitment ritual, or a mimetic display for entertainment, we shall never know, but it is likely to indicate the former existence of both activities.[55]

Golghaire Banside, The Lament of the Otherworld Women, and lamenting as a whole, also represent an area rich for further investigation. There is an interesting myth of origin about funeral wailing contained in the story of Táin Bó Fraích. When Fraích is injured and detained at the Connacht fort of Ailill and Medb, the goddess Boand ('Boyne'), who is his aunt, together with her female companions, three times fifty of them, are heard (*sic*) lamenting as they arrive at Cruachan wearing purple tunics and green head-dresses. They depart again with Fraích and their wailing is heard as they make their way (*a ngol ac dul úad*) back to the lios. It is mentioned at the end of the story that from that occasion the lamenting of the bansíde (*golgaire ban síde*) became known to the musicians of Ireland (*áes ciúil Hérenn*).[56]

Another interesting technicality is included in the ninth-century story of the Battle of Moytura (*Cath Maige Tuired*). During the battle between the Tuatha Dé Danann and the Fomorians, Rúadán, a member of the latter group, was attacked by a spear and subsequently died in the presence of his father and the Fomorian assembly. His mother Bríg then came to lament her son (*Tig Bric [ocus] cáines a ma*c). At first she shrieked, in the end she wept (*Éghis ar tos, goilis fo deog*). And the story ends: 'Then for the first time weeping and shrieking were heard in Ireland. (Now she is the Bríg who invented a whistle [*feit*] for signalling at night.)'[57]

It is not my intention to deal at length here with the enormous topic of funeral lamenting. Much remains to be done on the medieval sources. I have included these references here primarily because they serve to illustrate their function as symbolic sound, and because it is evident, in the latter case, that not all of the utterances fall within what is normally construed as 'music', i.e., fully-developed melody, or even what might be classed as chanting or intoning. It is an excellent illustration of the risks involved in drawing too firm a line between categories of intentional human sound, thereby overlooking important aspects of their psychological import.[58]

As a final example, the *craebh ciúil*, or 'branch of music', a stick with (usually three) metal balls (presumably bells), the poet's branch, was used as a symbol of office, shaken to announce the beginning of proceedings, or to calm the crowd into silence.[59] At *Fled Bricrind*, or Bricriu's feast, when the company began to quarrel loudly, Sencha, poet and chief advisor to King Concobar Mac Nessa, stood up, shook his branch, and all of the Ulster people gathered there fell silent to hear him.

The poet's staff or *crann chiuil* appears to have been more than a symbol his activities, but also informed as to his relative status in his profession. In the Dialogue of the Two Sages (*Agallamh an da Shuadh*), reference is made to a gold branch as symbol of the chief poet or *ollamh*, a silver branch for the second-grade poet of *anradh*, while all other poets carried one of bronze.[60] The reference to metals of varying degrees of value is of course indicative of rank.

Similarly, one notes the reference in the law tract, the *Senchus Mór*, whereby fines are imposed for stealing

> a bell [*cloc*] from the necks of cattle: i.e., privileged cattle, i.e. which sounds from the necks of cattle, i.e. which makes privileged cattle of them, i.e. it is about them every night, or depending from their necks that they may be known, i.e. the fine which will be paid to a person for taking the privileged cattle in distress from him, is to be paid by him for making privileged cattle of them before the arrival of the time of their being exempted from being taken in distress from him.[61]

The use of something similar to a sounding gong is also referred to in *Tochmarc Eimire* ('The Wooing of Emer') where Concobar is described as commanding silence in his court by striking the red bronze post of his couch with a silver stick, and using his royal wand[62] to strike a silver plate which hung above him and reached to the roof of the palace.

The symbolic presence of such a sounding instrument is surely echoed in the importance attached to clerical bells, horns and stringed instruments, particularly when associated with saints. But these matters take us into other topics which will be dealt with in greater detail below. The purpose in mentioning them here is to underline the interdependent meanings and associations of objects and aural-physical experiences across different contexts, and the associated symbolism of their reproduction in mimetic behaviour.

3. SOUND SYMBOLS OF EARTHLY POWER AND RANK

Pre-Norman Irish society was characteristically 'heroic', consisting of social groups within areas dominated by a dynastic overlord (or *ríg*). Far from being self-contained or stable, these political rulers were constantly vying with one another for land and power in both monastic and secular institutions, there being little to separate these interests, for the same families were usually in control of both, abbots and kings often being of the same blood. It was a society which depended on farmer-soldiers, an agricultural-warrior society, where survival depended on increasing one's lands in order to maintain control of one's property; to stand still was to lose, for someone else was gaining. Group cohesion among the established was court-based in the sense that a household was ruled by a king with a retinue of advisors (historians, jurists, priests), craftsmen, warriors, agricultural labourers, and their extended families. But it was not a court society in the later sense in which that term is generally used, implying a settled court with a power monopoly in the hands of a single ruler, with relative pacification of the surrounding territory resulting in long-term stability, such as first manifested itself, in European terms, in eleventh-/twelfth-century France and subsequently England. No one person had the monopoly of power in pre-Norman Ireland (though many attempted it, and some nearly achieved it, as in the case of Brian Bóroime in the early eleventh century).

A society which depends on its warriors for survival also depends on leaders who are close to the action, on leaders who themselves are in constant fear for their physical safety. In such a situation there is less scope for developing elaborate administrative structures and codes of conduct and sentiment, such as extended rituals, refinement of table manners and styles of dress, or the patronage of artistic pursuits such as painting, sculpture and music. The kind of monopoly of wealth and power required to plan and produce, say, the Gothic cathedrals of France or the Palace at Westminster – or the music which was performed in them – depended on long-term stability of political rulers, strong defence of the marches, which were a long way from the centres of urban life, the time and the resources to train specialist craftsmen, reserves of capital to pay them, and leisure time to enjoy their products. Elaborate court ceremonial and attendant rituals accompany this gradual civilizing or pacification process, a process which remains fundamental to explaining all other processes, all social structures, without which there can be no deeper understanding of social behaviour, the arts included. Social context is no mere accompaniment or background framework of reference: it is of the essence in any analysis.

Members of a warrior society, such as characterised pre-Norman Ireland, depended on land ownership for social status, and on honour as a code of conduct between its members. The Old Irish law tracts and mythological tales all emphasise the importance of personal honour as a symbol of reliability and credibility. Social rank was legally defined in terms of property and 'honour-price', the latter referring to a scale of fines which could be claimed for various kinds of injury from third parties. A society in which property and honour are determinants, essentially, of one's very security and existence in law, demands a very public manifestation of status. In order to maintain that monopoly of power one needs to display it constantly in order i) to ward off other contenders from attempts to undermine it, and ii) to maintain loyalty among one's followers by providing for them to their satisfaction so that they will not be tempted to take their allegiance elsewhere.

In Gaelic Ireland, as in other warrior as well as court societies, occasional displays of 'conspicuous consumption' were essential to this process. Feasts and large assemblies represented an important part of power maintenance, demonstrating the generosity of the king who provided food and drink, and all manner of entertainment, to show off his wealth and to sustain his following. To bolster his status, he employed historians, poets, musicians all of whom served him, literally, by 'paying court' in the form of genealogies and other historical materials tailored to the glorification of his family and forebears, poetry and songs of praise, brilliance in instrumental performance which won the admiration of audiences, and so on. In addition to the kingly élite, there was also a separate class of *briugu*, the highest class of commoner, whose sole function was to honour the code of hospitality towards those who came to avail of it, according to their rank, failing which a *briugu* lost status and became the butt of satire and ridicule.[63]

With hospitality and public display invariably come all the attendant symbols of status including music and other entertainment. And so it is no surprise to find in the literary sources the same kinds of information on status for musicians as for other members of society. The most telling comments concern their rank, which is defined according to the instruments they play which, in turn, inform as to their respective public rôles.

As long established also elsewhere in Europe, an Irish court musician was invariably a string player (on *cruit*, more rarely *timpan*). According to one Old Irish law tract, the *Uraiccecht Bec* or 'Small Primer', he enjoyed professional standing recognised in law as equivalent to the highest grade of independent commoner or 'cow freeman', that of a superior *bó-aire* (i.e., entitled to an honour-price, compensation for injury, of four cows).[64] In some tracts it is allowed that he enjoyed this status whether or not in the employ of a court, and that he was free to travel about as he wished. Players of a wind instrument known as *cuisle* also appears to have been ranked fairly high among the entertainers but they, together with other less specialised musicians and general entertainers such as *cronánaig*, whistle-players (*fedánaig*), equestrians who perform acrobatics on horse-back, spear-jugglers (*clesamnaig*), buffoons (*fuirseoiri*), podicicinists (*brugedoiri*) and practitioners of 'mean' (i.e., base) arts in general, had no status unless officially attached to a patron. In other words, compensation for any injury done them was due only to their patron, thus rated according to his status alone. Another tract known as the *Crith Gabhlach* underlines the relative status of the members of a king's court by describing their seating order in the assembly hall. Next to the king at the eastern end sit his unforfeited hostages and visiting guests, next to them the king's poets, followed by his *cruit*-players. At the other end of the hall, in the south-east part near to the door are seated the players of *fedán* and *corn* as well as jugglers and other entertainers.[65]

The scribes of both the twelfth-century Book of Leinster and the late-fourteenth-century Yellow Book of Lecan provide an additional insight into this system of grading. Both of these sources contain an imaginary sketch of the great banqueting hall at Tara as it might have been in the days of King Cormac Mac Airt.[66] Although the later manuscript provides more detail, both sources contain depictions of seating arrangements and portions of meat due to all those present at the king's table, according to their rank. In the centre aisle are three hearths, a cauldron, a candlestick, and a lantern; the long tables are arranged two deep on either side. In the Book of Leinster version we observe *cruit*-players seated at the left-hand outer table between horsemen and judges; they are due pigs' shoulders, along with deer-stalkers, fifth-grade poets, champions, master wrights, and their successors. *Timpán*-players are included with *cruitiri* in the Yellow Book of Lecan drawing.

Cuislennaigh are seated at the left-hand inner table towards the top end, next to the schoolteachers, and in line with the string-players. This group is served the shin portions, as are *Aire Desa*, fourth-grade nobility, and chess-players, soothsayers, and druids. *Cornairi* and *buinniri* are seated further down at the same table nearer to the door between builders and wrights on one side and engravers on the other. These musicians (in the same position but on the inner table in the YBL) are due cheering mead[67] – on a par with cooks. *Fedánaig* and *cronánaig* are listed also among general entertainers in a gloss in the *Uraiccecht Bec*, but not specifically in the drawings. It is noteworthy that while only string-players are classified as freemen, *cuislennaig* are on a par with school-teachers, while all of the musicians included in the diagram occupy positions superior to buffoons (*fuirseoiri*) and conjurors (*clesamnaig*), who are entitled to pig's shin bones, king's fools (*druth*), back bones, and satirists (*cainte*) – podicicinists (*brigedoiri*) are also included in the Yellow Book of Lecan – and cordwainers, shoulder fat.

The laws also provided for compensation of a more immediately practical nature whereby, according to the *Senchus Mor* glossator, a *cruit*-player is entitled to requisites such as his tuning key (*crand glésta*[68]), strings, etc. during his time of playing. (The Book of Aicill provides interesting information on compensation for various kinds of physical injury, including the loss of the top of a finger. In the case of a *timpán*-player,[69] if his nail was cut off he was entitled to a 'wing nail' (presumably a quill plectrum).

Within the feudal social system an individual with unfree status might acquire franchise by practising a skilled trade. Therefore not only *cruit*-players but also smiths and physicians were classed as freemen according to the maxim of law, '*is ferr fer a chiniúd*' ('a man is better than his birth').[70] However, although we are lacking information on the genealogies, and even the individual identities of all but a handful of musicians, the usual pattern of recruitment was on the basis of heredity, as in other professions:

> Let the *corn*-player's son carry the *corn* . . . let the cleric's son take to
> the circuit, joyfully singing the psalms [*do gabáil co suairc na salm*]
>
> Let the *cruit*-player's son carry the *cruit*: that will not harm either of them
>
> The son of the *timpán*-player of the strings [*mac an timpánaig na tét*]:
> let him play a pleasant tune [*issé a bés gabáil grés nglan*][71]

Chieftains' courts provided open house to travelling musicians and poets who received hospitality and gifts in return for their services of entertainment. The subject of a poem was often, not surprisingly, that of praise for the host. This emphasis on hospitality, and loss of face for its absence, gave much power to poets and musicians right up to the end of the Gaelic order at the close of the seventeenth century (a pattern which was adopted also by Anglo-Irish and English families who had long become acculturated within Irish feudal society, acting as hosts and patrons just like the Gaelic lords, their homes similarly functioning as centres of 'court'-like activities).[72]

From the numerous references to music instruments and related activity found within Irish literary sources we may form some idea as to the importance attached to entertainment at the courts; but the kind of music it was, stylistically or structurally, and the precise nature of the instruments, eludes us, for no accounts are sufficiently detailed. We are thus heavily dependent upon comparative information from British and Continental manuscript and art historical sources for suggestions and implications as to possible instrumental types, a situation far from tenuous as the extent of Irish contact with people from several parts of Europe is attested in many fields of enquiry (paleography, literature, archaeology, architecture, ornamental design and other art-work). But it is impossible to establish whether there were characteristically Irish instruments in existence during the Early or High Middle Ages. We may assume a great diversity of regional styles throughout the whole West European area although it is not accurate to speak of the 'medieval Irish harp' unless we speak in general typological terms, since we know nothing precise about any harps from Ireland of that time. Unfortunately, Irish, Welsh and medieval English literature are not specific enough to inform us on these matters but twelfth- and thirteenth-century French romances abound in such references. In one of the numerous Tristan stories from a French thirteenth-century manuscript, King Marc recognizes the visiting harper, Helyot, and sees from the style of his instrument that he comes from the Kingdom of Logres. Extraordinary accomplishments are praised in Gottfrid von Straßburg's verse narrative of the Romance of Tristan, where the hero is credited with performing songs in Irish, Welsh, Latin, French and German, which might well also imply as many distinctive styles and timbres.

The question of ranking and social function of music instruments – or rather of their players, of whose social networks an instrument is symbol – is central to any investigation of medieval European music history. At the English and French courts as well as within the German-speaking principalities, trumpeters commanded the highest status, probably because the performance of their office affirmed the authority and presence of the ruler (whether indoors at ceremonial occasions or outdoors). Players of stringed instruments, such as various forms of lute and harp, were often accorded the status of second rank, being members of the courtly retinue who were required to provide music for indoor convivial gatherings such as banquets, or for more private occasions such as the diversion or consolation of an individual in the bedchamber. At a lower level were various other unattached minstrels, some of whom occasionally gained access to court audiences but otherwise entertained at fairs, at peasant weddings, and at outdoor spectacles or tournaments. Consistently, the most reviled group were beggars who often performed on hurdy-gurdies, accompanied dancing bears and otherwise performed feats of acrobatics and juggling wherever they were tolerated.

At the Irish courts, as elsewhere, musicians were there to honour, to entertain, to form part of the retinue of symbolic power and display on behalf of kings, hospitallers and bands of young warriors on occasions of feasts, hostings, leisure-time activities, and when on journeys. Although the narrative tales are ostensibly mythological and were recited for entertainment, they inform us greatly about the reciters and their patrons. Exaggeration in accounts of personal valour or misfortune seems to have been an important convention. Detailed descriptions of super-human deeds and heroic attitudes inform us as to likely codes of the time. And there are numerous references to music: music which soothes, music which assists the casting of spells, music for tricking enemies, for praising gods; stringed instruments with golden tuning pegs and silver strings. The most common characteristics alluded to in the Irish manuscripts are weeping music, laughing music, and sleeping music, classifications of great antiquity which have been observed in disparate cultures and civilizations. But of course this is insufficient as an explanation for their continued use in an Irish context, or indeed contexts, for their meaning and significance are bound to have changed over time. As they occur in the literature, they are usually performed for the purpose of confounding an enemy or aiding a pair of lovers (e.g., in order to plot an escape), comforting and healing the sick, wounded warriors, tired kings and women in labour, as well as in general leisure pursuits. They were also performed also on the occasion of *Samhain* or Hallowe'en, the beginning of the Celtic New Year, which became christianised as All Souls'.[73]

Musicians were also necessary to military campaigns and royal progresses; accompanying the warriors with brave martial music, vocal sounds, battle-cries and drones, as well as the sounding of wind instruments producing terrifying sounds to put the enemy at a psychological disadvantage. Geoffrey Keating, in his History of Ireland, provided a description of threefold sounding of wind instruments before commencement of a feast in the banqueting hall at Tara:

> the first time for the entry of the shield-bearers of the nobility and the hanging of each shield in its appropriate place, the second time for the entry of the shield-bearers of the leaders of warriors and the hanging of their shields, and the third time for the entry of all the guests.[74]

Classical commentators on warfare practices among the continental Celts, for example, the Greek Poseidonios, wrote *c*80 BC (several centuries before these manuscripts were copied) about the barbaric nature and harsh sounds of the Celtic war-horns which he termed *salpinx* (plural, *salpinges*). Polybius (*c*200 BC–*post* 118 BC), a Greek writer on the Battle of Telamon, described the terrifying effect on the Roman army of the din and clamour created by large numbers of Celtic trumpeters and horn-blowers, and by the war-cries of the entire Celtic army. He also added that there was great fear inspired by the appearance and gestures of the finely-built, naked warriors in the front rank, and by their leaders who were richly adorned with gold.[75] An interesting comment on psychological insight is provided in the Irish account of the Civil War of the Romans, which is a free adaptation of Lucan's *Pharsalia*. On one occasion Caesar's troops were said not to have needed the additional excitement-arousal provided by their military instruments (listed as *stuic, sturgana, cuirn, cuislenna catha*), 'for their work and their duty were supporting them'.[76] The use of large metal instruments as symbols of prestige is long established in Ireland and can be traced to the Bronze Age. Their precise function has eluded us so far, but their symbolic significance as objects of high prestige is borne out by examination of their technology and the costly materials with which they were made.[77] Horns of wood are also known from the early middle ages, including instruments associated with clerical practices, a topic to which I shall return in the next section.

Wind instruments were not only instruments of war and court ceremonial, however. In the *Táin Bó Fraích*, there is an account of magical horns. Fraích, the human son of an Otherworld woman, went on a mission to woo Findabair, daughter of Ailill and Medb, monarchs of Connacht. His hosts caused him a severe illness by inducing him to enter a pool where he was attacked by a water-monster. His horn-players (*a chornairi*) went ahead to the fort whereupon the melting plaintiveness of their music causes thirty of Ailill's dearest friends to die of rapture.[78] It may reasonably be assumed that here something more elaborate than signalling instruments was in question (though not necessarily producing melody as we might understand it). In Fraích's retinue were also other professional entertainers whose duty it presumably was to provide services while camped for the night. The party was preceded by three buffoons (*druith*[79]), wearing coronets; it also included seven horn players (*cornaire*) with instruments of gold and silver, wearing many-coloured clothes and white shirts; three *cruit*-players, each with the appearance of a king from the style of his dress, his arms and his steed.[80]

This description is one of the most elaborate in terms of detail, and needs to be presented more fully. The instruments referred to as *cruit* were carried in bags of otterskin, ornamented with coral over which was more ornamentation of gold and silver. The bags were lined on the inside with white roebuck skins, these in turn overlaid with black-grey strips of skin.[81] White linen cloths were wrapped around the strings. The frames of the instruments were decorated in gold, silver and *findruine* with figures of serpents, birds and greyhounds. As the strings vibrated, these figures 'went around the men', in other words, appeared to move and dance with the movement of the instrument and the vibrating strings. The musicians played the three strains of weeping, laughing and sleeping music, just as they had done when Fraích's mother was in labour, reflecting the sequence of her emotions of pain, joy and rest, and soothing her in the process.

The Tale of Donn Bó also refers to Fergus's retinue which included players of *cruit, cuisleann* and *corn*. On the eve of the Battle of Magh Rath, Congal Claen, Prince of Ulster, was put to sleep by the gentle sounds of the *cuisleann ciuil* and by playing of *cruit* and *timpan*, according to a late twelfth-century version.[82]

As though to emphasise the importance of hospitality, good manners, and the ongoing need to maintain one's reputation, the tale of Bres from Cath Maighe Tuired provides an excellent example of a cautionary tale, one which bears out all that has been discussed so far. Bres is typified as the personification of incompetent kingship who loses honour by failing to offer hospitality and because he does not have regard for the arts. The Tuatha Dé Danann complain that they were never offered ale when they visited his house, nor on any occasion did they encounter his entertainers there. They never saw his poet (*a filidh*), his bards (*a mbardan*), or his satirists (*a cáinte*), or his *cruitire* or his *cuslendaib*, or his *cornaire*, or his *clesamhnaig* or his *ónmide* (fools). 'They did not go to contests of those preeminent arts. Nor did they see the warriors proving their skill at arms before the king, only Oghmai mac Etnae who fetched the firewood'![83]

4. SOUND SYMBOLS OF SUPERNATURAL POWER

In an informative article, Peter Crossley-Holland[84] explores this constant
theme of Irish saga literature with reference to the Dagda's *crot* from the
Battle of Maige Tuired, a mythical contest between the Tuatha Dé Danann
(whose three gods were Lugh, the Dagda himself and Ogma) and the
Fomorians. Crossley-Holland suggests that one of the symbolic meanings of
the three kinds of music concerns the seasons of winter (weeping), summer
(laughing) and autumn (sleeping). His discussion ranges more widely into
the topic of cosmology, the harmonious ordering of the universe and of
nature (represented here in analogy with sound), and the importance of the
sun (the Dagda was the Sun god) as ruler of all of this. In addition to any
long-term explanation of such symbolism, it needs to be understood as an
inherited metaphor in the hands of genealogists and historians who embellished the tales of conquest and valour in order to suit the particular version
of the past which they wished to present.

Since, as McCone reminds us, '[t]he greatest battle was between the clerics and the pagan druids',[85] it is not surprising that the topic of music, and
the feats of musicians, also occur in a Christian context. For example, St
Brigid visited the King of Munster to beg the release of a prisoner. The king
was absent and she asked his friends to play on the instruments (*'citharizate
nobis citharis vestris'*) which were hanging on the walls. They replied that
all the court *cithara*-players were absent; but she performed a miracle so
that the gathered guests found that they too were able to play.[86]

The wearing of a prayer as a talisman about the neck was surely also a
transference from pre-Christian practice. The greatest rivals to the Christian
clergy were the druids since they too had power to commune with the
Otherworld, and thus represented an alternative belief-system with control
over the minds and hearts of would-be converts. The relative unacceptabili-
ty of 'magical incantations' and other powers associated with the chanting
of non-Christians is counter-balanced by the exceptional promotion of private prayer, including litanies, in early medieval Ireland. One cannot but be
struck by the emphasis on counting and repetition,[87] and on the very earth-
bound, physical tangibility of prayers such as the 'breastplate' or Lorica of
Laidchenn, and the fact that there are accounts of people actually wearing a
prayer around the neck as a form of protection. In a version of the story of
the Vision of Mac Conglinne there is a conversation between the latter and a
phantom who tries to tempt him to partake of a magnificent feast, with references to placing a cheese in the shape of a gospel around his neck, to
which MacConglinne replies that he will put his own paternoster around the
phantom's neck, 'and neither greed nor hunger can visit him round whom it is
put'.[88] One could hardly imagine a more materialised use of symbolic sound

than to wear an utterance on one's person. The emphasis on repetition of Christian prayer as a kind of mantra does, I would venture to suggest, appear to connect quite convincingly with its having replaced (or countered) other kinds of 'spell'. Similarly the singing of hymns also served as a protection against bad luck. Carney observes, in his discussion of the poems of the eighth-century Blathmac, that the poet 'has a reverent perception of the mystery, the awesomeness, and the power of the chanted word' and that these and other religious texts (in this case hymns of devotion to Mary) 'are conceived of as a breast-plate and helmet against evil powers'.[89]

Rather like the christianisation of incantations, in order words the process of adaptation of non-Christian prayer to Christian prayer, non-human, sound-producing instruments seem to have been similarly 'converted', being very much part of the regalia of saints and holy men, and appearing to match their awe-inducing symbolic power in secular society. A story from the life of St Mac Creiche, purporting to relate an incident from the sixth century, well illustrates this. Along with pestilence and other misfortune, the people of the region of Inchiquin, Co. Clare, were tormented by a monster and they appealed to a group of holy men to use their powers to save them. One day, as the monster chased the local herds of cattle, the clergy led by three saints attempted to scare off the monster by sounding their bells (*cloicc*) and their *ceoláin*[90] and making a great noise with their reliquaries and their croziers, followed by the local people who shouted in assistance.[91]

Saints' bells were preserved as religious relics for many centuries, in some cases special shrines were made, just as they were made also for books and other objects, in order to house them safely. Some of these shrines, such as the *Cathach* ('Battler') of St Columba and the Shrine of St Mogue (*Breac Maedóic*) were carried into battle as a form of symbolic protection. The latter, which is pictured on the dustjacket of the present publication series,[92] served as a talisman in various kinds of contest.[93] It may even be that the harp-playing figure was intended to represent the saint himself for, as we have remarked above, clerics were known to travel about with a small stringed instrument on which they used to accompany their own singing. A late recension of Gerald of Wales's *Topographia hibernica* adds to the stock of information on this practice. Since it is a late addition to the *Topographia*, we cannot be certain that it originated from Gerald or his circle; in any case, the reference is in the past tense. Nevertheless, it serves as grist to the mill of a credible and reasonably accredited, even if not positiviely verifiable, practice:

> Thus it was that bishops and abbots and holy men in Ireland carried their *citharas* about and delighted in playing pious music upon them. Because of this, St Kevin's *cithara* is held in no mean reverence by the natives and until this day is regarded as a great and sacred relic.[94]

A tale from the Book of Lecan also refers to this practice.[95] One is struck too by representations on the Irish high crosses where some images of musicians performing on instruments are clearly intended to represent clerics, just as is seen on the Shrine of the Stowe Missal.[96]

Other tales from these sources concern fear of the supernatural powers embodied in saints' horns.[97] In the *Topographia* there is an account of a poor Irish mendicant in Wales who always carried St Brendan's bronze horn about his neck as a relic. He held it out to be kissed (an Irish custom, according to Gerald) by members of an attendant crowd, whereupon it was snatched by a priest named Bernard.[98] Bernard blew the instrument and was struck down with a double sickness within the hour, losing the powers of speech and of memory. Gerald claimed that he met him some days later and witnessed the fact that the priest no longer knew the psalms by heart and required assistance with elementary literacy, in contrast to his previous skills.

A variant of this story is given in Gerald's *Descriptio Cambriae* where the case concerns St Patrick's horn of bronze. The saint's instrument was held in such respect that nobody ever dared blow it until one day, when it was being carried about the neck by a bearer at a funeral, it was held out to be kissed. Bernard, in this version, suffered an immediate attack and had to travel from Wales to Ireland in order to seek a cure from St Patrick himself. His recovery was only partial. Such tales should be viewed as evidence of the power – wished-for or otherwise – of clerics. They suggest parables intended to warn unbelievers and those unwilling to respect the authority of the cloth. Their magico-mythical associations are strongly suggestive of a christianisation of pagan fears.[99]

As discussed above, certain wind instruments used in battle and other military manoeuvres had the power to inspire fear and dread of their owners' fighting skills in all potential victims. Similar accounts of clerical use of horns – and other instruments – is also therefore likely to be an accurate reflection of local practices. It is probably no coincidence either that not only bells and stringed instruments but also horns appear to have been used as a liturgical instrument in the Irish church. A horn recovered from the bed of the River Erne and dating to the eighth/ninth century bears decoration similar to that found on bells and (sacred) buckets of the period. It is made of two pieces of yew, a sacred wood, lapped together with bronze fittings. The location of the find is close to two ancient monastic sites. The hypothesis is further attested by annalistic references to horns with metal fittings and precious stones which were the property of the monasteries of Clonmacnoise and Derry; there are also other references to such objects being included among church treasury in twelfth-century Ireland.[100] Although we lack any precise accounts of the function of these instruments, further evidence for their clerical use is demonstrated on the ninth/tenth-century Irish high crosses, the Cross of

Muireadach at Monasterboice, Durrow Cross, and the Cross of the Scriptures at Clonmacnoise. In all three cases a horn-player is depicted on the side of the Just in scenes from the Last Judgement/Christ in Glory. In Monasterboice, where there is exceptional attention to detail, the horn-player joins with a string-player in leading the assembled clerics in singing from a book, possibly the Psalter or a collection of hymns. The choir is represented by tonsured monks in robes. The Durrow carvings feature a horn player behind whom is seated a lyre-player; while Clonmacnoise features a horn-player on either side of Christ.[101] In these cases the horn is not curved but straight with a bell-shaped terminal, closely resembling the River Erne find (its length is 58.5cm).[102] A curved horn is included among the instruments played (the others are a harp and a set of triple pipes) by a group of three cowled ecclesiastics on a tenth-century cross slab at Ardchattan, Argyll, Scotland.[103]

There is clearly much more investigation to be carried out on this topic; but it might be worth considering several interrelated points when attempting to understand the supernatural associations of horns: horns were not only sounding instruments; they were also used as vessels (as alternatives to a situla or bucket) for containing the sacred oil for anointing priests[104] (and monarchs). It is possible that this association of sanctity applied equally to both uses of the horn. And furthermore, sacred unction was part of the inauguration of kings in many ancient societies. A parallel set of functions applied to an instrument made of buffalo horn, the *corn buabhaill* or *benn buabhaill*, in Irish mythological sources. The former term was more usually applied to its use as a drinking vessel, from which the king drank his ale; the latter when used as a wind instrument as a preliminary to battle, or as a warning signal of some kind. One occasion of ale-drinking was the ritual of newly-anointed kings. Nobody else was permitted to drink from the king's horn, a sacrosanct symbolic object.[105]

While one cannot reconstruct the sounds which may have been produced on horns, whether simple signals, soft or loud drones, whether sounded together at different pitches; but clearly they were highly prized and held in awe.

5. SOUND SYMBOLS OF SAINTLINESS, GOOD AND EVIL

Medieval Irish literature, as it comes down to us, is essentially an exercise in political propaganda, including an emphasis on preaching Christian morality. It represents a revised version of Irish pre-Patrician history whose function it was to complement the post-Patrician period which was dominated and controlled by 'a highly trained, highly self-aware mandarin class . . . the worlds of native and ecclesiastical learning had merged long before the bulk of the surviving texts were redacted – a matter which is of very considerable consequence.'[106] And so there is a moral tale embedded within every event, adapted to the rightful, One-God-centred world view, in which those who conform represent the established on earth and the elect in the next world. All others are cast in the role of outsiders, non-believers, untrustworthy, and damned. Part of the challenge of incorporating the native mythology or 'pre-history' within the new order involved explaining pre-Christian practices in terms of ignorance and subsequent renunciation as a result of enlightenment, or of resistance which could only be relegated to the world of evil and the devil, depending on the nature of the event. Here too, music (and other symbolic sounds!) were used to drive home the message. An example is provided by the eighth-century legal tract *Cóerus Béscnai* in which the question is posed, 'how many feasts (*fleda*) are there?' The tripartite response, in descending order of status of the medieval Irish estates of Church, refers to a godly feast, a human feast and a devilish feast. The devilish feast

> . . . is given to sons of death (*do macaib báis*) and bad people, i.e. to buffoons (*do druthaib* . . . possibly originally *druídib* 'to druids') and satirists (*7 cáintib*) and begging poets (*7 oblairib*) and farters[107] and clowns (*7 fuirseoraib*) and bandits and pagans (*7 geintib*) and whores (*7 merdrechaib*) and other bad people. For every feast that is not given for earthly exchange, and is not given for heavenly reward, that feast belongs to the devil.[108]

One is reminded of the ranking order of musicians and other entertainers discussed already. In this case the tale serves to reinforce a clerical twist on the situation, with status accruing to those who pay their dues to the church in the form of a 'godly feast', and to those clients who honour their lord in the form of a 'human feast' such as hospitality, while stigmatizing those who fail in their obligations, among whom are all manner of outcasts, damned on earth (and presumably in the hereafter) by their 'devilish feast'.

A similarly colourful account, relying even more heavily on symbolic sound (!), is provided in the tale concerning the Cenél nÉogain king of Tara, Fergal mac Máel Dúin (d.722) and his two sons and successors, the warlike Áed Allán (d.743) and the pious Níall Frossach (d.778). It is preserved in the so-called Fragmentary Annals of Ireland which survive in the form of a transcription dating to 1643 from an original dating perhaps to the beginning of the fifteenth century. When the sons came to visit their father, he wished to test their characters and so after they were fed and entertained he went to the houses in which they were lodged. In the case of the elder son,

> . . . it was very foul indeed inside that house. There were buffoons (*fuirseoiri*) and satirists (*cainteadha*) and horseboys (*eachlacha*) and

jugglers (*oblóiri*) and oafs (*bachlaigh*) roaring and bellowing there (*ag beceadhoig 7 acc buireadhaig ann*). Some were drinking, some sleeping, some vomiting, some playing a *cuisle* (*dream occ cusleannaigh*), some whistling (*dream oc featcuisigh*). *Timpán-* and *cruit*-players performing (*Timpanaigh 7 cruithiri ag seanmaimh*); a group was boasting and arguing.

Whereas in the younger son's house,

[Fergal] heard nothing there but thanksgiving to God for all that they had received, and sweet, quiet *cruit*-playing (*cruitireacht ciúin bínd*) and poems being performed in praise of the Lord (*duana molta an Coimdeadh 'ga ngabail*).[109]

The good musician is the Christian, law-abiding servant; the evildoer consorts with those who do not control their behaviour, are debauched, physically ugly, serving those like themselves (and like Satan).

The image of the good musician, and music which is acceptable within the strictly ordered society of church and court, is a constant theme in both literature and iconography. Here, as in other aspects of medieval Irish society, we err if we attempt to draw clear and mutually-exclusive distinctions between clerical and secular life, or between Latin and Gaelic culture or, for that matter, between church and secular music. They merge like a seamless garment, and once again, we are reminded of the need for caution in over-categorizing on the basis of morphology when the processes of human interaction provide a far more reality-congruent index of social behaviour. The last example illustrates this well. We observe that a *cruit* is mentioned in both situations; and so it is not the instrument itself which is good or evil, but what is played on it and in what circumstances. However, the reference is embellished with lists of other musicians and entertainers of low social standing, along with beggars and whores. Their stigmatization is underlined also in the Hall of Tara sketch where, along with buffoons etc., they are entitled to consume the poorest parts of the pig.

In the Life of St Brendan of Clonfert from the fifteenth-century Book of Lismore, an account is given of a young cleric who entertained the monks on his *cruit* during dinner, following which he went to play for Brendan, abbot of the monastery. The saint, however, filled his ears with wax, explaining that he had been visited seven years before by a bird (the Angel Michael in disguise) who performed for him such heavenly music that he could not longer listen to wordly music. However, as a concession he allowed the cleric to play the 'three strains' (*trí hadhbuinn*) for him, assuring him that he would be rewarded in heaven for that playing.[110]

Here is a clerical sanctioning of the good musician, the holy man of God, rewarded by the saint. Brendan, however, is superior to other humans, and so does not have need of any earthly pleasure. St Maelruain of Tallaght (d.792), similarly, resisted such temptation, according to his Life in a fifteenth-century source written in Late Old Irish of the early ninth.[111] The section actually commences with the observation, 'Also Maelruain did not approve of listening to music' (*cotsecht fris ceola*). This is exemplified by reference to a holy man, the anchorite Cornan of the Glen who lived in south Leinster and was a player of the *cuisle*. He regularly received gifts from Maelruain and wished once to play a tune for him (*adpand do seinm don cleiriuch*). But Maelruain instructed the messenger to tell him that his ears were not for earthly music (*ceolu talman*) so that they 'may be lent to the music of heaven' (*ceoli nime*). This is a point of relative sanctity, therefore; some clerics perform (secular) music, but self-denial is a sign of greater holiness. Interesting also is the reference to a wind instrument in this context, as it is rarely personalised or contextualised. Furthermore, the anchorite in question has been identified by Plummer as Cronan of Glen Aosa mentioned in the Martyrology of Donegal for February 26.[112]

There are variants of this parable also in the tale of Cas Corach, the son of one of the Tuatha Dé Danann chiefs who arrived at the King of Ulster's court dressed as a minstrel, carrying his *timpán* on his back.[113] His purpose was to make the acquaintance of Cailte Mac Ronáin, in order to learn from him new songs and stories to add to his own repertory. Cailte received him warmly and introduced him to St Patrick. The saint, delighted with his playing (which included religious music in praise of the King of Heaven),[114] heard his confession of faith and assured him of his place in heaven on that account and on account of his superb playing. Then preaching a homily, he assured him, 'heaven is thine, and may thy art be one of the three last arts by which a person shall realise his benefit in Erinn; and though the unwelcome which may be intended for a man of thy art, when he has played his music and [told] his stories, may be great, he shall not be any longer unwelcome; and the professors of thy art shall be at all times the couch fellows of kings, and they shall be prosperous provided they be not lazy'.[115]

The christianisation of Ireland's past, including her musicians, is exemplified also in the tale of Donn Bó. When the Leinstermen's emissary found Donn Bó's head on the battlefield, performing a *dordfhiansa* for his king, the former wished to take the head with him (presumably so as he could perform for the enemy court). Donn Bó's head retorted that he preferred that nobody should take him away except for Christ, the Son of God. He then reluctantly agreed provided that an undertaking was given to reunite his head with the rest of his body – presumably so that he would be able to respond to the Call of Judgement. (Is this an attempt to counter certain battle practices?)

We note in the story of Brendan and the monk, as also in other sources, that string playing and entertainment were not the exclusive preserve of the laity, nor of professional secular musicians. Clerics are referred to as string players, particularly in their function of travelling missionaries going about with a small *ocht-tédach* (eight-stringed) attached to the girdle. Monastic centres included schools and so employed musicians together with teachers of other subjects. Here one may assume that alongside teaching of stringed instruments and singing, instruction in chant was also involved. Perhaps only those intended for the monastic life were taught to specialise in chant, but instruction on instruments would hardly have been confined to sacred music. Similarly, those musicians who served in the secular courts were likely also to have been familiar with chant and 'pious music' such as hymns and psalmody. The story above refers to the younger son engaged in singing pious songs in praise of the Lord.

A reference in the tract on taboos of kings includes both those things to be avoided (*gessa*) and those which were lucky to do (*buada*). In the case of the King of Munster, one of his *buada* was to chant the Passion at Lent in Cashel (*coigital chésta Corguis hi Caissil*).[116] There is also a tale concerning Colm Cille's receiving and entertaining the poet, Cronán. When the latter had departed, the saint was asked by his followers why he had not asked his visitor for a poem sung 'with modulation', (i.e., varying pitch, in other words, not spoken).[117] The saint explained that he foresaw the man's imminent death and so it would have been most inappropriate. In this case, it does not seem to have been linked with the impropriety of light-hearted entertainment as such, but represents rather the saint's sensitivity to his fellow humans, as well as his prophetic gifts. (There is a clear parallel between this tale and that of Donn Bó, who would not entertain the court on the eve of a battle which he knew would lead to disaster for the gathered company.)

However, another reference, in the *Amra Coluim Cille*, describes the saint's contrition at having taken pleasure in the performance, referred to as *aidbse*, by the poets of Ireland in his honour, following his blessing of their craft at the Synod of Droim Cet.[118] But here the emphasis appears to be less on the medium itself and more on the message, that of praise from the poets of this world: the saint is advised, rather, to give heed to the judgement of God, but of course it carries resonances for the entire activity of secular entertainment and the desirability of humility.

The most vivid and consistent representation of the good musician is to be found in the numerous carvings of Biblical scenes which still survive on early medieval Irish ecclesiastical monuments in stone and metal. For a long time there has been ongoing controversy as to whether the images on the high crosses, in particular, represent a older 'native' or a more recent continental (i.e., Carolingian) influence. Apart from the fact that many of the scenes are based on biblical accounts, there are some for which a clear, definitive interpretation is impossible. The apparently unprecedented concentration of activity in the production of these images appears to coincide with the development of Carolingian biblical iconography, on stone, glass, and on more portable objects such as ivory, which strongly suggests influence from beyond the sea, whether through travelling Irish missionaries, trade, or importation of foreign craftsmen. There are many aspects to this complex question, however, which are not amenable to an either/or, native/foreign dichotomist approach. For example, there are details of clothing, of armour, of figural representation which require detailed comparative analysis in order to trace their history and associations. And here a close examination of how musicians are portrayed is indeed revealing. It has been a common tendency to regard all musician-images as representing the biblical King David, author of the Psalms and Old Testament Prophet. This has become almost a knee-jerk reaction not only among medievalists, but among many musicologists who continue to undervalue the importance of iconography as a source for the history of music, preferring to cling to the old positivist mythology that some kind of technical description of notated repertories has a monopoly on scientific value, while its absence renders other evidence worthless. The importance of allusion, of myth, of metaphor, to an understanding of music, or any other aspect of human-social behaviour, is every bit as important as, and perhaps more reality-congruent than, reams of Pythagorean discourse or clerical praise and dispraise, because here we begin to build an image of actual processes at work.

While some of the instruments may be modelled on treatises and therefore not related to any known object, there is much on the Irish (and Scottish) monuments which reveals local knowledge. Furthermore, several of the scenes depict a musician where there is no such reference in the biblical source.[119] It may be that David is held up as the model in the carvings: the good musician who sings the praises of God and does not consort with evildoers. But that does not mean to say that the figure is necessarily intended to be interpreted as David in all cases. A realistic Irish scene may be interposed in a local adaptation of biblical stories. The church is marking its territory by enabling certain kinds of musicians and music-making while excluding others, in a similar way that stones with pre-Christian associations were marked with a cross in order to bring older customs within the new fold, thereby disempowering the old order of druids, pantheists and pagans.[120] This iconographic offensive is directly paralleled by the taking over of the mythological tradition by recasting it in a Christian mould. We have very clearly-directed interpretations, but we also observe elements of local norms and practices which existed before as well as during the process of christianisation.

The carving of representations of musicians, particularly string players, is so long attested in Europe that it would be very myopic indeed to suggest that these images came into being, as it were, from nowhere. European warrior-aristocracies, from as far back as the Bronze Age, have customarily engaged the services of string players to sing and accompany accounts of noble deeds and songs in praise of their prowess. There are lyres depicted on funeral stelae of warriors in Zaragoza, Spain (ninth–eighth century BC), and Brittany (c70 BC), as well as in illustrations in situla art from Urnfield and La Tène Hungary and Austria (seventh century BC). Diodorus Siculus (born during the reign of Caesar Augustus, 27 BC–14 AD) commented on the use of such instruments by the continental Celts who had instruments 'resembling [Greek and Roman] lyres' which they used in the accompaniment of eulogies and satires sung by lyric poets.[121] This practice is further attested by lyres found in early medieval warrior graves from Saxon Germany, Viking Scandinavia and Russia, and Anglo-Saxon England. The heroic-age warrior and his personal poet laureate, along with everybody else, were recast in the Christian mould to serve the heavenly Lord. On the basis of comparative evidence, it seems at least possible that carvings or some kind of pictorial representation of musicians may well also have been carried out in pre-Christian Ireland. Perhaps this was done on wood or other perishable material.[122] But the realism of instruments and of the contexts of music-making represented in stone carving in Ireland, and on some monuments of south-west Scotland (Argyll, an Irish region), indicate local norms which are in striking contrast to contemporary and even somewhat later English and continental European sources which tend to emphase stock images taken without much understanding or attention to detail from late antique sources, in particular, music treatises and philosophical discourse. This seems to have occurred in Ireland only to a limited extent; and so the Irish sources are exceptionally rich and early in their potential for informing on actual practices.

That said, however, the purpose of these representations was overwhelmingly exemplary. The good musician was modelled on David; and this parallels so much else in early Irish literature which takes the Bible as its starting point: the Old Testament for pre-Patrician, pre-Christian society; the New Testament for post-Patrician Ireland with its clerical and lay authorities united in their religious affiliation, and in their concern for the maintenance of earthly power. Such a view of the iconographic record bears out McCone's own theory about the literature and serves to clarify the motivation and purpose behind these monuments.

6. FUTURE AGENDA

There is insufficient space to deal more fully with many related practices: some of them have been merely outlined above; others must await another occasion. Certain well-known topics, such as lamenting the dead, are widely attested and need to be developed, ideally, within a wider sociological framework. A more comprehensive survey along those lines would include all uses of organised sound as a marker of circular and linear time. Circular time, the repetitive acts of day, week, month, season and year, was ordered, for example, by the use of bells to signal moments in the daily cycle of work, prayer, eating, and relaxation; the chanting of the Office symbolically marked the course of the twenty-four hour day; day- and night-time activities, seasonal labour etc. were symbolised by animal bells, calls, songs, cries and other rituals associated with craftsmen such as smiths, builders, masons, agricultural labourers, hunters, fishermen; traders; travelling clerics and pilgrims; seasonal festivities for spring and harvest, and for the summer and winter solstices (later subsumed within the Christian calendar, though retaining pre-Christian elements); saints' and other liturgical feasts; processions; pilgrimages; fairs, including kings' royal assemblies (political meetings) as well as days of public festivity were accompanied by stringed and wind instruments mark certain festivities and their associated rituals of hospitality and entertainment. Linear time includes life-cycle rituals: birth (we remember the tale of the three kinds of music performed for Fraích's mother while she was giving birth), initiation, betrothal, death; age-group rituals such as the activities of members of the Fian; initiation rites for kings accompanied by music on *corn* and *stoc*, followed by court entertainment; elaborate lamentations for the dead, particularly that of warriors and kings, and on occasion of loss in battle. There has been been little attention accorded to the subject of women's music in medieval Ireland, that is, music performed by women for the purpose of entertainment and leisure. Clearly women were associated with lamenting the dead.[123] What other evidence there is is not extensive, because the usual context for it is in the sphere of private life and informal household activities. It is worth mentioning the *grianán* where women sat and did handiwork such as embroidery to the accompaniment of a sweet-stringed *timpán*. There are also occasional references to individual women musicians, whether professional or amateur: for example, the fairy musician in *Aisling Oengusso* who played a *timpán* to which Oengus slept.[124] Interestingly, I have not come across references to women performing on other instruments, not even a *cruit*. In spite of the close association of *cruit* and *timpán* in the hands of male professionals, a certain distinction seems to have been observed in the case of women; though the paucity of information makes such speculation difficult to develop any further. The Fragmentary Annals of Ireland contain an entry for the year 689 concerning the slaying of Diarmait of Mide about which a woman satirist (*bancháinte*) is said to have sung on an occasion of the Fair of Tailtiu, clearly a reference to a professional performer.[125] It is likely that more information can be brought to light with further research on this topic.

A Latin song from *c*600 attributed to St Columbanus is very suggestive of actual singing of worksongs. Although Carney may be correct in proposing that it represents a metaphoric exhortation to his monks to persevere in their Christian faith, like men steering a boat in rough weather,[126] it would seem unreasonable not to regard it as modelled on such a song from real life, given its use of the refrain, '*Heia viri! nostrum reboans echo sonet heia!*' (Heave, men! And let resounding echo sound our 'heave'!) in the first four strophes, changing to '*Vestra, viri, Christum memorans mens personet heia!*' (You men! remember Christ with mind still sounding 'heave'!) for strophes five to eight.[127]

The musical equivalent of putting new wine into old bottles is a generally established custom, in this case, of encouraging piety where thoughts of the secular world might intrude. From some seven hundred years later, we have the *carmina* of the Richard Ledrede (Bishop of Ossory 1317–*c*1361) who set a number of popular songs of the period to new, devotional texts in order to encourage his clerics to piety. Unfortunately, no notations survive in the manuscript, but the form of the texts provides useful insight into current popular singing.

From all that has been discussed above, a picture clearly emerges of a society more in touch with the wider world than is suggested by much of the writing heretofore on Irish music, or by the 'nativist' standpoint which has so dominated the field of medieval Irish studies. In terms of the narrative literature, the associations of music with the emotions, the role of string players at court, the use of instruments as a symbol of office in military and civilian life, the variety of music instruments, the overtly Christian moralising, including the good musician and his devout practices, are all paralleled in the other European vernaculars as well as in medieval Latin literature.

With regard to liturgical music, although there is no direct Irish evidence prior to the twelfth century,[128] it is clear that chant, psalmody and hymns were taught from the outset in Irish ecclesiastical centres in order to serve the requirements of the liturgy. How this was done, who the teachers were, we shall probably never know. It is likely that it was assisted with accompaniment or some kind of support on a stringed instrument. A tantalising comment from Jonas, one of Colombanus's biographers and a member of his community in Bobbio, actually refers to the saint's having set out instructions for the performance of chant.[129] Unfortunately no further information has been forthcoming in any source. It appears likely that hymns and psalms were sung antiphonally as well as responsorially; but again the lack of any more precise information makes it impossible to chart the course of development of a *schola cantorum* as such, or of cantors.

The activities of Irish churchmen in Britain and continental Europe between the sixth and ninth centuries are well attested. Their outstanding skills as teachers of grammar in Carolingian centres can be observed in surviving documents. However, their direct involvement in music instruction is not so clear in spite of accounts such as occasionally come to light. For example, in the seventh century, Gertrude, daughter of Pepin, mayor of the imperial palace, and abbess of Nivelles in Brabant, is said to have invited St Foillan and St Ultan, brothers of St Fursa, to instruct her nuns in psalmody.[130] Sedulius Scottus and John Scotus Eriugena taught grammar and philosophy in Liège and Laon, respectively. In 841, Moengal (Marcellus), another Irishman, became master of novices at the school of St Gallen. Among his pupil were the famous Notker Balbulus (840–912) of sequence fame, and Tuotilo who used to compose tropes, accompanying himself on a *rotta*. Much has been made of this by some writers (e.g. Harrison, *inter alia*)[131] motivated by a Celticising desire. The oldest liturgical sequences stem from the north-west French region, not, it must be emphasised, from Ireland itself.[132] What is overlooked here is the very cosmopolitanism of these monks, without which they would surely not have been engaged in employment abroad during a period of Romanising reform. Clearly, in a general sense, Irish (and Anglo-Saxon) influence was fundamental in continental education of the time; just as there was extensive cultural interchange between Irish, Irish-trained British, and English-trained British monks in the seventh and eighth centuries. But as with Insular manuscript decoration, it becomes very difficult to separate the strands in many instances. And indeed, because the oldest evidence often points in the direction of Ireland (e.g., private prayer, litanies, liturgical drama), the 'magic bag' tends to bulge somewhat with the wishful thinking of those who see Irish invention and innovations in every reference.

However, there is equally a tendency to veer in the opposite direction and to deny the extent of possible Irish influence. Fleischmann, for example, in his article on 'Music of the Celtic Rite'[133] opted for Anglo-Saxon England as ' . . . [t]he main source of litanies', rather than discussing the actual processes of transmission from available evidence and ongoing debate. Similarly, he rejected Stäblein's case for a possible Irish connection for a number of melodies which may perhaps retain evidence of characteristically Irish poetic, and therefore melodic, structure, on the grounds that 'the occurrence of a chant in an Irish manuscript is not in itself sufficient to prove its Irish origin'.[134] This statement has been accepted at face value by Brannon,[135] though perhaps both writers miss the point, because of a preoccupation with the idea of ultimate origins. The fact is that the features are decidedly non-Roman and it may well be that they represent some element of Irish practice which was subsequently absorbed into more general West-European practice. They may represent elements which resulted from a fusion of Irish and Latin poetry, aspects of which therefore are indirectly Roman. This is not to deny the usefulness of Stäblein's observation in identifying these features; but it would represent an isolationist or insularist view to seek to place some notionally pure Irish melody or melodic structure in bipolar opposition to all others, particularly given the late date of those sources discussed by Stäblein (thirteenth century).[136]

Obviously, it would be incorrect to reject the possibility of identifiably Irish characteristics, for example, in the early evidence for private prayer,[137] in certain hymns, etc. But matters were evolving and mixed. After all, the Christian church was Roman at base, and Mozarabic and Gallican influences are noticeable features of Irish liturgical practice. This is not to deny, but only to seek clarification in a very complex weave of multidirectional influences. For example, Stevenson, in her recent review of the problematic, notes that some of the earliest surviving liturgical records of features generally regarded as Hiberno-Latin are preserved in English manuscripts, Irish collections having been subject to so much more destruction, it would appear.[138]

The interdependence of Latin and Gaelic learning and culture makes it likely that education in all subjects, including music, would have included both traditions, even if those opting for a clerical training might have specialised more in chant. Members of the nobility studied in monastic schools in other parts of Europe too, up to the time of the foundation of the universities in the twelfth century. One wonders about cross-fertilization of influences in repertories, styles, aesthetics, teaching methods. Only recently, McCone[139] has argued for the presence of a strong Latin influence even in certain forms of Old Irish poetry (called *reitoiric*, 'rhetoric'), long deemed to represent archaic, pre-Christian practices. Surviving treatises are not plentiful in Irish versions; but from knowledge of the Latin authors known to early medieval Irish scholars, in particular glosses and commentaries, it is evident that monks were familiar with the heritage of scholastic music theory. This does not necessarily have any bearing on *musica practica*, of course; but is a part of the cultural and intellectual history of European music.

Irish monks had knowledge of the Church Fathers at an early date. The writings of the Spanish author, Isidore of Seville (d.636), were known in seventh-century Ireland along with Cassiodorus (*c*485–*c*580), Augustine (354–430), and his younger contemporary, Martianus Capella (*fl.* ?early fifth century) – very early in European terms. Clearly more work needs to be done on specific topics covered by Irish glosses on the Bible, as well as patristic and late antique writings. So far, only two sources have been addressed with reference to music.

An Old Irish treatise on the Psalter has been interpreted as a comment on existing Irish practice, when in fact it merely explains the Old Testament text by writing the term *cruit* in the margin near to the term *instrumentum musicum*.[140] In other words, it is not conclusive, although there is reason to believe that the commentator may have been linking local practice with Old Testament use, as occurs in many instances in early Irish literature. We do have other evidence in Irish sources for the use of lyres by clerics in the performance of sacred music. Accompanied singing of sacred songs is well attested elsewhere also, for example, in the case of Tuotilo in ninth-century St Gall, and the tenth-century English St Dunstan. It was also an established teaching method to use a stringed instrument in chant instruction.[141]

Eriugena's commentaries on Martianus Capella's *De nuptiis Philologiae et Mercurii* led Münxelhaus[142] to opine that not only does the former show considerable departure from other commentators by adding some ideas of his own, but he refers to observed practice of music, *musica practica*, which she assumes to have a bearing on Irish affairs. This rests on flimsy ground, for there is no indication from his words that Eriugena had any particular region in mind. Furthermore, Münxelhaus believes that he implicitly refers to polyphonic practices because of his analogy of the sounding together at different pitches of organ pipes, and of voices of a choir, in order to explain the theory of the Harmony of the Spheres. Again, this is not proof of anything beyond experimentation with pitch combinations, consonance and dissonance, and measurement of tones. The organ in Eriugena's time is not known to have been used in performance, being technically too limited for this purpose, and confined to demonstrating music theory. Even the detailed description of the famous organ built at Winchester in the mid-tenth century has been thought by McKinnon to be exaggerated. Organs were not in use as full developed music instruments until much later.[143] The reference to the choir is indeed more thought-provoking, but does not prove anything beyond demonstration of a principle. Unfortunately Münxelhaus becomes somewhat preoccupied with the idea of discovering older references to polyphonic practice, forgetting in the process that what is generally referred to by this term is a technically elaborated, consciously structured form of composition which was developed in liturgical music in twelfth-century Paris. It needs to be emphasised that the sounding together of two or more pitches should not be regarded as anything strange or new in the history of human music-making and it is more than likely that all kinds of performance, of accompanied song and of two or more instruments and/or voices were practiced in Ireland and elsewhere in northern and southern Europe.

Apart from the questions of regular liturgical practice in Mass and Office, there is evidence of Irish use of liturgical drama from eighth- and ninth-century Northumbrian sources with distinctly Irish characteristics.[144] Similarly, the lament tradition, well-attested in the vernacular mythological literature, and reflected *inter alia* in the 'Lament for the death of Colm Cille' and in the eleventh-century 'Eve's Lament',[145] should rightly form part of the study of the long-term history of Latin and vernacular *planctus* in the mainstream

European tradition. Towards the other end of the chronological spectrum are the British and Continental liturgical offices for Irish saints, which have never been surveyed as a whole, and of which further examples will no doubt come to light in the course of time.[146]

Whether our concern is with liturgical or secular practices, it seems wise to redirect our attention to processes of social behaviour rather than seeking isolates and treating them out of context. The course of this topic is extremely far-reaching and all aspects must be taken into account when endeavouring to document it. Two major processes of (internal) acculturation have been overlooked; they merit separate treatment, and the work has barely commenced.

First of all, the Scandinavian influence in the towns and cities of Ireland, especially since their christianisation (by the English church from Canterbury) in the tenth century. Regarding secular music, Fleischmann and Gleeson[147] refer to the visitation of entertainers from Iceland to the court of the Hiberno-Norse kings in Dublin in the tenth century; while I have examined and reported upon a number of instruments and associated fragments from Scandinavian and Hiberno-Norman Irish urban centres.[148]

Secondly, the Anglo-Norman settlement, which introduced French- and eventually English-speakers into Ireland in large numbers. This undoubtedly included imported repertories of singing and dancing, of which two *chansons de geste* are now the only surviving record.[149] Liturgical manuscripts representing the new accommodation are relatively late, and have long been ignored as they were deemed to be merely a copy of Sarum Use. Fortunately, these Irish sources are now beginning to be accorded the kind of scholarly attention which they merit.[150]

Despite the Viking incursions in the eighth–ninth centuries, the establishment of Anglo-Norman rule in the 1170s, and the large-scale ecclesiastical reforms of the twelfth century in conformity with centralising Roman practices, many older aspects of Irish artistic and cultural life continued until the seventeenth century, when the Elizabethan plantations contributed to the ultimate decline of the political power of the Gaelic chieftain ascendancy. Following the formal establishment of English administration in Ireland under Henry II, rather than Ireland becoming anglicized in any uniform or totalising way, the new French- and English-speaking settlers engaged in patronage of Gaelic harpers and poets just like the longer-established chieftains. However, they also introduced other types of artistic expression, particularly in the form of English rites, to the new ecclesiastical centres which they established (such as the cathedrals in Dublin). And so alongside the Use of Sarum, the cathedral choir schools, and Corpus Christi processions in urban centres, the culture of the old Gaelic courts continued to flourish.

One of the implicit aims of this paper has been to examine what is commonly referred to somewhat schizophrenically as the 'Irish' and 'European' dimensions of Irish cultural history, with particular emphasis on the history of music behaviour, in the context of a theory of civilizing processes. This apparent duality is viewed as one of the long-term results of being peripheral to other centres (and thus subject to limited mutual influence) while at the same time having a strong sense of local identity because of relative distance and hence a slower pace of convergence. Needless to say, more questions and problems have been raised here than have been resolved; which is how it should be, since our view of the past changes according to our experience of the present. The two are interdependent: perceptions of the past are our perceptions, based on our knowledge and experience. The greatest wish which I, for one, have for work of this nature is that we be willing to change and develop our views of these topics. Materials we have in great abundance, but they can only be sifted within the wider framework of comparative evidence, and in an open-minded way.

It is necessary, from a music-historical perspective, to revisit the extensive corpus of Old and Middle Irish and Hiberno-Latin poetry, as well as to re-assess narrative literature containing interpolated lyric. Only with systematic work like this can we begin to assess the potential scope for further study. Too often, the potential for such information is overlooked by inadequate translation or lack of attention to the possibilities. Even while searching materials in existing editions of the literature, time and again one comes across mis-translations of terms for instruments, and rarely, even in well-indexed works, does one find terminology relating to music and sound in general, which again points up the lack of awareness of the importance of this topic, not only – let it be emphasised – to serve the needs of more specialist, technical, musicological enquiry, but also to enhance upon the rich evidence for a major part of Irish social and intellectual history. I hope the present essay will go some way to making a convincing case of this plea, contained, as it is, in the Shrine of St Mogue.

NOTES

1. An account from *Adomnan's Life of Columba*; see A.O. and M.O. Anderson, *Adomnan's Life of Columba*. Edinburgh: Thomas Nelson & Son, 1961, 288–9; *ibid.*, rev. M.O. Anderson, OUP 1991, 70–71.

2. I gratefully acknowledge receipt of a *Music and Letters* Award and assistance from the Dublin office of the British Council in support of library and archive visits.

3. James Carney, *Medieval Irish Lyrics* with *The Irish Bardic Poet*. Portlaoise: The Dolmen Press 1967/R1985, 67–73.

4. Literally, 'is singing a sweet *sian'*, a tune or strain.
5. Literally, 'drone'.
6. Literally, 'lament'.
7. Literally, 'playing' or 'performance'.
8. Kuno Meyer (ed. and trans.), *Four Old Songs of Summer and Winter*. London: David Nutt, 1903, 11, str.6.
9. 'The Dialogue of the Old Men', or the 'Colloquy of the Ancients', a twelfth/thirteenth-century narrative composition about the Fianna in old age, some of whose members survived to witness the coming of St Patrick. (See n.50.)
10. One is reminded also of the modern Irish phrase, *'abair amhrán dom'* ('sing me a song'): one 'says' rather than 'sings' a song, presumably indicating emphasis on its narrative function rather than on its style of delivery.
11. Kim McCone, *Pagan Past and Christian Present in Early Irish Literature*. Maynooth: An Sagart 1990/repr. 1991, 256.
12. Donnchadh Ó Corráin, Liam Breatnach and Kim McCone (edd.), *Sages, Saints and Storytellers. Celtic Studies in Honour of Professor James Carney*. Maynooth Monographs 2. Maynooth: An Sagart 1989, xv.
13. '. . . the worlds of native and ecclesiastical learning had merged long before the bulk of the surviving texts were redacted – a matter which is of very considerable consequence' (Ó Corráin quoted in McCone (as n.11), 28).
14. Aron Gurevich, *Medieval Popular Culture, Problems of Belief and Perception*; transl. J.M. Bak and P.A. Hollingsworth. Cambridge and Paris: Cambridge University Press/Éditions de la Maison des Sciences de l'Homme 1988/repr. 1992, xviii.
15. Peter Brown, *The Cult of the Saints. Its Rise and Function in Latin Christianity*. Chicago and London: University of Chicago Press and SCM Press, 1981, 30.
16. *ibid.*, 31.
17. *ibid.*, 33.
18. I use this term not in any derogatory sense of value judgment, but rather in its accepted sociological meaning of long-term human-social development. For further discussion, see the seminal study by Norbert Elias (published originally in German, 1939), *The Civilizing Process, I, The History of Manners*. Oxford: Blackwell, 1978; *II, State Formation and Civilization*. Oxford: Blackwell, 1982.
19. J.R. Tolkien, 'Welsh and English'. In *Angles and Britons*. O'Donnell Lectures. Cardiff 1963, 29.
20. This should not be read as 'English' in the narrow sense, but rather as an indication of 'Insular' use.
21. See Hortense Panum, *Stringed Instruments of the Middle Ages*, rev. and ed. Jeffrey Pulver. London: William Reeves 1940/1971, 93 and 102.
22. The likely presence in Ireland of English harpers, of harpers in an Anglo-Norman tradition, should not be overlooked either, as we are reminded from some of the entries in the Dublin Guild Merchant Roll. One of the names, that of Thomas le Harpur, is even accompanied by an outline sketch of a harp. See Philomena Connolly and Geoffrey Martin edd., *The Dublin Guild Merchant Roll, c1190–1265*. Dublin: Dublin Corporation 1992; the sketch is reproduced in the frontispiece. Hiberno-Norman settlers in other Irish walled towns are sure to have included instrumentalists. Though we have so far uncovered no

surviving instruments, the practice of composing *chansons de geste* in Hiberno-Norman settlements further attests to the likelihood of such practices.

23. See Ann Buckley, 'Music-related Imagery on Early Christian Insular Sculpture: Identification, Context, Function', *Imago Musicae/International Yearbook of Musical Iconography* 8 (1991), *passim*. In further explanation for the continuation of the predominant association of the small 'medieval' harp with Ireland, it should not be overlooked, of course, that professional harping continued in the so-called 'Celtic fringe' of Ireland, Scotland and Wales well into the early modern period, and was then self-consciously revived. Hence it is understandable that harps in general became symbolic of nationalist sentiment and small-nation assertiveness within the Atlantic Archipelago. But we need to exercise great caution in order not to project these much more recent sentiments onto another time, another place, a very different Other.

24. This problem arises notably with studies of the monophonic repertories such as lai and sequence, in particular their early history, as well as other non-Roman materials such as litanies, acclamations etc. It is discussed more fully in the first chapter of my forthcoming book, *The Old French Lyric Lai to c.1300. A Comparative Study of French and Latin Monophonic Song*.

25. For discussion of some of the problems, see Ann Buckley, 'Boundaries in the Field – what do they serve? A review of the landscapes of historical musicology and ethnomusicology'. In Ann Buckley, Karl-Olof Edström and Paul Nixon (edd.), *Proceedings of the Second British-Swedish Conference on Musicology: Ethnomusicology (Cambridge, 5–10 August 1989)*. Skrifter från Musikvetenskapliga Institutionen, Göteborgs Universitet, no. 26; Musikmuseets Skrifter 21: Göteborg 1991, 39–59.

    Discussion of a so-called 'New Musicology' along the lines of 'New History' and 'New Archaeology' are still relatively undeveloped. Peter Jeffery has attempted to explore some of the issues, nailing his colours to the mast with a rather arresting subtitle: see Peter Jeffery, *Re-Envisioning Past Musical Cultures. Ethnomusicology in the Study of Gregorian Chant*. Chicago and London: The University of Chicago Press 1992. In spite of his pioneering and persuasive case for new approaches to the history of plainchant, however, he does not take the potential application of ethnomusicological methods very far, beyond indicating his general concern at the need for more contextual studies. Indeed, his appraisal of presumed consensus and achievements in the field of ethnomusicology is rather idealising, since scholars who undertake research within that subdiscipline rarely develop an interest in historical perspectives; equally rarely do they address European art music or its long-term development processes. My own preference is for an emphasis on social-scientific, dynamic, action-orientated discussion, rather than on setting up ever more static, functionalist categories and classifications. Regardless of (sub)disciplinary labels, which rarely in themselves lead to any resolution of problems, behaviour-centred questions need to be kept uppermost if we are to gain any understanding of process, which is, after all, what is central to human-social life in all its forms of communication.

26. I am in process of developing the many topics of this presentation into a book-length study on Music in Medieval Ireland.

27. McCone (see n.11), 2–3.

28. Reinhold Hammerstein, *Macht und Klang. Tönende Automaten als Realität und Fiktion in der alten und mittelalterlichen Welt*. Bern: Francke 1986.

29. *ibid.*, 87 (my translation).

30. See also Gurevich (as n.14), 72 for information on more widespread cults of trees, water and stones in German and Scandinavian pre-Christian practices. Also John Walter Taylor, 'Tree Worship', *The Mankind Quarterly* 20 (1–2), 1979, 79–141.

31. This is not the place to explore organisation of sound among non-human animals. Clearly there are no zero-points; and some animals appear to have an understanding and sense of intentionality as, for example, in signals of warning and other communication in differentiated birdsong, and among higher mammals, in particular. But no animal is as complex or as cerebrally organised as the human animal, or as equipped with capacities for memory and foresight: and here is the essential distinction in behavioural terms, and therefore the cut-off point for what is usually termed 'music'. For further discussion of these theoretical issues, see Ann Buckley, 'Music and Humanisation as long-term Process'. In Marcel Otte (ed.), *'Sons Originels'. Préhistoire de la Musique. Actes du Colloque de Musicologie, 11–12–13 Décembre 1992*. Études et Recherches Archéologiques de l'Université de Liège, no. 61. Liège 1994, 275–285.

32. Loss of control in situations of heightened excitement is of course still encountered, for example, among certain religious sects, at pop concerts, etc., once again reminding us that differences from non-Western, or past Western societies – in other words, between various human groups – are not absolute. But the essential difference remains one of attitude and belief in the supernatural power of music, determined by a lower level of relative autonomy, or self control, on the part of groups of individuals in less technologically advanced societies. In the case of supernatural beliefs, external control on the individual is greater, thereby producing fear and expectation of submission to the forces of greater power. More scepticism, and concomitantly less belief in the supernatural (and less external control), produces more individual assertiveness (and more self-control).

33. See Anderson (as n.1), 1961, 288–289 and n.11; 1991: 70–71 and n.83. The later edition uses slightly different wording. The editors note that Ps. xliv of the Vulgate is equivalent to Ps. xlv of the English version of the Psalter.

34. Francis J. Byrne, *Irish Kings and High Kings*. London: Batsford, 1973/R1987, 27.

35. McCone (as n.11), 73, quoting *Senchas na Relec*.

36. S.J. Connolly, *Priests and People in Pre-Famine Ireland 1780–1845*. Dublin and New York: Gill and Macmillan/St Martin's Press, 1982, 136.

37. See Connolly *ibid.* for a further account.

38. Kathleen Hughes, *Early Christian Ireland. An Introduction to the Sources*. London: The Sources of History Ltd. in association with Hodder and Stoughton, 1972, 128.

39. Tadhg O'Donoghue, 'Advice to a Prince', *Ériu* 9(i), part 1 (1921), 46 and 51 § 9.

40. *ibid.*, § 10.

41. Whitley Stokes, 'The Battle of Allen', *Revue Celtique* 24, 1903, 49–51.

42. *ibid.*, 55–57; cf. Eugene O'Curry, *Manners and Customs of the Ancient Irish*, III, Lectures XXX–XXXVIII. London and Dublin: 1873, 311.

43. Stokes *ibid.*, 59, n.5.
44. or *cruinsech* as one version has it (Stokes *ibid.*, 63 and n.2). I have not found any explanation, or other instances, of this term.
45. Stokes *ibid.*, 61–63; cf. O'Curry *ibid.*, 311–312.
46. Fergal McGrath, *Education in Ancient and Medieval Ireland*. Blackrock: Skellig Press, 1979, 117.
47. See O'Curry (as n. 42), 376 and discussion in the following section below.
48. *ibid.*
49. *ibid.*, 378.
50. *ibid.*, 379–80; Whitley Stokes and Ernst Windisch, *Acallam na Senorach*. Irische Texte 1. Leipzig 1900, 11. 760–3; Myles Dillon, *Stories from the Acallam*. Medieval and Modern Irish Series 23. Dublin: Dublin Institute for Advanced Studies, 1970, 12–13.
51. See McCone (as n.11), 205ff for further references. Also Stephen O. Glosecki, 'Wolf Dances and Whispering Beasts: Shamanic Motifs from Sutton Hoo?' *The Mankind Quarterly* 26 (3–4), Spring/Summer 1986, 305–319.
52. The Hungarian dance, *verbunkos*, and its Romanian equivalent *bărbunca*, now more or less confined to the mimetic arts of folkloric music and dancing, derives from the German term *werben* – to recruit.
53. Breandán Breatnach, *Folk Music and Dances of Ireland*. Dublin and Cork: The Mercier Press 1971/rev. 1977, 38–39.
54. This is the assessment of Helen Roe, recorded on the information card accompanying the book-cover which is housed in the National Museum of Ireland, Dublin.
55. The scene on the cover includes a group of five men in the lower part, clearly engaged in dancing. One figure holds a sword aloft, another his arms akimbo; two figures hold the ends of a withy between them, one of whom also raises aloft a round object. The fifth figure holds a similar round object in both hands, apparently beating it rhythmically. There are other indications on the cover which suggests tales of adventure, or scenes from the life of a knight – a knight on horseback slaying a dragon (perhaps St George?), an eagle, a boar, Maltese crosses, and an IHS logo. Such knightly iconography common in European history of Middle Ages. It is not beyond the bounds of possibility that the cover once enclosed a text on such a topic.
56. Wolfgang Meid, *Táin Bó Fraích*. Medieval and Modern Irish Series 22. Dublin: Dublin Institute of Advanced Studies 1967, 9–10.
57. Elizabeth A. Gray (ed.), *Cath Maige Tuired: the second Battle of Mag Tuired*. Irish Texts Society 52. Naas: Irish Texts Society 1982, 56–57, § 125.
58. O'Curry (as n.42), 380ff, lists several other terms associated with particular kinds of vocal utterance: *Duchand*, and the related term, *luínneog*, as well as *esnad gúba*, sighing or mourning in grief, *logairecht*, a vocal funeral cry, *sámhghúbhla, sian / sianan, sirechtach, adbond, trírech*. A full investigation of these would extend far beyond the scope available here. But I mention them as one more aspect of this multifaceted topic which has yet to be addressed.
59. *ibid.*, 313ff.
60. *ibid.*, 315.
61. *Ancient Laws of Ireland*, 6 vols. Rolls Series. Dublin and London: 1865–1901, 1: 123, 143.

62. For discussion of the ritual status of the king's wand or *slat*, traditionally made of hazelwood, see Byrne (as n.34), 22.

63. See Katharine Simms, 'Guesting and Feasting in Gaelic Ireland', *Journal of the Royal Society of Antiquaries of Ireland* 108 (1978), 76 and *passim*.

64. See *Ancient Laws* (as n.61), V, 106–109; also Eoin MacNeill, 'Ancient Irish Law. The Law of Status or Franchise', *Proceedings of the Royal Irish Academy* 36 C (1923) 16, 280.

65. *Ancient Laws ibid.*, IV, 339; MacNeill *ibid.*, 306.

66. For facsimile reproduction and transcription of this idealised scene see O. Bergin and R.I. Best (edd.), *The Book of Leinster* I, Dublin: Dublin Institute for Advanced Studies, 1954, 116–117; and (for the *Yellow Book of Lecan*) R.A.S. Macalister, *Tara. A Pagan Sanctuary*, London: Charles Scribner's Sons, 1931, 64–65. For discussion and translation of the accompanying texts (including transcriptions of both schemes) see George Petrie, 'On the History and Antiquities of Tara Hill', *Transactions of the Royal Irish Academy* 18 (1839), 196ff.

   There are many propagandist tales about Cormac Mac Airt, including teachings and wise sayings attributed to him (for example, *Tecosca Chormaic*, the Teachings of Cormac), since he was the legendary ancestor of the Uí Néill and the Connachta. In order to enhance this lineage and its claim to political hegemony in Christian Ireland, Cormac is depicted as a convert even before the arrival of St Patrick. See above, p. 29.

67. ' . . . not a flatulent kind', according to the accompanying poem in the Book of Leinster (see Petrie *ibid.*, 202).

68. Literally, a 'tuning tree', no doubt because they were made of wood, at least in some cases. The same term was presumably applied to metal tuning keys.

69. One should not view these technical terms too strictly, particularly as *cruit* and *timpan* were often, though not always, used interchangeably. Therefore it is likely that compensation may have been intended for players of both types of instrument. It should be remembered also that a *cruit* referred to a lyre before harps were introduced and it is no longer possible to pinpoint precisely when this may have occurred.

70. See Byrne (as n.34), 175.

71. O'Donoghue (as n.39), 49 and 54 §§ 29–31.

72. See also Simms (as n.63), 67.

73. For further discussion of the symbolism of this and other tales about the magico-mythical powers of music, see Section 4 below.

74. The terms used by Keating are *fear an stuic* for the instrumentalist, and his instrument variously as *stoc* and *barr buabhall*. The account is obviously too close to our interest here to exclude it purely on grounds of Keating's lack of credibility. Although his great History of Ireland (*Foras Feasa ar Éirinn*), completed in 1633 or 1644, was based on documents no longer extant, apparently governed much by his own emotional commitment to the subject, it is best if at least we acknowledge his inclusions in the absence of other evidence, while, however, remaining open to the possibility of their being unfounded. For the above account, see Patrick S. Dineen, *Keating's Foras Feasa ar Éirinn*, II. Irish Texts Society VIII. London: Davit Nutt, 1908, 253.

75. See James J. Tierney, 'The Celtic Ethnography of Posidonius', *Proceedings of the Royal Irish Academy* 60 C 5 (1960) 189–275 for a collation of these references.

76. Whitley Stokes (ed. and trans.), *In Cath Catharda. The Civil War of the Romans.* Irische Texte, 4th ser., 2. Leipzig 1909, 430–1, ll. 5909–5913. The reference to *cuislenna catha* ('warpipes') is interesting. It occurs here in an early seventeenth-century source when the use of such an instrument was well-established in Ireland (as we know also from the account of John Derricke, Elizabethan civil servant and traveller). The medieval history of this instrument is not clear. See John Derricke, *The Image of Ireland; with a Discoverie of Woodkarne.* London 1581; repr. with the notes of Sir Walter Scott. Edited with Introduction by John Small. Edinburgh: Adam and Charles Black 1883, pls. 2 and 9.

77. Long and short horns are found in many parts of Bronze and Iron Age Northern Europe, in particular, Southern Sweden and Denmark, Germany and Ireland, though distinctive regional differences have been noted, suggesting separate development. For further discussion, see Peter Holmes and J.M. Coles, 'Prehistoric Brass Instruments', *World Archaeology* 12(3), February 1981, 280–286; also Cajsa S. Lund, 'The "phenomenal" bronze lurs'. In Cajsa S. Lund, *The Bronze Lurs*, Second Conference of the ICTM Study Group on Music Archaeology, II, Publications issued by the Royal Swedish Academy of Music no. 53, Stockholm 1986, 9–50.

78. Meid (as n.56) 8, § 20; cf. Byrne (as n.34), 19. O'Curry (as n.42), 382, gives sixty, from another source.

79. But see McCone (as n.11), 221 for a comment on the attested confusion between the terms *drúth* (buffoon) and *druí* (druid), resulting in difficulty in interpreting certain sources.

80. O'Curry (as n.42), 219ff; Meid (as n.56), 4, ll. 95–99.

81. For a recent study of harp bags see Martin van Schaik, 'The Harp Bag in the Middle Ages. An Iconographical Survey'. In *Proceedings of the International Historical Harp Symposium, Utrecht 1992.* Utrecht: STIMU 1994, 3–11.

82. John O'Donovan (trans.), *The Banquet of Dún na nGédh and the Battle of Magh Rath.* Dublin: Irish Archaeological Society. 1842, 168; cf. Ann Buckley, 'What was the tiompán? A study in ethnohistorical organology: Evidence in Irish Literature', *Jahrbuch für musikalische Volks- and Völkerkunde* 9 (1978), 62, and *passim* for other references.

83. Gray (as n.57), § 36.

84. Peter Crossley-Holland, 'Myth and Music in Ancient Ireland', *The Mankind Quarterly* 21(4), Summer 1981, 377–391.

85. McCone (as n.11), 220ff.

86. See Aloys Fleischmann and Ryta Gleeson, 'Music in ancient Munster and monastic Cork', *Journal of the Cork Historical and Archaeological Society* 70(2), no. 202, (1965), 81.

87. See Kathleen Hughes, 'Some Aspects of Irish Influence on Early English Private Prayer', *Studia Celtica* 5 (1970), 53 for a reference to Patrick in his Confession: 'My spirit was moved so that in a single day I would say as many as a hundred prayers, and almost as many in a night'. In Hughes's opinion 'the habit of constant and repeated prayer belongs to the very oldest stratum of Celtic Christianity'.

88. See Kuno Meyer, *The Vision of MacConglinne*. London: David Nutt 1892, 80–81.
89. Carney (as n.3), 49. For further discussion see Fleischmann and Gleeson (as n.86), 87 and *passim*. For a wide-ranging discussion from a more sociological perspective, see Brown (as n.15), *passim*, and Gurevich (as n.14), *passim*.
90. *Ceolán* appears to have been a small bell, usually described as a clerical accoutrement from which was produced a faint, tinkling sound.
91. O'Curry (as n.42), 332. See Fleischmann and Gleeson (as n.86), 88, n.44 for an account of Conall Clogach ('Conall, the Belled'), so-called because he was cursed by St Colm Cille who struck thrice nine bells against him. One is reminded also of tales of St Patrick banishing the snakes from Ireland – a common theme in early Christian hagiography, although, to my knowledge, these do not necessarily include references to any kind of organised sound to add to the miraculous power. Cf. the case of St Marcellus in Jacques Le Goff, *Time, Work, and Culture in the Middle Ages*, transl. Arthur Goldhammer. Chicago and London: The University of Chicago Press 1980, 159ff, where there is discussion of dragons and serpents as a topos in medieval saints' Lives.
92. Which judicious editorial decision will no doubt have a beneficial effect in the battle of the marketplace!
93. See Byrne (as n.34), 21.
94. See J. Dimock, *Giraldi Cambrensis Opera*. Rolls Series V. London 1867, 155.
95. Fleischmann and Gleeson (as n.86), 92; cf. O'Curry (as no.42), 74.
96. See Ann Buckley, 'Musical Instruments in Ireland from the ninth to the fourteenth centuries. A review of the organological evidence'. In Gerard Gillen and Harry White (edd.), *Irish Musical Studies I: Musicology in Ireland*. Blackrock: Irish Academic Press, 1990, plate XIV.
97. Details and full Latin text may be found in Ann Buckley, 'Music in Ancient and Medieval Ireland'. *A New History of Ireland*, I, Oxford: The Clarendon Press (forthcoming). For full texts and further discussion see Paul J. Nixon, 'Giraldus Cambrensis on Music: How Reliable are his Historiographers?' In Ann Buckley (ed.), *Proceedings of the First British-Swedish Conference on Musicology: Medieval Studies, 11–15 May 1988*. Publication issued by the Royal Swedish Academy of Music no.71. Stockholm 1992, 264–89.
98. There is a marginal illustration of this scene in one of the *Topographia* MSS, Cambridge University Library, Ff.1.27, fol.46r (late thirteenth/early fourteenth century). The instruments are large, curved horns, possibly made of wood since the illuminator painted them dark brown. A similar instrument, dating perhaps to the ninth century, is housed in the National Museum of Ireland. Its context has unfortunately not been recorded. See Buckley (as n.23), fig. 42.
99. The Christian rites of exorcism and excommunication, with 'bell, book and candle', are late survivors of these older practices. They relate to the wider topic of sound as an element in warding off evil. More generally, the use of bells, horns and other sound tools as votive offerings needs to be explored further as longer-term processes of association, memory and transmitted practice. It impinges on a number of issues concerning human interaction by means of

symbolic sound, involving psycho-emotional, physical and other social bonding against, or in communion with, a group-perceived non-human force.

100. See the note by Raghnall Ó Floinn in Michael Ryan (ed.), *Treasures of Ireland. Irish Art 3000 b.c.–1500 a.d.* Dublin: Royal Irish Academy 1983, 185.

101. See Buckley (as n.96), pls VI, VIII, X; also *ibid.* (as n.23), figs. 7, 8 and 13.

102. The topic of liturgical horns is discussed, with all the relevant illustrations, in Buckley (as n. 23).

103. See Buckley *ibid.*, fig. 19. This south-west region of Scotland was dominated by the Irish or 'Scotti' since the Dal Riata of Antrim displaced the Pictish inhabitants in the fifth century. Argyll remained part of the Irish political structure for several centuries.

104. See Buckley *ibid.*, Section 4.2, 'Anointment of David', for further discussion on Insular iconography of this topic.

105. A gloss in the Irish laws known as Heptads lists the theft of a buffalo horn as a crime since, as a 'foreign curiosity', it was difficult to replace (*Ancient Laws* (as n.61), V, 221). Though this may refer to quite another context, i.e., not the precious ritual object, it does nonetheless point to the relative rarity value of buffalo horns, an aspect which would also enhance its symbolic role as a sacred, untouchable, perhaps terrifying object. Cf. also Glosecki (as n.51), *passim* for discussion of the ritual use of horns in Anglo-Scandinavian and Baltic societies.

The representation of clerics holding (perhaps exchanging?) horns on the Cross of Scriptures, Clonmacnoise is however perhaps related to the common later medieval symbol of land tenure whereby (elaborately carved ivory) horns represented a contract (see Buckley (as n.23), Section 3.2). There are surviving Irish examples, for instances, the Kavanagh 'Charter' Horn in ivory and brass which became associated with the kingship of Leinster. See Ryan (as n.100), 184–185, which includes an illustration.

106. Ó Corráin quoted in McCone (as n.11), 28.

107. This craft seems to have been generally enjoyed in the Irish courts as elsewhere in medieval Europe. The fact that it was associated with humour and low-class entertainment (but nonetheless within the courts) is one more feature of long-term civilizing processes whereby bodily functions were gradually privatised and associated with shame and embarrassment if inappropriately engaged in (cf. Elias (as n.18), I, *passim*) – a process emphasised by the emotional release provided by grotesque and humour-inducing performers. Gothic manuscript iconography is packed with drawings of figures in positions associated with such activities, often making use of music instruments in order to reinforce the point – for example, the clasping of a shawn (a reed instrument) between the buttocks. For discussion of such sources from an art-historical perspective, see Michael Camille, *Images of the Edge. The Margins of Medieval Art.* London: Reaktion Books 1992.

I am not aware of any study of the profession of podicicinist, which no doubt can be traced at least as far back as the Roman circus. Petrie (as n.66), 203–204, n.52, felt it inappropriate even to translate the gloss in the Yellow Book of Lecan poem, but had recourse instead to a quotation from Dante's *Inferno* ('*Ed egli avea del cul fatto trombetta*')! The Irish manuscript has: *Fuirseoiraigh .i. do níad an fhuirseoracht ar a mbealaibh – brigedoiri .i. do niad in bruigedoracht ag a tonaibh* (Belchers, i.e., they belch with their mouths – Farters, i.e., they fart with their rear ends). However Petrie did add that he had heard of a manor in England 'said to have been formerly held by the tenure of a *saltus*, a *sufflatus*, and a *crepitus ventris*, enacted in the presence of the king' (*ibid.*), clearly a humorous and somewhat more exacting variant of a peppercorn rent!

Evidence for this practice up to modern times in western Europe is provided by the highly successful career of the French (aptly-named) Petomane from the early part of the twentieth century. His particular achievement was said to have been his ability to perform popular tunes to order in this manner. Thus apart from the relevance of such symbolic behaviour to the study of the social uses of sound in the wider sense (in this case, via a corpophone), it also has a bearing on music history in the narrower sense because of its incorporation (!) of popular music of the day.

108. McCone (as n.11), 222.
109. Joan Newlon Radner, *Fragmentary Annals of Ireland*. Dublin: Dublin Institute of Advanced Studies 1978, 60–61, §177. Radner translates this as 'the singing of praise songs to the Lord', but there is no specific reference to 'songs' here. Cf. McCone (as n.11), 222 who reproduced Radner's version. I have restored the terminology of the original source in respect of all of the instrumentalists, and corrected mistranslations of *timpanaigh* which both Radner and McCone give as 'drummers' (cf. n.143 below).
110. Whitley Stokes (ed. with trans. and notes), *Anecdota Oxoniensa. Lives of the Saints from the Book of Lismore*. Oxford: Clarendon Press 1890, xii–xv.
111. See E.J. Gwynn and W.J. Purton, 'The Monastery of Tallaght', *Proceedings of the Royal Irish Academy* 29 C 5 (1911), 131, § 10.
112. *ibid.*, 166.
113. See Stokes and Windisch (as n.50), 98, ll. 3453ff. That version varies somewhat from the details provided in O'Curry (as n.42), 325; details from both O'Curry's version in the Book of Lismore and that of Stokes and Windisch (who used MS Laud) have been included here.
114. Stokes and Windisch version.
115. O'Curry (as n.42), 325.
116. See Hughes (as n.38), 188; Myles Dillon, 'The Taboos of the Kings of Ireland', *Proceedings of the Royal Irish Academy* 54 C 1 (1951), 14–15, § 3.
117. '"Cur", aiunt, "a nobis regrediente Cronano poeta aliquod ex more suae artis *canticum* non postulasti *modolabiliter decantari*?"' (Anderson (as n.1), 298; my emphasis). McGrath (as n.46), 228 renders this as 'sung . . . to musical accompaniment' in his section on 'Harp accompaniment to the Chant', but the source refers neither to chant nor to the use of an instrument. However, if a stringed instrument were used, it would most likely have been a lyre.
118. McGrath, as n.46.
119. I am in the course of preparing a paper on this topic, entitled 'Music and biblical imagery on medieval Irish monuments'.
120. See discussion in Section 2 above.
121. For details, see Tierney (as n.75) 251, §31.

122. We must not forget, for example, in Cogitosus's description of Brigid's monastery, the paintings which covered the altar screen of her church. For further discussion and bibliographic references, see Buckley (as n.23), Introduction.
123. This problem underlines further the need to maintain a very broad perspective on definitions of 'music', as argued in the early part of this paper. Such organised sound as lamenting the dead is central to the field of music history, but it is never defined as 'music' in any shape or form by those who make use of it. This is as true of antique and medieval societies as it is of parts of the contemporary world where such practices continue to exist, for example, in Eastern Europe where I am conducting an extensive field project, including the documentation of laments and other rituals for the dead.
124. See Buckley (as n.82), 56ff for further discussion.
125. See Radner (as n.109), 38–39, § 103.
126. See Carney (as n.3), xvi.
127. Carney *ibid.*, 8–10.
128. The oldest example of transcribable notation is the polyphonic colophon autograph by the scribe, Cormac, in London British Library MS Add. 36929, a twelfth-century Irish psalter.
129. See Bruno Krusch (ed.), *Ionae Vitae Sanctorum Columbani, Vedastis, Iohannis.* Hannover 1905, 158.
130. McGrath (as n.46), 233. These materials require further investigation. Suffice it for the present to mention that it was a fashion in Carolingian monasteries to adopt Irish saints and religious teachers as their 'mythistorical' founders.
131. See E.J. Dobson and F. Ll. Harrison, *Medieval English Songs*, London: Faber and Faber, 1979, 86ff.
132. For further discussion of this problem, see Michel Huglo, 'L'Organum à Landévennec au IXe siècle', *Études Celtiques* 23 (1986) 191–192: 'If the Insular [teachers] – Scots and Irish – played an indisputable rôle in the initiation of the élites of the Continent – particularly in grammar and computistics – it is often difficult to disclose and to gauge the importance of their contribution to the elaboration of the quadrivial sciences in the schools of the Empire' (my translation). The quadrivial sciences (*Quadrivium*) refer to Arithmetic, Music, Geometry and Astronomy which, together with the *Trivium* of Grammar, Rhetoric and Dialectics made up the Seven Liberal Arts of the medieval school system.
133. Aloys Fleischmann, 'Celtic Rite, Music of the', *The New Grove Dictionary of Music and Musicians.* London: Macmillan, 1980, 4, 52–53.
134. *ibid.*, 52. See Bruno Stäblein, 'Zwei Melodien der altirischen Liturgie'. In H. Hüschen (ed.), *Musicae Scientiae Collectanea. Festschrift für Karl Gustav Fellerer zum 70. Geburstag.* Cologne: Arno Volk 1973, 590–597.
135. Patrick Vincent Brannon, *A Contextual Study of the Four Notated Sarum Divine Office Manuscripts from Anglo-Norman Ireland.* Ph.D. diss., Washington University, 1990. UMI Dissertation Services no. 9103125: Ann Arbor 1994, 15–17; *ibid.*, 'The Search for the Celtic Rite. The TCD Sarum Divine Office MSS reassessed'. In Gerard Gillen and Harry White (edd.), *Irish Musical Studies 2: Music and the Church*, Irish Academic Press: Blackrock, 37, n.10.
136. Isobel Woods has observed chants with similar features in Scottish sources, which strengthens Stäblein's case without undermining my own pleadings. See Isobel Woods, '"Our awin Scottis Use": Chant Usage in Medieval Scotland', *Journal of the Royal Musical Association* 112(1), 1987, 21–37.

137. See Hughes (as n.87) *passim.*
138. See F.E. Warren, *The Liturgy and Ritual of the Celtic Church.* Second Edition with a new Introduction and Bibliography by Jane Stevenson. Studies in Celtic History ix, Woodbridge: Boydell and Brewer, 1987, lxxx.
139. McCone (as n.11), 35ff.
140. *Pace* Fleischmann and Brannon. See Aloys Fleischmann, 'References to Chant in Early Irish MSS'. In S. Pender (ed.), *Féilscríbhinn Tórna.* Cork: Cork University Press, 1952, 47, and *ibid.* (as n.133), 53; cf. Brannon cf. (as n.135), 1994, 15. For further discussion of these sources, see Buckley (as n.23), Section 4.3.
141. Cf. Huglo (as n.132), 189.
142. Barbara Münxelhaus, 'Aspekte der Musica Disciplina bei Eriugena'. In R. Roques (ed.), *Jean Scot Erigène et l'Histoire de la Philosophie. Actes du Colloque International 561.* Paris: CNRS 1977, 253–262; *ibid.*, 'Der Beitrag Irlands zur Musik des frühen Mittelalters'. In H. Löwe (ed.), *Die Iren von Europa im frühen Mittelalter.* Stuttgart: Klett-Cotta 1982, ii, 630–638.
143. Unfortunately, Brannon (as n.135) 1993, 15, 1994, 14 and n.21, has reproduced an error, long ago corrected by Fleischmann (see Fleischmann (as n. 140), 1952, 48), concerning the presumed destruction of organs at the Irish Church of Cluain Cremha. The original source is an entry for the year 814 in the Annals of Ulster. Fleischmann, who traced the cause of the error, noted that the reference, *organ Cluain Cremha*, was glossed *direptio* in the margin, a translation of the Irish term *organ* ('destruction') which has been misconstrued as referring to organs by a number of writers ever since. The Old and Middle Irish term *organ* can refer to a music instrument or to some kind of organised sound in one or, usually, more parts (like the Latin term *organum* from which it is derived); but clearly not in this case. It is indeed regrettable that only the source cited by Brannon (Warren (as n.138), 126 and n.4), now very much out of date, was republished, in its original 1881 version, without correction of this error. But it also underlines the critical importance of checking the original source and having due regard, in particular, for the complexities of medieval Irish (and other) terminology.

In a not too dissimilar vein of Celtic optimism, William Leslie Sumner (*The Organ. Its Evolution, Principles of Construction and Use.* London: Macdonald, 1973, 35), referred to the sixth-century Irish saint, Maildu(l)f, founder of the monastery at Malmesbury, as a maker of organs. It appears that nothing was beyond the bounds of possibility (or credibility) where these ingenious Irish monks were concerned! Although Sumner does not state whether the source was in Latin or in Irish, or supply its date, it may be that it represents one of the many fantastic feats attributed to those hero-saints (perhaps paving the way for St Dunstan (*c*924–988) who did provide an organ for Malmesbury, and who was a known performer on several instruments, including a lyre). However, it is also possible that the term which Sumner saw, whether the Latin *organum* or Irish *organ*, was intended as a general term of reference to an instrument of music – perhaps in this case, even a stringed instrument – that is, assuming that the reference actually states in some form that which Sumner reports. Having said that, it is equally important to mention that the late history of antique (i.e., hydraulic) organs is very opaque indeed; but it should be remembered that they were used on occasions of jubilation and display, to heighten the excitement of gladiatorial combat and to lend further intensity to imperial acclamations, not for performing melodies as we understand them. The adoption of (wind-driven) organs in the West is not attested before 757 when one was presented to Pepin III by the Byzantine Emperor Coroticus. For at least two centuries it seems to have been confined to palace use only. It is not known to have entered the precincts of church or monastery before the tenth century. For recent discussion see James McKinnon, 'The Tenth Century Organ at Winchester', *The Organ Yearbook* 5 (1974), 4–19; Hammerstein (as n.28), 85ff.

Brannon's study contains other errors which can ill be afforded in this neglected, often over-indulgent, field of Irish music historiography. He appears unaware of the extent of recent debate on Gerald of Wales's references to instruments. Apart from the general inadequacy of the translation upon which he relies, he even renders Gerald's *timpanum* (*timpan*, an Irish stringed instrument) as English 'tabor', a drum, an error exposed by O'Curry over a century ago (see O'Curry (as n.42), 363). For recent studies of the medieval Irish *timpan*, see Ann Buckley 'Notes on the tiompán in Irish literature', *Studia Instrumentorum Musicae Popularis* 5. Stockhom: Musikmuseet 1977, 84–90; also *ibid.*, (as n.82) and *ibid.*, 'Timpan/Tiompán', *The New Grove* and *The New Grove Dictionary of Musical Instruments*, ed. S. Sadie, London: Macmillan 1980 and 1986 (respectively).

An appraisal of the many pitfalls and problems in the history of Geraldine music-historical commentary, together with all relevant quotations (in Latin and English translation), is provided in Nixon (as n.97), *passim*.

144. D.N. Dumville, 'Liturgical drama and panegyric responsory from the eighth century? A re-examination of the origin and contents of the ninth-century section of the Book of Cerne', *Journal of Theological Studies*, N.S. 23 (1972), 374–406.

145. See Carney (as n.3), 72–75.

146. See, for example, Jean Leclerc, 'Documents on the cult of St Malachy', *Seanchas Ardmhacha* 3 (1959) 318–336; also David Hiley, 'Rouen, Bibliothèque Municipale, MS 249 (A.280) and the Early Paris Repertory of Ordinary of Mass Chants and Sequences', *Music and Letters* 70 (4), 1989, 471–472, 481–482, for a source of sequences in honour St Laurence O'Toole from the collegiate church of St Laurent at Eu where the saint died in 1180. There are some notated fragments in the Vienna Schottenkloster, probably dating to the thirteenth century, containing devotions to Irish saints (including Patrick, Brigid, Columba, Kilian), which appear to be linked to the Vienna monastery's founding community at Regensburg.

147. as n.86, 93.

148. Instruments from Hiberno-Norse and Hiberno-Norman Irish sites have been discussed in the following articles of mine: 'Notes on the Archaeology of Jew's Harps in Ireland', *North Munster Antiquaries Journal* 25 (1983) 29–35; 'Jews's Harps in Irish Archaeology'. In Cajsa S. Lund (ed.), *Second Conference of the ICTM Study Group on Music Archaeology*, Stockholm: Publications issued by the Royal Swedish Academy of Music no.53 (Stockholm 1986), I, 49–71; 'A Ceramic Signal Horn from Medieval Dublin', *Archaeologia Musicalis* 1 (1987)

9–10; 'A Viking Bow from 11th–century Dublin', *Archaeologia Musicalis* 1 (1987) 10–11; 'Musical Instruments from Medieval Dublin – a Preliminary Survey'. In E. Hickmann and D. Hughes (edd.), *The Archaeology of Early Music Cultures: Proceedings of the Third International Conference of the Study Group on Music Archaeology*, Bonn: Verlag für systematische Musikwissenschaft 1988, 145–162; 'Sound Tools from the Waterford Excavations' [typescript] 1991; 'An archaeological survey of musical instruments from medieval Ireland'. In Franciszek Rożnowski (ed.), *Miscellanea Archaeologica Thaddeo Malinowski Dedicata*, Sorus: Słupsk-Poznań 1993, 65–72. cf. also n.96.

149. See Hugh Shields, 'Carolling at New Ross, 1265', *Ceol* 4(2) (1973) 34–36; *ibid.*, 'The Walling of New Ross: a thirteenth-century poem in French', *Long Room* 12–13 (1975–6), 24–33. Also Joseph Long, 'Dermot and the Earl: who wrote "The Song"?' *Proceedings of the Royal Irish Academy* 75 C 13 (1975) 263–272; Alan Bliss and Joseph Long, 'Literature in Norman French and English', *A New History of Ireland II: Medieval Ireland 1169–1534*, ed. Art Cosgrove. Oxford: The Clarendon Press, 1987, 715ff.

150. See Brannon (as n.135); Máire Egan-Buffet and Alan J. Fletcher, 'The Dublin *Visitatio Sepulcri* Play', *Proceedings of the Royal Irish Academy*, 90 C 7 (1990), 159–241; also Frank Ll. Harrison, 'Polyphony in medieval Ireland'. In E.M. Ruhnke (ed.), *Festschrift Bruno Stäblein*. Kassel: Bärenreiter, 1967, 74–79. For a full list of medieval sources containing music notation (including fragments), see Buckley (as n.97), Appendix. Brannon (1994, 42–43), provides a list of all of the Irish Sarum manuscripts.

REFERENCES

Anderson, A.O. and M.O. *Adomnan's Life of Columba*. Edinburgh: Thomas Nelson & Son, 1961. Rev. Oxford: Oxford University Press 1991.

Ancient Laws of Ireland. 6 vols., Rolls Series. Dublin and London 1865–1901.

Best, R.I. and O. Bergin (edd.), *The Book of Leinster* I, Dublin: Dublin Institute of Advanced Studies, 1954.

Bliss, A.J., The inscribed slates at Smarmore, *Proceedings of the Royal Irish Academy* 64 C 2 (1965) 33–60.

Bliss, Alan and Joseph Long, Literature in Norman French and English, *A New History of Ireland II: Medieval Ireland 1169–1534*, ed. Art Cosgrove, Oxford: The Clarendon Press, 1987, 708–736.

Brannon, Patrick Vincent, The Search for the Celtic Rite. The TCD Sarum Divine Office MSS Reassessed. In G. Gillen and H. White (edd.), *Irish Musical Studies 2: Music and the Church*, Blackrock: Irish Academic Press 1993, 13–40.

—— , *A Contextual Study of the Four Notated Sarum Divine Office Manuscripts from Anglo-Norman Ireland*. Ph.D. diss., Washington University, 1990. UMI Dissertation Services no. 9103125. Ann Arbor, Michigan 1994.

Breatnach, Breandán, *Folk Music and Dances of Ireland*. Dublin and Cork: The Mercier Press 1971/rev. 1977

Brown, Peter, *The Cult of the Saints. Its Rise and Function in Latin Christianity*. Chicago and London: The University of Chicago Press and SCM Press, 1981.

Buckley, Ann, Notes on the tiompán in Irish literature, *Studia Instrumentorum Musicae Popularis* 5, Stockholm: Musikmuseet, 1977, 84–90.

—— What was the tiompán? A study in ethnohistorical organology: Evidence in Irish literature, *Jahrbuch für musikalische Volks- und Völkerkunde* 9 (1978) 53–88.

—— Timpan/Tiompán, *The New Grove* and *The New Grove Dictionary of Musical Instruments*. London: Macmillan 1980 and 1986, respectively.

—— Notes on the Archaeology of Jew's Harps in Ireland, *North Munster Antiquaries Journal* 25 (1983) 29–35.

—— Jew's Harps in Irish Archaeology. In Cajsa S. Lund (ed.), *Second Conference of the ICTM Study Group on Music Archaeology*, Stockholm: Publications issued by the Royal Swedish Academy of Music no. 53, Stockholm 1986, 1, 49–71.

—— A Ceramic Signal Horn from Medieval Dublin, *Archaeologia Musicalis* 1 (1987) 9–10.

—— A Viking Bow from 11th–century Dublin, *Archaeologia Musicalis* 1 (1987) 10–11.

—— Musical Instruments from Medieval Dublin – a Preliminary Survey. In E. Hickmann and D. Hughes (edd.), *The Archaeology of Early Music Cultures: Proceedings of the Third International Conference of the Study Group on Music Archaeology*, Bonn: Verlag für systematische Musikwissenschaft, 1988, 145–162.

—— Musical Instruments in Ireland from the ninth to the fourteenth centuries. A review of the organological evidence. In Gerard Gillen and Harry White (edd.), *Irish Musical Studies I: Musicology in Ireland*, Blackrock: Irish Academic Press, 1990, 13–57

—— Boundaries in the field – what do they serve? A review of the landscapes of historical musicology and ethnomusicology. In Ann Buckley, Karl-Olof Edström and Paul Nixon (edd.), *Proceedings of the Second British-Swedish Conference on Musicology: Ethnomusicology (Cambridge, 5–10 August 1989)*. Skrifter från Musikvetenskapliga Institutionen, Göteborgs Universitet, no. 26; Musikmuseets Skrifter 21: Göteborg 1991, 39–59.

—— Sound Tools from the Waterford Excavations [typescript 1991].

—— An archaeological survey of musical instruments from medieval Ireland. In Franciszek Rożnowski (ed.), *Miscellanea Archaeologica Thaddeo Malinowski Dedicata*, Słupsk–Poznań: Sorus 1993, 65–72.

—— Music and Humanisation as long-term Process. In Marcel Otte (ed.), *'Sons Originels'. Préhistoire de la Musique. Actes du Colloque de Musicologie, 11– 12–13 Décembre 1992*, Études et Recherches Archéologiques de l'Université de Liège, no. 61. Liège 1994, 275–285.

—— Music in Ancient and Medieval Ireland. In *A New History of Ireland* 1, Oxford: The Clarendon Press (forthcoming).

___ Music-related imagery on early Christian Insular sculpture: identification, context, function, *Imago Musicae/International Yearbook of Musical Iconography* 8 (1991).

—— *The Old French Lyric Lai to c.1300. A Comparative Study of French and Latin Monophonic Song*. New edition and study. 3 vols. Lucca: Libreria Musicale Italiana (forthcoming).

Byrne, Francis J. , *Irish Kings and High Kings*. London: Batsford, 1973/R1987.

Camille, Michael, *Images on the Edge. The Margins of Medieval Art.* London: Reaktion Books 1992.

Carney, James, *Medieval Irish Lyrics* with *The Irish Bardic Poet.* Portlaoise: The Dolmen Press 1967/R1985.

Connolly, Philomena and Geoffrey Martin (edd.), *The Dublin Guild Merchant Roll, c1190–1265.* Dublin: Dublin Corporation 1992.

Connolly, S.J., *Priests and People in Pre-Famine Ireland 1780–1845.* Dublin and New York: Gill and Macmillan/St Martin's Press 1982.

Crossley-Holland, Peter, Myth and Music in Ancient Ireland, *The Mankind Quarterly* 21(4), Summer 1981, 377–391.

Curran, Michael, *The Antiphonary of Bangor.* Blackrock: Irish Academic Press 1984.

Derricke, John, *The Image of Ireland; with a Discoverie of Woodkarne.* London 1581; repr. with the notes of Sir Walter Scott. Edited with Introduction by John Small. Edinburgh: Adam and Charles Black 1883.

Dillon, Myles, The Taboos of the Kings of Ireland, *Proceedings of the Royal Irish Academy* 54 C 1 (1951), 1–36.

—— , *Stories from the Acallam.* Medieval and Modern Irish Series 23. Dublin: Dublin Institute for Advanced Studies. 1970.

Dimock, J. , *Giraldi Cambrensis Opera.* The Rolls Series 5. London 1867.

Dineen, Patrick S. (ed. and trans.), *The History of Ireland by Geoffrey Keating, D.D. Volume II, containing the first book of the History from Sect.l XV to the End.* Irish Texts Society 8. London: David Nutt, 1908.

Dobson, E.J. and F. Ll. Harrison, *Medieval English Songs,* London: Faber and Faber 1979.

Dumville, D.N., Liturgical drama and panegyric responsory from the eighth century? A re-examination of the origin and contents of the ninth-century section of the Book of Cerne, *Journal of Theological Studies,* N.S. 23, (1972), 374–406.

Egan-Buffet, Máire and Alan J. Fletcher, The Dublin *Visitatio Sepulcri* Play, *Proceedings of the Royal Irish Academy,* 90 C 7 (1990), 159–241.

Elias, Norbert, *The Civilizing Process, I, The History of Manners.* Oxford: Blackwell, 1939/R1978.

—— , *The Civilizing Process, II, State Formation and Civilization.* Oxford, Blackwell, 1939/R1982.

Fleischmann, Aloys, References to Chant in Early Irish MSS. In S. Pender (ed.), *Féilscríbhinn Tórna,* Cork: Cork University Press 1952, 43–49.

—— , Celtic Rite, Music of the, *The New Grove Dictionary of Music and Musicians.* London: Macmillan 1980, 4, 52–53.

—— and Ryta Gleeson, Music in ancient Munster and monastic Cork, *Journal of the Cork Historical and Archaeological Society* 70(2), no. 202, (1965), 79–98.

Gerbert, Martin, *De cantu et musica sacra a prima ecclesiae aetate usque ad praesens tempus.* St Blasien, 1774/R1968.

Glosecki, Stephen O., Wolf Dances and Whispering Beasts: Shamanic Motifs from Sutton Hoo? *The Mankind Quarterly* 26 (3&4), Spring and Summer 1986, 305–319.

Gray, Elizabeth A. (ed.), *Cath Maige Tuired. The Second Battle of Maige Tuired.* Irish Texts Society 52. Naas 1982.

Gurevich, Aron, *Medieval Popular Culture. Problems of Belief and Perception*; transl. J.M. Bak and P.A. Hollingsworth. Cambridge and Paris: Cambridge University Press/Éditions de la Maison des Sciences de l'Homme 1988/R1992.

Gwynn, E.J. and W.J. Purton, The Monastery of Tallaght, *Proceedings of the Royal Irish Academy* 29 C 5 (1911), 115–179.

Hammerstein, Reinhold, *Macht und Klang. Tönende Automaten als Realität und Fiktion in der alten und mittelalterlichen Welt*. Bern: Francke 1986.

Harrison, Frank Ll., Polyphony in medieval Ireland. In E.M. Ruhnke (ed.), *Festschrift Bruno Stäblein*. Kassel: Bärenreiter, 1967, 74–79.

Hiley, David, Rouen, Bibliothèque Municipale, MS 249 (A.280) and the Early Paris Repertory of Ordinary of Mass Chants and Sequences, *Music and Letters* 70 (4), 1989, 467–482.

Holmes, Holmes and J.M. Coles, Prehistoric Brass Instruments, *World Archaeology* 12(3) (1981), 280–286.

Hughes, Kathleen, Some Aspects of Irish Influence on Early English Private Prayer, *Studia Celtica* 5, (1970) 48–61.

——, *Early Christian Ireland. An Introduction to the Sources*. London: The Sources of History Ltd. in association with Hodder and Stoughton 1972.

Huglo, Michel, L'Organum à Landévennec au IXe siècle, *Études Celtiques* 23 (1986) 187–192.

Jeffery, Peter, *Re-Envisioning Past Musical Cultures. Ethnomusicology in the Study of Gregorian Chant*. Chicago and London: The University of Chicago Press 1992.

Kenney, James F., *The Sources for the Early History of Ireland: Ecclesiastical. An Introduction and Guide*. Dublin: Pádraic Ó Táilliúir 1979.

Krusch, Bruno (ed.), *Ionae Vitae Sanctorum Columbani, Vedastis, Iohannis*. Hannover, 1905.

Leclerc, Jean, Documents on the cult of St Malachy, *Seanchas Ardmhacha* 3 (1959), 318–336.

Le Goff, Jacques, *Time, Work, and Culture in the Middle Ages*, transl. Arthur Goldhammer. Chicago and London: The University of Chicago Press, 1980.

Long, Joseph, Dermot and the Earl: who wrote 'The Song'? *Proceedings of the Royal Irish Academy* 75 C 13 (1975) 263–272.

Lund, Cajsa S., The 'phenomenal' bronze lurs. In Cajsa S. Lund (ed.), *The Bronze Lurs*, Second Conference of the ICTM Study Group on Music Archaeology II, Publications issued by the Royal Swedish Academy of Music no. 53, Stockholm 1986, 9–50.

Macalister, R.A.S., *Tara. A Pagan Sanctuary*. London: Charles Scribner's Sons, 1931.

MacNeill, Eoin, Ancient Irish Law. The Law of Status or Franchise, *Proceedings of the Royal Irish Academy* 36 C 16 (1923), 265–316.

McCone, Kim, *Pagan Past and Christian Present in Early Irish Literature*. Maynooth: An Sagart 1990/R1991.

McGrath, Fergal, *Education in Ancient and Medieval Ireland*. Blackrock: Skellig Press, 1979.

McKinnon, James, The Tenth Century Organ at Winchester, *The Organ Yearbook* 5 (1974), 4–19.

Meid, Wolfgang, *Táin Bó Fraích*. Medieval and Modern Irish Series 22. Dublin: Dublin Institute of Advanced Studies 1967.

Meyer, Kuno (ed. and trans.), *The Vision of MacConglinne*. London: David Nutt, 1892.

Meyer, Kuno (ed. and trans.), *Four Old Songs of Summer and Winter.* London: David Nutt 1903.

Münxelhaus, Barbara, Aspekte der Musica Disciplina bei Eriugena. In R. Roques (ed.), *Jean Scot Erigène et l'Histoire de la Philosophie. Actes du Colloque International 561*, Paris: CNRS 1977, 253–262.

—— , Der Beitrag Irlands zur Musik des frühen Mittelalters. In H. Löwe (ed.), *Die Iren von Europa im frühen Mittelalter*, Stuttgart: Klett–Cotta, 1982, ii, 630–638.

Nixon, Paul J., Giraldus Cambrensis on Music: How Reliable are his Historiographers?' In Ann Buckley (ed.), *Proceedings of the First British-Swedish Conference on Musicology: Medieval Studies, 11–15 May 1988.* Publication issued by the Royal Swedish Academy of Music no. 71, Stockholm 1992, 264–289.

Ó Corráin, Donnchadh, Liam Breatnach and Kim McCone (edd.), *Sages, Saints and Storytellers. Celtic Studies in Honour of Professor James Carney.* Maynooth Monographs 2. Maynooth: An Sagart 1989.

O'Curry, Eugene, *Manners and Customs of the Ancient Irish*, III. London and Dublin: 1873.

O'Donoghue, Tadhg , Advice to a Prince, *Ériu* 9 (i), Part 1 (1921), 43–54.

O'Donovan, John (trans.), *The Banquet of Dún na nGédh and the Battle of Magh Rath*. Dublin: Irish Archaeological Society 1842.

Panum, Hortense, *Stringed Instruments of the Middle Ages*, rev. and ed. Jeffrey Pulver. London: William Reeves 1940/R1971.

Petrie, George, On the History and Antiquities of Tara Hill, *Transactions of the Royal Irish Academy* 18 (1839) 125–232.

Praetorius, Michael, *Syntagma Musicum*. [1619] II: *De organographia*, trans. and ed. David Z. Crookes. Oxford: Clarendon Press 1986/R1991.

Radner, Joan Newlon, *Fragmentary Annals of Ireland*. Dublin: Dublin Institute of Advanced Studies 1978.

Rimmer, Joan, *The Irish Harp*. Cork and Dublin: The Mercier Press 1969/1984.

Ryan, Michael (ed.), *Treasures of Ireland. Irish Art 3000 B.C.–1500 A.D.* Dublin: Royal Irish Academy, 1983.

Shields, Hugh Carolling at New Ross, 1265, *Ceol* 4(2) (1973) 34–36.

——, The walling of New Ross: a thirteenth-century poem in French, *Long Room* 12–13 (1975–6), 24–33.

Simms, Katharine, Guesting and Feasting in Gaelic Ireland, *Journal of the Royal Society of Antiquaries of Ireland* 108, 1978, 67–100.

Stäblein, Bruno, Zwei Melodien der altirischen Liturgie. In H. Hüschen (ed.), *Musicae Scientiae Collectanea. Festschrift für Karl Gustav Fellerer zum 70. Geburtstag*, Cologne: Arno Volk 1973, 590–597.

Stokes, Whitley (ed. with trans. and notes), *Anecdota Oxoniensa. Lives of the Saints from the Book of Lismore*. Oxford: Clarendon Press 1890.

Stokes, Whitley, The Battle of Allen , *Revue Celtique* 24 (1903), 41–70.

—— (ed. and trans.), *In Cath Catharda. The Civil War of the Romans*. Irische Texte, 4th ser., 2. Leipzig 1909.

Stokes, Whitley and Ernst Windisch, *Acallam na Senorach*. Irische Texte 1. Leipzig 1900.

Sumner, William Leslie, *The Organ. Its Evolution, Principles of Construction and Use*. London: Macdonald 1952; rev. 1973.

Taylor, John Walter, Tree Worship, *The Mankind Quarterly* 20 (1–2) 1979, 79–141.

Tierney, James J., The Celtic Ethnography of Posidonius, *Proceedings of the Royal Irish Academy* 60 C 5 (1960) 189–275.

Tolkien, J.R., 'Welsh and English'. In *Angles and Britons*. O'Donnell Lectures (Cardiff 1963), 1–41.

Van Schaik, Martin, The Harp Bag in the Middle Ages. An Iconographical Survey. *Proceedings of the International Historical Harp Symposium, Utrecht 1992*. In Martin van Schaik (ed.), *Aspects of the Historical Harp*, Utrecht: STIMU 1994, 3–11.

Warren, F.E., *The Liturgy and Ritual of the Celtic Church*. Second Edition with a new Introduction and Bibliography by Jane Stevenson. Studies in Celtic History ix, Woodbridge: Boydell and Brewer, 1987.

Woods, Isobel, 'Our awin Scottis Use': Chant Usage in Medieval Scotland, *Journal of the Royal Musical Association* 112(1), 1987, 21–37.

Traditional Music and Irish Cultural History

RÍONACH UÍ ÓGÁIN

This essay addresses certain aspects of Irish traditional music and the history of Irish culture. In the first section it draws on early Irish literature as a source in illustrating the role of music in Irish cultural history. The second section deals with an era in which traditional music, song and dance have become established and where outside influences have been absorbed on many levels to form a native tradition corpus. The final section concentrates on the social and aesthetic functions of music in contemporary Irish life, functions which have been dictated to a large degree by all the aspects of history that influence and shape attitudes to culture.

1. THE DEVELOPMENT OF CULTURAL FORMS

Irish traditional music has always been a particularly vital aspect of Irish culture. In the last decade in particular, Irish music has achieved a high degree of international popularity and has become a powerful vehicle for establishing links with other countries and cultures. It is, of course, a vibrant means of communication. Clearly song, music, dance and related material are all part of Irish music or of Irish musical culture. Although they overlap, they are also individual aspects of a general corpus. The word 'Celtic' has been applied to Irish music and it introduces a question to which there may be several complicated answers; although it is debatable whether the Irish could be described as blood-Celts, their music may possibly have some kind of 'Celtic' source but there is no evidence to support this theory.

In tracing the development of these cultural forms, some of the earliest available sources provide a great deal of information towards understanding the importance and the role of music in early Irish tradition. The term *teinm laída* (illumination of song) has been well-documented in the Irish metrical tracts as one of the qualifications required by aspiring poets who had to undergo a rigorous and long course of training. Chanting was also one of the prerequisites in the education of a poet. The terms *díchetal* (verbal noun of *can*) and *cetal* (cantation) are also used in this context and underline the importance of the qualification. They appear in these instances to be technical terms and along with *imbas forosnai* (knowledge which illuminates) are associated together and related to the art of the poet.[1]

In early Irish literature the human voice is emphasised as a form of musical expression and frequently this expression takes on a magical significance. In both the literature and in oral tradition, Fionn Mac Cumhaill is one of the most celebrated heroes, originally as a 'divine figure symbolising wisdom',[2] and his close association with song and chant indicates their special role in early Ireland. One of Fionn's many talents was his ability to produce *ex tempore* rhetoric and this included automatically the ability to chant these rhetorics. The word used to denote his chanting was *díchetal*, and was seen by the eighth to the ninth-century writers as a term appropriate to Fionn's magical wisdom.[3] Chanting appears to have been closely associated with ritual in the Fenian material, as implied by the phrases *díchetal de chennaibh colla* (chanting from the extremities of the body) and *cetal na haisnéise* (chanting of prophecy). *Teinm laída* features in a story found in Cormac's glossary, an Old-Irish glossary compiled by Cormac Ua Cuileannáin, King-Bishop of Cashel in the tenth century. Here, the character Lomna, Fionn's fool, was killed and his head taken away while his body was left behind. Later, Fionn was asked to identify the body, whereupon he put his thumb into his mouth and chanted *teinm laída*, and said it was Lomna's body.[4]

Chanting in early Irish literature was practised in extreme circumstances and conveyed the special, magical associations of music. The belief in the power of music is illustrated in the story of the Battle of Allen found in the fourteenth to fifteenth century manuscript of the Yellow Book of Lecan and elsewhere. Fergal, son of the high-king of Ireland and Donn Bo, an excellent reciter of poetry and saga, are killed in battle against the Leinstermen. One of the victorious Leinstermen is sent to the battlefield to fetch a man's head.

> Baethgalach, a valiant Munsterman, volunteers, and as he comes near to where Fergal's body lies, he hears a voice and sweet music (apparently resembling that of an orchestra). He learns that a head in a clump of rushes is addressing him: 'I am Donn Bo,' says the head; 'I have been pledged to make music to-night for Fergal.' The head consents to allow itself to be taken on condition that it is afterwards brought back to its body. Baethgalach promises, and returns to the feast with the head, which is then placed on a pillar in their midst. Baethgalach orders the head to make music for them, as it has been wont to for Fergal. But Donn Bo . . . sings a sweet melody, but so plaintive that the Leinstermen weep bitter tears, and presently the same warrior takes back the head of Donn Bo to his body, and fits it to its trunk.[5]

Other instances occur in the early Irish sagas where the heads of dead sages chant, for example the head of Cúchulainn's father chants a lament in the Tain Bo Cuailgne.[6]

These happenings are clearly pre-Christian performances: among the rites abolished by Patrick was the *teinm laída*, as heathen offerings were involved in its performance. The concepts of magic, rhythm and incantation were interlinked. Meaning took second place to the chanting and the sound of the performance conveyed its purpose in onomatopoeic, alliterative form.[7] Rhythm in poetry is termed *rosc* and has a secondary meaning, a short poem, ode or chant once again conveying the proximity of the spoken rhythmic word to music along with the special nature of these forms. The overlap of pre-Christian and Christian tradition in Ireland is conveyed in words like *cetal*, which has the meaning of spell or incantation in a literary context, and in a biblical and ecclesiastical context has the meaning chanting or reciting psalms or chants (DIL 1968, 155) – *díchetal . . . druadh do chetal fair* and *cetal ind sailm*.[8] This use of *canaid* (sings, recites) in both the literary and ecclesiastical sense, once again indicates the context associations of the word 'chanting'.[9]

Although the nature of the music which accompanied the chanting is lost to us, it is certainly relevant that in modern Irish today the words '*abair amhrán*' are used when asking someone to sing. This communicates the importance of the text. The word *amhrán* was originally used to describe a poem composed in *amhrán* metre which was based on vowel assonance as opposed to syllabic metre. *Amhrán* then became the descriptive term for a song. Music was accepted as a force which had an inherent, divine power. The Fianna had their own musician, Aillén, and when he played his harp, the music was so powerful that it put to sleep everyone who heard it. The only exception to this was Fionn who had magical protection against the enchantment.

As to the tunes or melodies themselves, there are no early documents to indicate form or sound, apart from the idea that chanting, rhythm and shouting were closely interlinked. The quality of the music played was evidently of great importance and the onomatopoeic *séis* denoted an air, strain or melody, and in compound forms also conveyed the perfection of harmonious and melodious sound. Also from the Latin *sensus*, but later than *séis* is *síansa*, conveying the allegorical or mystical nature of music and meaning melody, harmony, a strain of music or the whistle of a weapon.[10] The word *port* used in modern Irish to describe a jig, or sometimes a general term for a tune, is comparatively late. The author of *Foras Feasa ar Éirinn*, the history of Ireland which was completed in the mid-seventeenth century, recounts a legend in which *port síthbhinn* plays a central part. Maon, who was also called Labhraidh Loingseach, was allured from France to Ireland when Moiriath, daughter of a king in west Munster, fell in love with him and the effect of music and song on his emotions was to set significant events in motion:

> Ollmhuighthear lé Craiftine Cruitire, oirfideach do bhí fán am soin i nÉirinn, ré dul 'n-a dhiaidh don Fhraingc agus iomad do ghréithibh geanamhla leis mar aon ré laoidh chumainn 'n-ar nocht sí díoghainne a dioghraise do Mhaon; agus sinnis port síthbhinn ar a chruit ar rochtain na Fraingce do Chraiftine an tan ráinig mar a raibhe Maon; agus gabhais an laoidh chumainn do rinne Moiriath inghean Scoiriath do Mhaon. Gabhais an oiread soin lúthghára ré hoirfideadh Chraiftine é go ndubhairt gur bhinn leis an laoidh is an port; agus ar n-a chlos soin da mhuinntir is do Chraiftine, do ghuidheadar rí Frangc fá chongnamh sluagh do thabhairt dó fá theacht dobhuain a chríche féin amach; agus tug an rí líon cabhlaidh dó .i. dá chéad ar fhichid céad; agus triallaid ar muir; agus ní haithristear a bheag da scéalaibh gur ghabhadar cuan ag Loch Garman.[11]

> She (*Moiriath*) equipped Craiftine, the harper, a musician who was in Ireland at the time, that he might go after him to France with many love-presents, together with a love-lay in which she set forth the intensity of her passion for Maon; and when Craiftine arrived in France, he played *a very sweet tune on his harp* (author's italics) when he came to where Maon was, and sang the love-lay which Moiriath daughter of Scoiriath had composed for Maon. He was so delighted with Craiftine's playing that he said he considered *the song and the tune melodious*; and when his followers and Craiftine had heard this, they besought the king of the French to give him an auxiliary force so that he might go and regain his own territory; and the king gave him a fleetful, that is, two thousand two hundred, and they put out to sea; and no tidings whatever are given of them till they put into harbour at Loch Garman.

In his study *Homo Ludens*, where the author examines the play element of culture, in which music holds a special position, Huizinga says that dancing is a particular and particularly perfect form of playing. This may explain to some degree the affinity between the word *damhas* for dance in modern Irish, and the use of the same word formerly to describe the frolicking of cattle emphasising the 'pure play' in the act of dancing.[12] In most of Ireland the same word *damhas* is used to describe human dancing which in some areas is equally known 'as *rince*. Both words *damhsa* and *rince* in modern Irish are borrowings and are first encountered in sixteenth and seventeenth century texts.

The word *dord* is used in modern Irish to denote a deep or bass humming sound and is a word of early origin. Unfortunately, as with so much else in music-related early Irish culture, we are left to surmise a great deal on the actual sound that was produced by the *dord*. It was doubtless a pleasant sound as the word, or a derivative, is used to describe variously mermaid's chanting, the song of a thrush and the belling of a stag.[13]

The *dord fiansa* appears to signify a kind of chant or refrain performed by the Fianna which was accompanied by a sound produced by striking together the shafts of their spears.[14] *Crann-Dord* also appears in this context and has been interpreted as a clashing together of wooden poles or spear handles as mentioned in *Táin Bó Cuailgne*.[15] It is most likely that *dord* would not be mentioned in the Fenian literature if it had not actually existed as Fenian lays are thought to mirror factual life, although the mirroring was retrospective, rather than current or directed towards the future.

The significance of music and its sounds is further illustrated by the numerous examples and varied applications of the word *ceol* and its derivative, and with this word we enter another aspect of the world of sound and its profound significance in early Irish tradition. Sweet sounding and melodious qualities are mentioned regularly. Compound words with *ceol* or a derivative also convey this regard for music's special aesthetic and mysterious qualities. *Leig don cheolchroidhe cuislinn* (from music's heart) is used in a descriptive sense as is, *is ciall dá gceolfhoghar* (they mean by their melody).[16] The earliest native Irish instruments mentioned in Gaelic literature include the *crott* , modern Irish *cruit* or *cláirseach* meaning a harp or lute, typically translating the Latin *cithara*. The regular occurrence of the Irish word in glosses and in early texts such as *Acallamh na Senórach* indicates the importance of this instrument and the respect accorded to its players, the *cruitti* who were graded according to expertise and had an *ard ollamh Ereann i ccruitirecht* as attested in the Annals of the Four Masters. The only entertainer who had independent legal status was the harpist, and this is an indication in itself of the regard in which the music of the harp and the harpist were held. Two other types of musician of a lower grade were referred to in legal tracts, the piper and the horn player, who were of a lower grade to the harpist, but were seen nonetheless to merit reference.[17] Yet another instrument which was mentioned with the *crott* in some texts was the *timpán*, a word which clearly derived from the Latin *tympanum*. It was apparently a stringed instrument and was frequently mentioned in conjunction with harp players and harp music,[18] although it did not achieve the same status as the harp. Also mentioned in early texts is the *feadán* (a musical pipe or whistle) which assumes great importance in the Fenian lore and once again interlinks music and magic. In one early tale, Aillén, a musician of the Tuatha Dé Danann, played sweet sounding music on the *tiompán* and on the *feadán*, but Fionn Mac Cumhaill had secret means of resisting the sleep induced by the music.

Early visual representations of musicians and their instruments assume a particular significance where other evidence of musical form, such as music notation, is lacking. A few representations in stone survive, like the figure on the tenth-century cross of scriptures at Clonmacnoise which shows a figure with three connected pipes in his mouth. The pipes are doubtless made of cane or reed and illustrate what must be some of the earliest instruments in Irish tradition, and more importantly portray the significant role of the musician in Irish society. Other illustrations in stone, most probably from the ninth and tenth centuries, depict a stringed instrument being played, and the eleventh century plaque attached to the shrine of St. Maodhóg clearly shows a harp with Irish characteristics.[19] However, on the whole, evidence is scant in relation to music type or form in early times, but the picture painted by the contemporary source material is one of an essential overlap between poetry and song, and a close association between magic, chanting, rhythm and song, which indicates the power of the poet or chanter and the esteem in which they were held.

2. THE FORMULATION OF A TRADITION CORPUS

Although a certain amount of knowledge is to be found, particularly in literary sources, relating to the role of music and song in Irish culture up to the sixteenth century, a clearly identifiable tradition corpus has emerged only in comparatively recent times. In the last five hundred years much more factual information is available to us about Irish culture in general, and about traditional music in particular.

The face of Irish music has changed substantially in the last five hundred years. Certain terms and words have changed meaning and been adapted to suit changes. Of course, the process of growth, change and the formulation of a music tradition corpus is, of its nature, gradual and not deliberately designed or contrived to produce a particular kind of music. It is largely an involuntary and unselfconscious creation. Although the earliest documented Irish traditional air occurs in the sixteenth century, it is probably, as is the case with so many other aspects of tradition, the documentation of what was earlier a purely oral tradition.[20] The same applies to the first Irish song – air and words combined – which was printed in the eighteenth century.[21]

Partly because of the strength of the manuscript tradition in the world of Irish poetry and partly because of the late appearance of music notation in the manuscript tradition, there has been a tendency to query whether or not the verse presented in manuscript form was sung to a given air or indeed, to any air. The answer is not simple, but the evidence suggests that some form of chanting or singing was the norm, and poetry and verse when married to music become song. A recent pertinent account by Liam de Noraidh, collector of music and song with the Irish Folklore Commission from 1940 to 1942, illustrates this 'singing of poetry':

> Lá dá rabhas i gcaidreamh mo charad Bean Uí Ríordáin (80 bl.) i mBaile Mhúirne, tharraing sí leabhar filíochta chuici féin – cnuasach filíochta Eoghain Ruaidh a bhí ann. Chrom sí ar fhéachaint tríd, agus in ionad na hamhráin a léamh b'amhlaidh a chanadh sí iad. Bhíodh fonn láithreach aici d'oireadh do mhéadar pé amhráin a thagadh faoina súile.[22]

> One day when I was in the company of my friend Bean Uí Ríordáin (80 yrs.) in Baile Bhúirne, she took up a book of poetry – it was a collection of Eoghan Rua's poetry. She began to look through it, and instead of reading the songs, she sang them. She had an air immediately that would suit the metre of whichever song her eye fell upon.

This was doubtless an inherited feature of traditional singing in Ireland and applied no less to the penny sheets or ballad sheets of songs mostly in the English language. These verses were described as 'song', but the name of an accompanying air was rarely suggested. It has been established for example, that of the two thousand odd broadside ballads in the collection of the National Library of Ireland, almost all of which are from the nineteenth century, 'less than two per cent of the items were directed to be sung to named airs'.[23] These broadsides were printed at a time in Irish cultural history when the Irish language was in decline and this decline has affected music, song and dance to the present day. Political and economic factors were part of the cause and effect of the changes. Songs in English were part of the traditional repertoire from the late seventeenth century onwards and these included English and Scottish ballads and also native Irish compositions. This meant that the decline of songs in the Irish language was paralleled with an increase in songs in English so that, in many instances, what had been a repertoire of songs in Irish became a bi-lingual repertoire. The English language and, with it, the English language song tradition, were closely associated initially with urban development, and this is certainly one of the reasons for the lack of international ballad tradition in the Irish language. The changeover in spoken language did not mean the automatic change and translation of song type. Most likely because of major social and economic change from the thirteenth century onwards, song in the Irish language took on a kind of rural or pastoral image which it maintains to some extent today. Insofar as narrative ballads are concerned, at least some of this vast body was adopted in the English language song tradition in Ireland and became an integral part of Irish musical culture.

Within the song tradition the nature of the songs which are composed and transmitted reveals a number of cultural characteristics. During the eighteenth and nineteenth centuries in particular, traditional music, song and dance developed identifiably Irish forms. The love-songs in Irish, which are undoubtedly a cornerstone of Irish song tradition, became established. Although they were composed, to a large extent, under the influence of an international literary renaissance of a much earlier period, they were, and still are, an especially Irish phenomenon in many other ways.[24] It is not possible to identify a single origin for the love-songs and neither is it possible to trace them to a period before the fourteenth century. There are many reasons for this. Clearly one reason is that the bardic schools flourished until the seventeenth century and only a small amount of documentation exists which indicate the nature of the vernacular song tradition. This latter tradition was so overshadowed by the more formal and structured manuscript composition and writing, that only some allusions survive in relation to a musical culture which is transmitted orally. This oral tradition itself must have changed a great deal over the years, so that by the time it became established it was moulded to suit a contemporary culture.

As we have seen, the harp was closely identified with Irish music, and the *uilleann* pipes rank probably in second place as regards instruments of a distinctly Irish nature. Although the pipes existed in Ireland in some form as early as the eleventh century, a particularly Irish form emerged only in the early decades of the eighteenth century. Other instruments became widespread in traditional music only in the last few hundred years. The most popular instrument of all, the fiddle, is an example of an instrument which was introduced to Ireland not earlier than the mid-seventeenth century, yet by the eighteenth century it was the dominant instrument. It was played chiefly for dancing, to which it was especially suited because of its flexibility.[25]

Some of the turmoil and diversity of Ireland's history – political, linguistic and ecclesiastical – is reflected in the musical tradition. As regards economical and social history, lilting, or *portaireacht bhéil* as it is known in Irish, played a dominant role in Irish dancing and music tradition, and its preponderance in particular districts illustrates how economic circumstances dictate, to a large extent, the presence or absence of musical instruments. Areas which were economically and socially disadvantaged and poor maintained their music and dance tradition through lilting. If we look at Conamara as an example of an impoverished area in the last century, musical instruments and, in particular, costly instruments like the *uilleann* pipes, were virtually non-existent and were not among the posessions of ordinary people. On the

Blasket Islands, in county Kerry, there is no recollection of an islander owning a set of pipes. But home-made fiddles were made, sometimes from wood which was readily available. Former Blasket Islanders remembered that a '*veidhlín*' was often made from driftwood and that at one time there were a number of home-made fiddles on the island, and also a number of shop-made ones.[26] Ironically, emigration brought its own rewards and the parcels which were sent home from the United States often gave recognition and scope to a musical talent at home where an accordeon, melodeon or concertina was included in the parcel sent home by the emigrant. Another aspect of Irish music is that it has been introduced, much of it through emigration, to other countries, especially to America, England and Australia, and has survived in a distinctly Irish form in these countries.[27]

In many instances, Irish culture has shown a remarkable ability to absorb new material and adapt it to its own. The free-reed instruments – melodeon, concertina and accordeon – found their way into the music of Ireland in the first half of the nineteenth century and were quickly married to the existing traditions.

There are numerous references to music and to musical instruments in Irish poetry in the seventeenth and eighteenth centuries and the role of a particular instrument is sometimes illustrated in song. Raiftearaí, the blind travelling poet and musician from county Mayo, praised the skills of one carpenter and craftsman, Seán Ó Braonáin of Creachmhaoil, county Galway:

> Tamboureen is cláirseach,
> French horn agus an clarinet
> an fife, an flute, an flageolet,
>   an fhidil agus an bow;
> seamsúr, boilg is mála,
> regulators is na heochracha,
> goití reed gan lucht ar bith,
>   drone, stoc agus dos mór.
> Aon ghléas ariamh dár dearnadh,
> a thabhairt chuige is níor mhiste leis,
> an hautboy is an spinet,
>   is a leagan os a chomhair,
> dulcimer is pianó
> is é a chuirfeadh i gcóir gach chuid acu,
> is ní fearr ná a dhéanfadh cuideachta
>   dá mbeadh sé i dteach an óil.[28]

> Tambourine and the harp,
> French horn and the clarinet,

the fife, the flute, the flageolet,
the fiddle and the bow;
chanter, bellows and bag,
regulators and the keys,
reeds flawless in appearance,
a drone, stock and bass drone.
Any instrument that was ever made
could be brought to him and he wouldn't mind,
the hautboy and the spinet,
and place them before him,
dulcimer and piano,
he would repair every part of them
and none better would keep you company
if he were in a public house.

Although little is known about dancing in Ireland prior to the seventeenth century, certain dance types are documented and there is an indication of their association with particular occasions. This is seen, for example, in a poem composed *c*.1687–1688, in celebration of James II accession to the throne of England where people are asked to dance *Rince an Chlaidhimh*, the sword dance, and *Rince an Ghadairigh* or *Ghaid*, the withy dance:

Déinidh rinnce is bídh go meanmnach
Is teinte cnámh ó shráid go falla agaibh
Ní nár síleadh tríd gach sparra libh
Rinnce an chloidhimh is rinnce an ghadaraigh.

Strike up the dance then, be jovial and jubilant,
And pile up your bonfires to fill up from street to wall;
Start at each city gate, what we ne'er hoped to see,
The dance of the sword and the dance of the withe again.[29]

The same two dances were danced by members of the O'Keeffe family before the death of their chief Dónall Ó Caoimh in 1669.[30] A dance entitled *An Rince Fada* seems to have been associated with occasions of public celebration and rejoicing.[31] Arthur Young's account of his journey to Ireland bears witness to some of the dances current in Ireland between 1776–1779:

Besides the Irish jig, which they can dance with a most luxuriant expression, minuets and country dances are taught, and I even heard some talk of cottillions coming in.[32]

The intimate relationship between songs and their music can perhaps best be understood in the songs which are regarded by singers and musicians alike as exemplary compositions. These include the pieces *Sliabh na mBan*, *Mainistir na Búille*, and *Anach Cuain*. Songs are primarily verbal in form and the air to which a song is sung is the emotional energy through which it is expressed. The song, therefore, dictates the musical interpretation, and the musical phrasing comes from the words of the song.[33]

The closeness of voice and music is recorded in a comment on the playing of the exceptionally talented Sligo fiddle player Michael Coleman. The speaker, Dick O'Beirne, talked about the flute players, melodeon players, and singers in the Killavil district in Sligo, all of whose music combined to shape the musical development of the young Michael Coleman:

> It was from this pooling of the genius of the older members of the great Killavil group that Coleman, through his genius for imitating and improvising, drew the unique inspiration in melody that sings like a voice through all his music.[34]

A great deal of what is considered most expressive in Irish traditional music, and especially in song, was composed at times of extreme deprivation and suffering by poets, singers and audience alike. Although intended for singing, the following verse from *An Bhláth-Bhruinneall* by Aindrias Mac Craith (An Mangaire Súgach) illustrates inherent aesthetic qualities and also communicates the entity of a song, words in music, as understood by the poet:

> A stóir dhil! mo stórsa tar aon tu,
> Mo stór tú go n-éagfad dar n-dóith;
> Is stór mé a stóir-dhil, gan tréada,
> 's gur dóith leo gur réic me gan fód;
> Beidheadh stór ag an stórach, ní baoghal di,
> Beidheadh bo-lacht gan baodhachas, 's fós,
> A stóir-dhil! do stórach, má thréigir,
> Gan stórach na rae 'gad am dheoig!
>
> Yours am I, my loveliest, wholly-
> O heed not the Blind and the Base,
> Who say that because of my folly
> I'll never have wealth, luck, or grace.
> How much the poor creatures mistake me!
> I'll yet have green acres and gold;
> But, O, if you coldly forsake me!
> I'll soon be laid under the mould![35]

This song may represent the thousands of love-songs composed during the troubled years of the eighteenth and nineteenth centuries. In this instance it is known that the county Limerick poet in question lived during times of hardship and also lived a reckless carefree life; he was at the same time, as Mangan said, 'perhaps the most melodious Gaelic poet of his day'.[36] The finest potential in a culture often finds its ultimate expression at a time when it is surrounded by, and under threat from, hardship or harshness. Here is an attempt at striking a balance between actual experience and inherited imagination. If song and music, primary vehicles of imaginative expression, were not available, then a sense of cultural hopelessness might well prevail. Where external, material, life may be difficult and challenging, culture often provides compensatory factors: conversely in times of affluence and physical comfort, there appears to be less challenge to the imagination, and a cultural dearth appears.

> At all times the vision of sublime life has haunted the souls of men, and the gloomier the present is, the more strongly this aspiration will make itself felt.[37]

Today, it may be argued that in many parts of Western Europe in particular where, physically and materially, life is extremely comfortable, the cultural imagination is, at best, unattractive. It has often developed into a form where violence, cruelty and a fascination with the grotesque and the morbid predominate in the creative world.

Perhaps it is true that only those who experience Irish music from within, active participators in the tradition, can comment in an entirely intimate and authoritative way on characteristics of Irish music. However, comments from those outside the tradition often help to identify characteristic features in a culture which are essentially 'Irish' because they are experiencing the tradition from without. The fact that Irish musicians were regarded as vastly more skilled than those of other countries was attested as early as the twelfth century by a Welshman who visited Ireland, namely, Giraldus Cambrensis, and the fact that he did not mention the kind of music they played indicates that its sound and form were in no way strange or foreign to him. Even in very recent times, the observation of a visitor can confirm an opinion or enhance a picture. In the middle of the nineteenth century, one William Irvine reported that:

> . . . a fiddler, a harper, or a piper was usually to be found in the small public houses attached to each of the Strawberry Beds, near the Phoenix Park.[38]

This is most likely the kind of comment that a local person would not make because they would regard the situation as too commonplace to merit mentioning. The response to an experience or experiences is often a key factor in determining the creation, development and ultimate retention of music and song, and the response is based in cultural experience.[39] Any particular piece of music has different meanings to different people, depending on the listener's background. The talented fiddle-player Mickey Doherty, from county Donegal, was renowned in the 1940s for his creative, virtuoso playing and one particularly artistic piece in his repertoire was entitled *The Hound after the Hare* which depicted in graphic musical representation the chase and capture of the hare.[40] This piece was held in high regard by the local community in Donegal during Mickey's lifetime, but today, it is a piece of music which is to a degree, in content and appeal, outside the culture of a rapidly increasing urban population. As part of my own work with traditional song, I have encountered on a few occasions a somewhat dismissive reaction to a declamatory, less ornamental style of singing traditional songs in Irish which existed in the early years of this century, a style which has by now disappeared and has been replaced by a more controlled, structured style of singing. This earlier style appeared strange to those who were more accustomed to contemporary styles and it is only when viewed, and heard, in a historical cultural context that such older material can be experienced and appreciated.

3. SOCIAL AND AESTHETIC FUNCTIONS

As observed by Huizinga, there is a semantic understanding between East and West in the meaning and use of the word 'play'. Musical instruments are 'played' in the Arabic, Germanic and Slavonic languages. It has been argued that there must be some deep-rooted psychological reason for so remarkable a symbol of the affinity between music and play, in relation to the use of the word play meaning 'fun'.[41] Modern Irish uses *seinm* for the playing of music and the word also means singing, warbling or chattering, all of which are pleasant, enjoyable events. Certain genres of music and song which have since disappeared had a function other than entertainment, but with changes in society these genres of music disappeared when they were no longer functional. One of the most striking examples of this kind of genre is the *caoineadh* or mourning for the dead. This cathartic performance over the corpse was strongly discouraged by the church, and as hospitals, funeral parlours and state services came to play a greater part in illness, old age and death, the *caoineadh* – along with its air and *ex tempore* composition – disappeared. In most instances, music, song and dance are particular-

ly social activities because of their inherent enjoyment factor. Other aspects
of tradition, such as calendar custom or patterns, provide enjoyment and
pleasant occasions, but their primary function is not necessarily to entertain.

Songs, and tunes to a lesser degree, may be badges of different social
groups and may express, for example, political feeling. Music is an aspect of
culture which is capable of rousing emotions in a particularly powerful way.

The chief function of music is to involve people in shared experiences
within the framework of their cultural experience.[42] For that very reason, it
mirrors a community's cultural past, present and future. In Ireland, the
Fenian lays, which were epic chants and not ballads, did not develop until
the twelfth century and were composed until at least the seventeenth century. Yet these lays were illustrative of a social life that had already disappeared at least fifty years before the time of their earliest composition in the
twelfth century. For example, artillery was in use in twelfth century Ireland
but is not mentioned in the Fenian material. These Fenian lays are part of a
literary heritage and have developed calcified forms in oral tradition and
perhaps this phenomenon of the Fenian cycle should be regarded as a general part of Irish culture and not as an isolated aspect of it. The language of literature tends towards a form which is about two hundred years behind the
spoken language. Druids and poets favoured 'ancient' sources and used
stereotyped formulae. The concept of antiquity assisted in developing the
belief in the special nature and value of music and song, a belief which has
survived to the present day.

In the contemporary situation Irish musicians, singers and dancers and
their audiences, value their musical heritage. This view has been supported
to varying degrees by official bodies over the years, but the most important
factor in the survival of the tradition is the high regard in which it is held by
those who perform it. Music has always been, and continues to be, a source
of cultural inspiration. People sense the uplifting nature of music and understand its special nature. The power of music for emotional release is long
attested to in the Irish literary tradition. In the mythic lore of the *Tuatha Dé
Danann*, the three musical feats which gave distinction to the harper were
not related to technique or beauty of playing as such, but rather to the emotional effect of the music on the listener, so that Dagda, the harper, played
the *goltraí* to produce weeping, *geantraí* to produce laughter and *suantraí* to
induce sleep.

Native Irish slow airs have always had a place of particular merit and distinction, due in no small measure to their potential emotional expression.
This esteem is a realisation that native airs and songs contain something
which is not part of the daily, humdrum existence. They are exceptional,
special, and make a powerful impact in particular when they are articulated
by especially talented musicians and singers.

This phenomenon of the exceptionally talented musician has been explained traditionally in a rational manner. The way in which it has been rationalised is the way in which people have always rationalised uncomprehended phenomena, that is, through a belief in magic. In Irish oral tradition there is a deeply rooted belief in the magical power of words and in the magical power of music. In early Irish literature, this power has been well documented in the oral and literary traditions, where it was believed that music and song could induce, for example, love or magic sleep, that song could provide protection on a journey, or that the flow of the cow's milk could be increased by song and music.[43] This general belief became a vital part of the tradition corpus at a later period. The musical genius of the fiddle players Michael Coleman and his brother Jim, was explained in the context of a supernatural experience. This account describes an occasion when the brothers were returning from a music session in Johnny Hunt's house in the Killavil locality in Sligo:

> The Coleman brothers set off home about midnight and they took a near way across the fields. And somewhere over in them fields there's an old fort supposed to be around two thousand years old, with a souterrain attached – an historical place, a strange place.
>
> They were supposed to have lost their way and found themselves in a beautiful garden with the loveliest trees they had ever seen, and the fields opened up into a large landscape. Instead of being afraid, it was joy. They had no fear. Jim was carrying a fiddle under his arm, and after a while they sat down and started to play the most beautiful music that ever was heard. All of a sudden the whole thing faded away from them: fear came over them and they went off home. They returned to Hunts' some nights after and their music, well there was a noticeable improvement in their music. The strange thing about it is, Michael never was known to tell the story. It was Jim that told it and I do know that Jim Coleman always had a terrible fear of the night.[44]

In Irish oral tradition, the music of the fairies is said to be of exceptional beauty and to have particular powers.[45] The fairies, or other world beings, sometimes grace the mortal world by conferring the gift of music on a human being. Implicit herein is the message that art of supreme beauty cannot be imitated as it has an inspirational or supernatural quality.

Here, we enter the realm of beauty. Huizinga discusses the concept of beauty in relation to enjoyment and the idea of play:

> . . . although the attribute of beauty does not attach to play as such, play nevertherless tends to assume marked elements of beauty . . .

> Mirth and grace adhere at the outset to the more primitive forms of
> play. In play the beauty of the human body in motion reaches its
> zenith. In its more developed forms it is saturated with rhythm and
> harmony, the noblest gifts of aesthetic perception known to man.[46]

Although the 'rhythm and harmony' mentioned here are not necessarily
describing music, they can certainly be applied to it readily as both are very
evident in the social context of music performance and related activities
where music introduces an enriching element. The beauty of music and song
is dependent to a large extent on the emotional impact of the performance
which depends in turn on the nature of the performance.

There is an understandable inclination to view music and music-related
activities as entities which are separate from other activities; Breandán Ó
Madagáin's comment to the effect that songs are not an independent entity
in themselves holds true, of course, for music and dance and other related
events. All are forms of human expression, and, as Breandán Ó Madagáin has
said, 'their vital context is the social life and culture of the community'.[47]
Certain facets of Irish life and culture are not only illustrated in song texts
but are highlighted by the emotional effect of the song. For example, emigration has taken a heavy toll on Irish families and continues to do so. Tom
Lenihan, Knockbrack, Miltown Malbay, County Clare, had a vast repertoire
of songs and ballads, and among them was a song called *The Christmas
Letter* from which the following is a verse:

> Then Kate, a stór, you're sleeping whilst my eyes is red with weeping,
> Yes, weeping for those little ones that's gone so far away.
> Will you read again that letter? somehow it makes me better,
> Oh, each time I hear the news of them that's in Americay.
> Oh, the kitchen here was full of them, but one by one the lot of them
> Sailed out across the great big sea to that land so far away;
> And now each little motion of that wild and dreadful ocean
> Falls heavy on a mother's heart this blessed Christmas Day.
>
> (IFC Tape TM 326/B/5)

Although the song may appear overly sentimental, it assumes a harsh significance viewed against the background of emigration from Ireland. Tom
Munnelly, song collector with the Department of Irish Folklore, has described
the effect on the listeners of this song:

> I myself have been in homes in West Clare at Christmastide and wit-
> nessed the impact of this song. The women listeners wept openly and
> the men shifted uncomfortably while making furtive attempts to wipe
> away their own tears before they were noticed.[48]

Another song entitled '*Máire Ní Mhongáin*' is full of sadness and is a song with which the Conamara singer, Sorcha Ní Ghuairim, identified. She said:

> Seo amhrán a bhfuil an-luí ag muintir Chonamara leis mar baineann an scéal atá ann dhóibh féin. Máire Ní Mhongáin bean a bhí ina cónaí thiar in aice le Baile na Cille a rinne é. Cailleadh an chéad fhear a bhí aici agus phós sí athuair. Ansin scaip an chéad chlann agus ó tharla go mbíonn bean i gcónaí i ndiaidh an chuid is sine den chlainn, bhí sí buartha brónach. Tá scéal gach máthar i gConamara ann a dtéann a gclann thar sáile. Dá chomharthaíocht sin, is minic a chonaic mé mná ag caoineadh agus an t-amhrán seo dhá ghabháil.[49]

> This is a song that people from Conamara enjoy a great deal because the story in it relates to them. It was composed by Máire Ní Mhongáin, a woman who lived near Baile na Cille. Her first husband died and she married again. Then her first family scattered and as a woman always favours the oldest members of the family she was sorrowful and sad. It tells the story of every mother in Conamara whose family emigrates. An indication of this is that I have often seen women crying while this song was being sung.

In the last hundred years a great deal of change has taken place in the field of Irish music, much of it part of a general homogenisation and technological progress. Irish music has been assimilating music and influences from other musical traditions. Clearly, this has affected both repertoire and style, among other things. These developments are not so much about change itself but about people's reaction to change, and how this finds expression in musical forms.

From the point of view of general human psychology, songs can be perceived as an illustration of words with sound. The lyrical love-songs in Irish which are designed for the ear are non-narrative in content and may have a visual emotional effect, and a person can be visibly moved and affected by a song or a piece of music. W.B. Yeats described, in a graphically appreciative manner, an occasion when he went to listen to Irish songs at a 'wide place on the Kiltartan-road' and depicted not only the atmosphere but the significance of the singing. He wrote:

> While I waited for the singers an old man sang the *Póraidh Glégeal* [*sic*] the praise of that country beauty who died so many years ago, and is still remembered, and spoke of a singer he had known who sang so beautifully that no horse would pass him, but must turn its head and cock its ears to listen. Presently a score of men and boys, and girls, with

shawls over their heads, gathered under the trees to listen. Somebody sang '*Sa Mhuirnín Dílis*, and then somebody else *Jimmy mo Mhíle stór*, mournful songs of separation, of death, and of exile. Then some of the men stood up and began to dance, while another lilted the measure they danced to, and then somebody sang *Eibhlín a Rúin*, that glad song of meeting which has always moved me more than other songs, because the lover who made it so long ago sang it to his sweetheart under the shadow of a mountain I looked at every day in my childhood. The voices melted into the twilight, and were mixed into the trees, and when I thought of the words they too melted away, and were mixed with the generations of men. Now it was a phrase, now it was an attitude of mind, an emotional form, that had carried my memory to older verses, or even to forgotten mythologies. I was carried so far that it was as though I came to one of the four rivers, and followed it under the wall of Paradise to the roots of the trees of knowledge and of life. There is no song or story handed down among the cottages that has not words and thought to carry one as far, for though one can but know a little of their ascent, one knows that they ascend like those old genealogies through unbroken dignities to the beginning of the world. Folk art is indeed the oldest of the aristocracies of thought, and because it refuses what is passing, trivial, the merely clever and pretty, as certainly as the vulgar and insincere, and because it has gathered into itself the simplest and most unforgettable thoughts of the generations, it is the soil where all great art is rooted.[50]

The status given to musicians, singers and dancers within their culture indicates to some extent the regard in which these traditions are held. In modern Ireland there are obviously many forces at work which influence attitudes towards Irish music. These forces are both internal and external, and are determined by economic, linguistic, sociological and many other factors. Music can express social attitudes and cognitive processes, but it is useful and effective only when it is heard by the prepared and receptive ears of people who have shared, or can share in some way, the cultural and individual experiences of its creators.[51]

We can look at and examine the music tradition in Ireland today and see what has survived from the past. This is an indication in itself of what has been valued. Some aspects may have been discarded or may have lost their function, and attempts may have been made to revive them or recreate them. One instance may serve to illustrate this point. The naming of an organised evening's dancing as *céilí* probably stems from a desire to use a native word to describe a comparatively recent social function. Formerly, *céilí* meant a visit or visiting, usually in the evening, and was thought suitable to apply to public dances when they were established at the turn of this century in Ireland.

In many instances we have been left with only the remnants of a tradition, and so it is much more difficult to say what has been discarded over the last few hundred years. In the twentieth century in relation to song in Irish, much of what has been discarded is associated with the disappearance of the Irish language in many counties. The demise of Irish includes the disappearance of a song tradition, especially songs with a local theme. The cultural values inherent in this song material have also disappeared. The songs which were the creation and expression of the *Gaeltachtaí*, cannot survive except in some artificial manner if the language in which they were first composed disappears as a spoken language. A recognition by song composers of different linguistic cultural values within Ireland may be found in the lack of translated songs, from Irish or from English, in the living singing tradition. As regards the English language song tradition in Ireland, the ballads, which are a part of the international song tradition, have almost disappeared. This is a change which has taken place over the last number of years. More and more, traditional singing in Ireland is in the hands, or rather the voices, of the outsider or of the revivalist. Much good work has been done over the years in collecting and documenting material to enable future generations to become familiar with traditional music and Irish culture.[52] It is certainly true to say that songs are not assimilated or acquired in the same way today as they were fifty years ago or even more recently than that. The concept of a purely oral tradition and of purely oral transmission is in the past. This holds true in all aspects of traditional music and song. Perhaps it is less so in dance, although the idea of 'instruction' is now a predominant feature in all aspects of the transmission of Irish musical tradition. Changes in performance and in methods of transmission have been accompanied by changes in style. It is important to note the reduction in distinct regional styles in instrumental music in this context. This is due in some degree to increased mobility, and to a more receptive approach to outside influences, and also to more access to these influences.

In order to assess cultural development and growth, perhaps one can look at some recent creations in the field of traditional music. A question often asked in relation to the singing tradition is whether new compositions are being created. The answer is that songs are being composed in Irish and in English. Some songs have taken on the role of socio-political comment as has happened, for example, in the case of compositions, in Irish, by John Beag Ó Flatharta in Conamara, or the songs of Fintan Vallely in English.[53] In the case of the former, this material has become part of the song tradition of Conamara, but although these recent compositions exist comfortably alongside other songs which are hundreds of years old, it is difficult to predict their survival for hundreds of years, as their relevance is immediate and their messages presented in an amusing, contemporary fashion. Comic songs usually disappear from tradition when the incident or humour ceases to be relevant to society.

As regards instrumental music and Irish culture, the most audible change is that fewer slow airs are played today. This has implications in relation to the expression of aspects of Irish culture through traditional music. The legacy of Irish music is no longer seen to include a substantial number of slow airs. One reason may be that music for dancing is much in demand due to the set-dancing revival. Another reason is, doubtless, the decline in the Irish language and its song tradition.

Obviously, social change has affected the performance situation of music and song. They are nowadays no longer associated with a domestic setting and are performed for the most part at festivals and formal occasions. This kind of public performance leads to a less intimate and less personal form of communication in music.

Ireland is renowned internationally as a country rich in its own expression of music and song. Groups or individual singers who are not 'traditional' in an absolute or purist sense, can still be said to reflect not only the importance of music and song in Irish culture, but also to articulate a sense of cultural history in their representation of Irish music. As the traditional musician and singer becomes ever more a part of the world of international music, involved in commercially – or culturally – contrived performances, Irish music and song are becoming more and more widely available both in Ireland and abroad. In keeping with the documentation of the scribes of the early centuries, who described in detail the importance of song and music in early Irish society and the power of that song and music, traditional music in Ireland, and all that it entails, is one of the most vibrant aspects of Irish culture today and in its many forms it is an unparalleled expression of the Irish imaginative tradition.

NOTES

1. Nora K. Chadwick, 'Imbas Forosnai', *Scottish Gaelic Studies*, Vol. IV, part 2 (1934–1942), (London *et al.*, 1935), 97–135. It has been argued elsewhere that the term *teinm laídi* means literally 'the chewing (or breaking open) of the pith'. Cf. Tomas O'Rahilly, *Early Irish History and Mythology* (Dublin, 1946), 336–40. A suggested interpretation is also 'breaking of the marrows' (?). Cf. Fergus Kelly, *A Guide to Early Irish Law* (Dublin, 1988), 44. I am indebted to Donall Mac Giolla Easpaig for his kind assistance with the early Irish language material. I would like to express also my sincere thanks to Bairbre Ní Fhloinn, Dr Anne O'Connor and to Dr Dáithí Ó hÓgáin, for their suggestions and generous assistance in the preparation of this essay.
2. Dáithí Ó hÓgáin, *Fionn Mac Cumhaill: Images of the Gaelic Hero* (Dublin, 1989), 25.

3. Dáithí Ó hÓgáin (as n. 2), 63.
4. Chadwick (as n .1), 118–19.
5. Chadwick (as n. 1), 123.
6. Chadwick (as n. 1), 125.
7. Cf. Dáithí Ó hÓgáin, *An File* (Baile Atha Cliath, 1982), 320, where a detailed study of the power of the poet in relation to satire is presented.
8. Myles Dillon et al. (edd.), *Contributions to a Dictionary of the Irish Language* [DIL] (Dublin, 1913–1975), 155 .
9. DIL (as n. 8), 55–56.
10. DIL 1953 (as n. 8), 208–209.
11. Seathrún Céitinn, *Foras Feasa ar Éirinn* (Geoffrey Keating, *The History of Ireland* Vol. II), ed. Rev. P. Dinneen (London, 1908),164–65. For earlier occurrences of this tale and an account of it see under *Labhraidh* in Dáithí Ó hÓgáin, *Myth, Legend and Romance* (England, 1990), 267–69.
12. John Huizinga, *Homo Ludens* (London, 1949), 164.
13. DIL (as n. 8), dodénta-dúus (1960), 357.
14. DIL (as n.13).
15. Eugene O'Curry, *Manners and Customs of the Ancient Irish*, Vol.III (Dublin and New York, 1873), 376.
16. DIL (as n.8), 1968 , 134–35.
17. Kelly (as n. 1), 64.
18. DIL (as n. 8) T-tnúthaigid 1943, 174; Breandán Breathnach, *Ceol agus Rince na hÉireann* (Baile Atha Cliath, 1989), 22.
19. Joan Rimmer, *The Irish Harp: Cláirseach na hÉireann* (Cork, 1977), 26.
20. Breathnach (as n. 18), 4–5: *'Cailín ó chois tSiúire mé'*, the well-known air *'The Croppy Boy,'* was published in *William Ballet's Lute Book* in 1594.
21. Breandán Breathnach, 'The First Irish Song Published', *Ceol: A Journal of Irish Music*, Vol. 5 , no. 1 (7/1981), 2–3. The original of the song *Sín síos agus suas liom* is in the British Library and bears no date but has been assigned to 1714.
22. Liam de Noraidh, *Ceol ón Mumhan* (Baile Atha Cliath, 1965), 10.
23. Alf MacLochlainn, 'To the air of . . . ', *Éigse Cheol Tíre* I (Dublin, 1972–73), 54.
24. Hugh Shields, *Narrative Singing in Ireland* (Dublin, 1993), 58–83; Uí Ógáin, 'The Love-Songs of Conamara', *Dal gCais* X (1991), 111–123.
25. For further reading on the role of the pipes and fiddle cf. Breandán Breathnach, *Folkmusic and Dances of Ireland* (Dublin, 1971), 73– 85.
26. Ríonach uí Ógáin, 'Ceol on mBlascaod', *Bealoideas* 56 (1988), 213.
27. The far-reaching influences of Irish music have been documented in Nuala O'Connor, *Bringing It All Back Home* (London, 1991).
28. Ciarán Ó Coigligh, *Raiftearaí: Amhráin agus Dánta* (Baile Atha Cliath, 1987), 59. For further information on the pipes as they appear in the Irish language song tradition, cf. Éamonn Brophy, 'The Song of the Chanter', *Dal gCais* X (1991), 95–101.
29. James MacErlean, ed., *Duanaire Dháibhidh uí Bhruadair*, Part III (London, 1917), 110–11. The editor and translator includes a footnote: There were dances known as the sword-dance and the withe-dance, but the words here contain an allusion to the wielding of swords and the hanging of traitors.

30. Breandán Breathnach, 'Dancing in Ireland to 1700', *Dal gCais* IV (1978), 106
31. Breandán Breathnach, 'Dancing in Ireland from 1700', *Dal gCais* V (1979), 39
32. Breathnach (as n.31), 40
33. In an unpublished lecture by singer and uilleann piper Éamonn Brophy, 5 May 1990, at the annual *tionol* of Na Píobairí Uilleann, the lecturer discussed in detail the playing of slow airs and the nature of the relationship between words and music in the playing of song airs. I am indebted to him for permission to refer to this lecture.
34. Harry Bradshaw, *Michael Coleman 1891–1945* (Dublin, 1991), 24
35. Translated by J.C Mangan in *Poets and Poetry of Munster* (Dublin, n.d.), 105–106
36. Mangan (as n. 35), 26
37. John Huizinga, *The Waning of the Middle Ages* (London, 1987), 36
38. William Irvine, *What they are doing in Ireland* (Manchester, 1859), 16
39. John Blacking, *How Musical is Man?* (London, 1976), 52
40. *The Gravel Walks* (Dublin, 1990), side1: 2
41. Huizinga (as n. 12), 158
42. Blacking (as n. 39), 48
43. Tom P. Cross, *Motif-Index of Early Irish Literature* (Indiana, 1952), 136, 145, 11, 210
44. Bradshaw (as n. 34), 27–28
45. The power of fairy music may be to the benefit or detriment of the listener. See for example W. G. Wood-Martin, *Traces of the Elder Faiths of Ireland*, vol. II (London, et al., 1902), 20–1. See also Cross (as n. 43), 254 and Sith Thompson, *Motif Index of Folk-Literature*, Vol. VI (Indiana, 1956), 531, 707, 730–731.
46. Huizinga (as n.12), 7
47. Breandán Ó Madagáin: 'Functions of Irish Song in the Nineteenth Century', *Bealoideas* 53 (1985), 132
48. Tom Munnelly, *The Mount Callan Garland* (Dublin, 1994), 86
49. Unbound manuscript in the Folk Music Section, Department of Irish Folklore. 1942. I am grateful to the Head of this Department for permission to consult and quote from archive material.
50. *An Claidheamh Soluis agus Fáinne an Lae* (Dublin, 13 July 1901), 281
51. Blacking (as n. 39), 54
52. Under the auspices of the Irish Folklore Commision, later the Department of Irish Folklore, a vast amount of material has been collected which contains priceless firsthand documentation on all aspects of Irish traditional music and cultural history. Among this material is for example song material in the Irish language from counties Tipperary and Limerick. Since 1974 Tom Munnelly, who has been a full-time collector with the Folk Music Section of the Department of Irish Folkore, University College Dublin, has collected and transcribed over 2000 audio-tapes of traditional singers throughout Ireland. The bulk of these recordings documents the English language song tradition in Ireland. The collection allows for unparalleled access to an aspect of the history of Irish culture which illustrates singer, repertoire, performance, style and other related aspects.

53. John Beag Ó Flatharta and others have composed and performed songs which are based in the culture of Conamara, but are highly relevant to other *Gaeltachtaí* also. The songs bemoan, some in country and western style, various social ills and among these are the scourges of emigration, unemployment and the potholes in the roads in Conamara. See for example *John Beag: Amhráin Ghaeilge* (CIC 084 Gaillimh: Cló Iar-Chonnachta, 1992) which contains tracks such as 'Na Blianta i Huddersfield'. For recent songs in English, see for example *Knock Knock Knock!* (Derry: UMFA Tapes 001, 1989) [Tim Lyons and Fintan Vallely] which contains songs like 'The Moving Statues'. Fintan Vallely has also composed numerous songs on political themes.

REFERENCES

John Blacking, *How Musical is Man?* (London: Faber & Faber, 1976).

Harry Bradshaw, *Michael Coleman 1891–1945* (Dublin: Viva Voce, 1991).

Breandán Breathnach, *Folkmusic and dances of Ireland* (Dublin: Mercier Press, 1971).

——'Dancing in Ireland to 1700' *Dal gCais* iv (Miltown Malbay: Dal gCais Publications, 1978) 103–07.

——'Dancing in Ireland from 1700' *Dal gCais* v (Miltown Malbay: Dal gCais Publications, 1979) 39–42.

——'The First Irish Song Published' Ceol: *A Journal of Irish Music* v no. 1 (7/1981) (Dublin: The Folk Music of Ireland Society, 1981) 2–3.

—— *Ceol agus Rince na hÉireann* (Baile Átha Cliath: An Gúm, 1989).

Éamonn Brophy, 'The Song of the Chanter' *Dal gCais* x (Miltown Malbay: Dal gCais Publications, 1991) 95–101.

Seathrún Céitinn, *Foras Feasa ar Éirinn*: Keating, Geoffrey *The History of Ireland* vol. ii, ed. Rev. P. Dinneen (London: The Irish Texts Society, 1908).

Nora K. Chadwick, 'Imbas Forosnai', *Scottish Gaelic Studies* vol iv, part ii (1934–1942), (London et al.: Oxford University Press , 1935) 97–135.

Tom P. Cross, *Motif-Index of Early Irish Literature* (Bloomington: Indiana University Publications, 1952).

Liam de Noraidh, *Ceol ón Mumhan* (Baile Átha Cliath: An Cumann le Béaloideas Éireann, 1965).

DIL *Contributions to a Dictionary of the Irish Language*, ed. Myles Dillon et al. (Dublin: The Dublin Institute for Advanced Studies, 1913–75).

The Gravel Walks CBÉ 002 (Dublin:Comhairle Bhéaloideas Éireann 1990).

Johan Huizinga, *Homo Ludens* (London: Routledge, Kegan, Paul, 1949)

—— *The Waning of the Middle Ages*, (London: E. Arnold & co, 1924, Penguin Edition ,1987).

William Irvine, *What they are doing in Ireland* (Manchester: A. Ireland & co, 1859).

Fergus Kelly, *A Guide to Early Irish Law* (Dublin: The Dublin Institute for Advanced Studies, 1988).

James MacErlean, ed. *Duanaire Dháibhidh uí Bhruadair* part iii (London: The Irish Texts Society, 1917).

Alf MacLochlainn, 'To the air of . . . ' *Éigse Cheol Tíre 1* (Dublin: The Folk Music of Ireland Society, 1972–73) 54–55.

James Clarence Mangan, *Poets and Poetry of Munster* (Dublin: Duffy & co, nd).

Tom Munnelly, *The Mount Callan Garland* (Dublin: Comhairle Bhéaloideas Éireann, 1994).

Ciarán Ó Coigligh, *Raiftearaí: Amhráin agus Dánta*, (Baile Átha Cliath: An Clóchomhar Teo, 1987).

Nuala O'Connor, *Bringing It All Back Home* (London: BBC Publications, 1991).

Eugene O'Curry, *Manners and Customs of the Ancient Irish* vol. iii (Dublin and New York: Williams & Norgate, 1873)

Dáithí Ó hÓgáin, *An File* (Baile Átha Cliath: An Clóchomhar Teo, 1982).

—— *Fionn Mac Cumhaill: Images of the Gaelic hero* (Dublin: Gill & MacMillan, 1988)

—— *Myth, Legend and Romance* (England: Ryan Publishing co, 1990)

Breandán Ó Madagáin, 'Functions of Irish Song in the Nineteenth Century' *Béaloideas* 53 (Baile Átha Cliath: An Cumann le Béaloideas Éireann, 1985) 130–216.

Tomás O'Rahilly, *Early Irish History and Mythology* (Dublin: The Dublin Institute for Advanced Studies, 1946).

Joan Rimmer, *The Irish Harp: Cláirseach na hÉireann*, (Cork: Mercier Press, 1977).

Hugh Shields, *Narrative Singing in Ireland* (Dublin: Irish Academic Press, 1993).

Ríonach Uí Ógáin, 'Ceol ón mBlascaod' *Béaloideas* 56 (Baile Átha Cliath: An Cumann le Béaloideas Éireann, 1988) 179–219.

—— 'The Love-Songs of Conamara' *Dal gCais* (Miltown Malbay: Dal gCais Publications, 1991) 111–23.

Nationalism and Irish Music

JOSEPH J. RYAN

How Grafton street has changed. A stroll through this attractive thoroughfare reveals how its recently pedestrianized paving has made it reminiscent of similar shopping precincts in Amsterdam, Copenhagen, and so many other European cities. The unversed visitor would today find difficulty in identifying this inanimate star of *Ulysses* as peculiarly Irish or central to a distinctive Dublin. And the dress of those who people the street would provide little assistance. This is an eclectic age: that mix of formal clothing, casual wear, the dress of protest, and current vogue for recreational apparel that the observer will discover in Grafton street is of the same diversity as in a fashionable centre of any major European conurbation. It is this very variety that provides the contrast with those attractive pictures of the street from the first decade of this century which show that familiar uniform of suit and hat for men and long and doubtless warm dresses for the women. The century has experienced a move from the uniform to the individual.

So it is with music. The variety of creative styles presented by the current school of indigenous composition is much the same as will be encountered in any fellow European city. Dublin and Ireland is at one with its neighbours displaying the same diversity, the same absence of assurance in a singular musical path that can be seen as either a strength or weakness depending on one's point of view. Just as with the physical landscape and the apparel of the people who give it life, there has undeniably been commensurate change in the perceptions of music.

UNIFORMITY AND DISTINCTION

This easy embrace of variety is what distinguishes the last decade of the century from the first. The century's opening was unwelcoming of eclecticism and there was a particular suspicion in Ireland where peripheral location has consistently sponsored a conservative outlook. Furthermore, in that chauvinistic age that emerged in the second half of the last century and extended into this, art was increasingly indentured to politics and music was for many valued as an abutment of a political outlook. In addition, it was

101

inconvenient in an age that valued uniformity that there was absence of consensus on what constituted Irish music. There is some irony here; an age that exhorted uniformity also required diversity, but it had to be a communal diversity, a uniform difference; the greater picture sought to comprise an assemblage of distinct images, and it was the purpose of each nation to make its peculiar contribution. A group desirous of being considered a nation – here signifying a people united in language, culture, and sympathy – would wish to make such a contribution but Ireland faced fundamental difficulties in this respect. Commentators would agree that the populace depicted in those early pictures of Grafton street would have been faced with a divided musical tradition; some were versed in the broader aesthetic of European art music and its more popular derivatives while a smaller number, given the urban location, would have had a musical allegiance to a traditional Irish note that was increasingly championed primarily for its very distinction from any universal culture. The former practice was a largely urban-based minority interest concentrated on a delimited group and suffering as a result of the poor level of musical literacy resultant on the low priority afforded music within the still-developing educational system. The latter was a living oral tradition intimately associated with the native language and traditional rural life which was inevitably threatened by increasing sociological change. It would be too simplistic to claim that the boundary between the two practices was absolute; an account of Carolan's work demonstrates that cross influence did occur, but in an age when there was a perceived necessity to aver a national way of life, a distinctive music possessed considerable practical and even political attractions. Happily such expediency did not last, but while it did an adversarial and exclusive mood dominated and there emerged in consequence a value system which sought to celebrate the indigenous and to disparage the cosmopolitan primarily in order to accent the distinction required by the tenets of nationalism. Those who walk in the capital's shopping streets today are not given to such reasoning; even the many buskers will demonstrate a variety of instruments and styles. There is today not only a willingness, but even a determination to break down barriers and to marry erstwhile distinctive styles with the result that music in Ireland now presents, albeit on a modest scale, the same stylistic multiplicity evident in neighbouring European nations.

NATIONALISM AND THE DIVIDED TRADITION

It is the bold contention of this paper that nationalism, the most potent political force in the modern era, is the crucial determinant on the course of music in Ireland in the past two centuries. The campaign to be accepted as an autonomous nation and the consequent claim for political sovereignty founded on that suit constituted the principal focus of public life for the duration. It is perhaps inevitable that such a powerful patriotic sentiment underlying a policy of national independence should hold sway in artistic matters; but it is the degree of influence that is telling. An observer's attention is drawn to this situation by the discrepancy between that celebration of the Irish as a most musical nation and the negligible creative output of Irish writers for the majority of the period in question. The eminent literary critic, Denis Donoghue, in a clear-eyed appraisal of Irish musical health made the point that

> There is in Ireland to-day no composer whose works an intelligent European musician *must* know.[1]

This assessment is irrefutable although it should be pointed out that it was made in 1955 and there has been welcome enterprise for change in the intervening decades. That Ireland, with its rich reputation, had descended to such artistic penury was largely the fruit of the puissant influence of nationalism on creative endeavour. There has in the past been too ready a willingness to attribute all deficiencies to a social and political condition resulting from a colonial history. Such a consequence undeniably plays a part, but as a people we are perhaps too ready to employ these incontestable practical difficulties in order to exonerate our own nation and its divided musical community for its failure to discover an earlier consensus for harmonious progress. The palliation also sits uneasily with the experiences of other aspiring nations in similar political circumstances. There is, furthermore, within Ireland the uncomfortable comparison with the impressive literary achievements of the same age which suggest that milieu alone cannot be held accountable for the sorry response of music.

No one could, however, gainsay the obstacles to musical activity in nineteenth-century Ireland. The salubrity of all high art had been undermined by the effects of the Act of Union which removed Dublin and Ireland from a central position in the affairs of these islands. The transfer of the political and commercial administration entailed the consequent departure of the very class that sponsored cultural activity. Music, which has always been an expensive art was especially enervated by the passing of patronage. An aristocratic art could not survive the passing of the aristocracy. Dublin became the 'deposed capital'[2] no longer of a significance sufficient to attract leading musicians from abroad. Nor, following the cultural displacement, was there sufficient audience at home to sponsor appreciable activity. The course of art music never recovered from this reversal through the whole century. Native musicians were forced abroad in order to pursue studies and subsequent

careers; the histories of Field, Balfe, Wallace, and later Stanford all testify to
the dearth of opportunity in Ireland. None of the infrastructure necessary to
a robust musical life existed in the country in the nineteenth century: there
was a poor standard of musical literacy; little educational opportunity; there
was consequently no ready audience; and there were but few concert venues.
Of these, by far the greatest limitation to the prospects of the art was the
want of a systematic scheme of music education. Here again nationalism
played a part; the debate over *what* was to taught was itself a factor in delay-
ing the emergence of a comprehensive design. Not until the middle of the century could Ireland boast of having its own specialized music school, which
was particularly necessary as the standard and availability of music in state
schools was poor. Music had little place at the primary level until the *Select
Committee of the House of Commons on Foundation Schools and Education
in Ireland 1835–6* recommended that vocal music be included as an option-
al subject on the curriculum of national schools because of its moral value and
civilizing influence.[3] It was to be the second half of the century before the
establishment of the Royal Irish Academy of Music and the municipal schools
of music in Dublin and Cork. The consequence of this sorry educational
record was that Ireland had neither the executants nor the discriminating public necessary to effect any substantial revival. The resultant want of a tradition of musical literacy is doubtless a major contributory factor in accounting
for the low priority afforded the art over many generations. It is embarrassing
in the light of such proud reputation to record that there is in Ireland little
consistent interest in matters musical. The narrative of music in the country
is a tale of heroic individual endeavour in the face of successive waves of
public enthusiasm which invariably fades to indifference. Accordingly, the
history is not the record of people and its art but of the commitment of individual labourers whose dedication and vision was responsible for providing
at least a modicum of music. It bears repeating that conditions were not
favourable to such enterprise; there were few opportunities to devote time
wholly to music in this period with limited openings for performers and the
rare few who sought to express themselves creatively required some paid
employment as there was little reward for original endeavour.

The negative implication of nationalism can be perceived from the fundamental question suggested above as to what constitutes Irish music. That
such a question could elicit controversy is revealing. A more liberal age and
outlook might proffer an inclusive definition but attitudes during the majority of the past two centuries were not as accommodating. Most students of
music in Ireland will readily identify the two principal schools of music outlined above. That a people should foster a folk music and a high culture
simultaneously is not at all unusual; the Irish experience is characterised by
the sharp division between the two, a rupture that lasted well into the current

century and one that proved inimical to the greater prosperity of the art. Other countries responded positively to this experience; Kodaly provides apposite evidence of a readiness to fructify art music through a synthesis of traditions and in so doing bestowed international recognition on a noble folk art. In Ireland there emerged no Kodaly or Bartok or Sibelius and the traditions remained compartmentalized. There was in reality little prospect of the emergence of such a figure in the absence of any congruous compositional praxis. In the wake of the Act of Union these disparate musics were increasingly championed as representative of a mode of life and were celebrated by some as much for their consocation as for their intrinsic worth. Adherents of the traditional practice spoke like Thomas MacDonagh of the 'Irish note';[4] it was here the very distinctiveness of the tradition that appealed. The celebration of this living culture, which was for many the only culture they knew, was advanced by others as a emblem of distinctiveness, valued precisely because it was different from the dominant European tradition of art music. In addition it was perceived in the pastoral ideal as concrete representation of a pure and natural life under violent attack from insidious modernism; for many who sought to preserve the traditional way their's was not only an advocacy of a nationalist petition but more fundamentally a genuine crusade to preserve a bastion of an inimitable quality of existence. Whatever the motive, the insular tendency engendered an exclusive view that held increasing sway in a parochial age.

That this pernicious division emerged and persisted is a result of the potency of the German romantic view of nationalism. Nationalism's greatest strength and the reason it has remained as a principal determinator in the affairs of humankind is its ability to adapt. It is precisely this polymorphic quality that affords the movement such lasting universal appeal. This particular romantic strain as advocated by Herder and modified by Fichte was embraced by Irish nationalists who saw in it an authoritative certification of their avowed political goal. But it was a leading graduate of this school, the apostle of Italian nationalism, Giuseppe Mazzini, who, in a review of the movement throughout Europe, proclaimed that Ireland could not lay claim to nationhood as it did not possess a distinctive culture, which was regarded as the prerequisite of every asseveration of autonomy. The Young Ireland movement had been formed in the image of Mazzini's initiatives that had inspired the rise of young nationalists throughout Europe. In common with *Giovine Italia* and its sister movements, the members of Young Ireland evinced the predisposition for cultural endeavour to become more political and populist during the 1840s. Yet Mazzini declined to include the Irish organisation in his People's International League established in 1847 to act as a parent body for nationalist campaigns throughout the continent. He sympathized with Ireland's case but felt that it did not plead for any distinct principal of life or system of legislation, derived from native peculiarities, and contrasting radically with English wants and wishes.[5]

The salient implication of Mazzini's perception was that nationalism entailed a popular and general consciousness of attachment to a nation which enjoyed common traditions and goals and employed a common language and that these conditions were not met with in Ireland. Such an assessment from such a man was a serious reversal and even if adjudged erroneous it served to demonstrate that an Irish intelligentsia had some way to go in convincing its fellow Europeans and nationalists that here dwelt a people possessed of a distinctive mode of life and expression. Much of the artistic energy of the second half of the nineteenth century was devoted to this task and the consequences for music were almost entirely deleterious.

Ireland's position as a compact island on the periphery of Europe gave it a creditable geographical claim to statehood but any advance towards greater self-determination would have little prospect of success without external influential support which was dependent on establishing an unambiguous claim to be considered a homogeneous nation. Hence, that small intelligentsia, comprising republicans and erstwhile unionists disillusioned by the consequences of the Act of Union, was faced with following the inevitable path prescribed by romantic nationalism: this directed that it was necessary first to establish the cultural case as the prerequisite to any consequent move towards autonomy. It was no enviable task to counter the perception that Ireland was but an extension of England; an objective visitor to any Irish urban centre must inevitably have had the impression that these islands shared a culture or, at best, that Ireland demonstrated a cultural varietal. As George Russell (AE) perceptively recorded:

> We stood for long in the shadow of a great tree which prohibited all but the most meagre growth of other life beneath its branches.[6]

Language was the most obvious badge of distinction and the increasing currency of English was the major source of concern to those desirous of establishing a separate cultural personality for Ireland. It was inevitable that support for the Gaelic tongue became central to the cultural debate; it was prized as a unique expression but also as the principal weapon in a cultural war. On a practical level the enduring concentration on the linguistic debate also occupied scare resources. But all other facets of life were enlisted in support of the claim to be considered distinctive. Music suffered in answering this call.

The practice of art music in Ireland was inevitably concentrated on urban centres and on an educated minority. In form and fashion it was no different from what one would encounter in any provincial English town. Irish cities and towns could not of course compete with London and even Dublin, previously regarded as the second city of an empire, could not in the nineteenth century match the more effulgent record of the previous century for the reasons outlined above. There was accordingly little activity and what activity there was was not distinctively Irish. An outside observer would have discovered little energy, all of a conservative nature, centred on a small portion of society concentrated in delimited geographical areas. As in so many cases where there is a lack of a musical infrastructure and dearth of instrumentalists, choral music was in the ascendancy. The record of music in Ireland in the nineteenth century is primarily a catalogue of choral enterprises with occasional addition of a celebrity concert. The popular music that was sponsored by a growing middle class was equally indistinguishable from that which could be encountered across the Irish Sea. Those who sought to establish a characteristic Irish note would clearly find no salvation in the practice of art music.

The impetus toward establishing a cultural claim for nationhood had also import for a fragile oral tradition. The ensuing expectations proved a heavy burden for a primitive heritage to bear. Traditional music was as slight as it was celebrated; the very life of the community in which it had thrived as a folkloric practice was threatened. The more obvious consequences of such as famine, flight from the land, and increasing urbanization have been well documented. But certain nineteenth-century movements had especial influence in hastening the inevitable alterations in musical direction. Changing practical circumstances resulted in the indigenous practice of music becoming centred on restricted rural areas where sociological conditions remained more constant. The ready adoption of the English language both by politicians and by the Catholic Church and the popular identification of the tongue as the medium of progress had inevitable consequences for a vocal musical tradition based on Irish. Emigration stole from small communities the younger generations necessary to preserve an oral tradition. This was the century of the great antiquarians and of impressive anthropological industry. The committed work of the collectors did much to combat the hostile situation of the time but their's was an early investigation of a wild and rude art unfamiliar even to many of their countrymen. While their industry served to record and inform, it could not alter the defining circumstances. The increasing rate of social change along with the combined forces of nationalism and its allied pastoral vision resulted in a celebration of the primitive and an understandable, if unrealistic, desire to capture and venerate what was increasingly realised to be an endangered emanation. It is however arguable that to take a snapshot of a living culture and to seek to preserve that moment with particular honour is inimical to the very growth of culture which, if it is a living entity and of a quality to survive, will inevitably continue to adapt in response to an ever-changing social environment. This move to define the tradition at a particular moment when it was, first, to be enlisted to evidence aesthetic individuality and, second, was perceived to be unable to withstand a pervasive dominant culture has had the effect for subsequent generations of confounding the question as to what precisely constitutes Irish folk music.

THOMAS MOORE

It is a moot point whether such a tradition could survive a wave of change; even in the early nineteenth century it was manifesting indication of contagion. Some of those most committed to the preservation and propagation of the indigenous heritage must have suspected as the twentieth century dawned that they were engaging with a radiant but moribund practice. It is in this respect worth considering the earlier contribution of the poet, Thomas Moore. Moore was as vilified after his passing as he was celebrated in living. A darling of society, he brought to wide attention one of the principal glories of the heritage: the abundant stock of beautiful melody. The song is the centre of the tradition and consequently the majority of airs lie within the singable compass of an octave or a twelfth. The loss of more ancient airs had left a preponderance of neoterical melodies while the architectonic construction of some attested the influence of Western European styles, often indicating that the melodies are of more recent derivation. More venerable airs were frequently asymmetrical in structure as was freely admitted by Moore:

> Another difficulty (which is, however, purely mechanical) arises from the irregular structure of many of those airs and the lawless kind of metre which it will in consequence be necessary to adapt to them. In these instances the poet must write, not to the eye, but to the ear.[7]

Moore was not slow to employ his mechanical means to bring the lawless to heel. His subsequent 'working' of the melodies has resulted in his memory being subjected to regular bouts of discredit and he indisputably offers an easy target. Anthony Cronin's summation of Moore as 'a bit of an embarrassment'[8] is one of the kinder verdicts and the critical assault continues even to the present. Moore has the distinction of raising the ire of both musical traditions but his sanitized versions of Irish melody brought Irish music into fashionable drawing rooms both in Britain and Ireland. Through dubious means he did more to propagate the nationalist cause than could any rebellion. He packaged a culture, or an element of a culture, in a wrapping that made it attractive and in so doing endowed succeeding generations of composers with the constraining association between Irish music and a particular kind of national sentiment. Moore also pointed to a revealing truism: what is important in the realm of propaganda is not essentially the product but the perception of the product. Such considerations were of moment in chauvinistic times. Later generations of musicians conversant with the Irish note have all had to grapple with this legacy and face the choice whether to engage with a pure tradition or to amend that heritage in order to proselytize and render it available to a much wider audience. A consequence has been a further rupture in the field of traditional music which persists to the present between what might be termed the preservers and the progressives.

THE VARIETY OF RESPONSE

Moore's success and the realization that it was achieved through the dilution of the heritage had another result: it convinced many who valued the tradition towards the adoption of an increasingly protectionist policy. This was a characteristically Irish reaction and distinguishes the history of music in this country from, for instance, that in Hungary or Finland. Individual creative musicians demonstrated a number of differing responses. Some, like Carl Hardebeck, Robert O'Dwyer, and Eamonn Ó Gallchobhair, who were active in the first half of this century, set themselves at odds with anything a dominant culture might have to offer and espoused a radical parochial line. They sought to build on the work of the great collectors of the nineteenth century with the dual ambition to preserve and to build from that tradition a characteristically national music. Despite being conversant with the broader aesthetic, Ó Gallchobhair sought to argue that it had nothing to say to an Irish audience that could not better be expressed through traditional music:

> . . . the Irish idiom expresses deep things that have not been expressed by Beethoven, Bach, Brahms, Elgar or Sibelius – by any of the great composers; and that where the vehicle used for the presentation of the Irish idiom is the vehicle of any of these men or their schools – then the Irishman is conscious of a clash of values, a struggle for mastery and he rejects the presentation as 'wrong'. And so I say that in no Irish art as much as in music does the Irish mind hold fast to the set of values fundamentally its own; and in no other art is the mind so conscious of the continued integrity of those values.[9]

One danger of asseveration is the correlated proclivity to denigrate. The efforts of those sympathetic to Ó Gallchobhair's view to give sustenance to the young shoots of a reemerging culture led to some indiscriminate pruning of the great tree casting the shadow. It is unfortunate but perhaps inevitable that some loss of objective appreciation is a consequence of a protectionist period. It would be more damaging if such an outlook were translated into educational policy. It should be recorded that official policy toward music, when such can be determined, has attempted to balance the requirement to preserve and record the folk tradition with an openness to the broader western heritage of art music.

That the traditional idiom is unsuited as the basis for a school of extended composition is a view given credence by the conscientious if ultimately unsuccessful essays in Gaelic opera by advocates of the insular approach. *Muirgheis* (1903) by O'Brien Butler and O'Dwyer's *Eithne* (1909), the two earliest Irish operas written under the influence of the newly emergent Gaelic League, are flawed works that earned only passing approbation. Both suffer in attempting to create a distinctive flavour from traditional elements which results in sectional conceptions lacking conviction. The failure of these and other works of the provincial school to realize a distinctive music further resulted in a switching of emphasis from creation to celebration. Energy was redirected from composition to preservation and even justification; there was little requirement to engage imaginative faculties when there was already a perfectly formed culture to extol. Culture thus became an historic concept; a pleasantly comfortable attitude for a conservative society but one ultimately antipathetic to a healthy aesthetic life.

However this represented but one view. One of the principal lessons bequeathed by the chronicle of music in Ireland is the persistent lack of coordination and direction. Division would appear to be an inherent part of our communal nature. A second response is represented by those such as the influential John Larchet who were more moderate espousing an approach consistent with the goal of establishing an ideal national classicism. Larchet was not possessed of a uniquely original voice; his authority came rather from his industry and from his essential contribution as a teacher in both University College Dublin and the Royal Irish Academy of Music where he instructed a whole school of composition for some four decades from 1921. It would be no exaggeration to state that the majority of Irish composers who emerged in the two decades following World War II were initially influenced by his guidance. This became the established approach to creativity in the middle years of the century. The principal and predictable problem faced by those ambitious to fashion a distinctive music founded on a folk idiom was that the very constitution of the tradition, with its linear character and small structure, left it unsuited as the basis of extended composition; folksong is simply not the stuff of extended composition; it fails the essential criterion that it is not capable of development. The emphasis on the indigenous idiom beguiled many of the first generation of musicians in the Free State to concentrate on producing arrangements and collocations of traditional airs. Indeed, a generous scheme launched by Radio Eireann in 1943 designed to encourage native composers was poorly rewarded with an endless supply of arrangements and undistinguished dance selections. A later generation of Larchet's students, principally Seoirse Bodley, had more success in seeking to construct a style not through direct quotation but from harnessing characteristic elements of the traditional practice. Larchet's academic colleague Aloys Fleischmann, professor of music in University College Cork from 1934 until 1980, demonstrated a progressive method moving from a path parallel with that taken by Larchet to an increasing espousal of the cosmopolitan outlook consistently advocated by Fred May and Brian Boydell. Born in 1911, May was in the vanguard of a tiny movement that paid no homage to national sentiment and proceeded bravely to write in a style consistent with the legacy of the Second Viennese School and in so doing present a third response to the challenge posed by nationalism. May and his followers were essentially to forge a response by ignoring the negative impact of the doctrine. Boydell was later to take a similarly uncompromising line even though both men were inevitably to suffer for engaging with a medium that would find little understanding, not to mention sympathy, with an audience unversed in its language. What critically distinguishes both these figures is not only their courageous artistic stand, but that they were the first composers of the modern era to study abroad and to have opportunity to be exposed to the most advanced current compositional approaches. May was the first to venture abroad studying in London at the Royal College of Music for three years with Gordon Jacob and Vaughan Williams before moving further to Vienna to study with Egon Wellesz, experiences which confirmed May as the least insular and consequently least understood Irish musical voice of his generation. His early orchestral works from the 1930s such as *Scherzo for Orchestra, Symphonic Ballad, Spring Nocturne*, and the impressive String Quartet in c minor are today remarkable not primarily for the originality of conception but for the contrast they provide with anything else being written by an Irish composer at that time. For most of his creative life May made no concession to popular expectation and his increasing frustration with the lot of music in Ireland, given voice though occasional articles in *The Bell*, evidences the price to be paid for artistic conviction. He did however have the satisfaction of knowing that he was first of a school that was to share his faith in the possibility of creating a distinctive voice without being insular or indentured to the past.

STANFORD AND THE EXOTIC

One additional creative disposition needs to be mentioned. That concerns
the treatment of a national flavour as an exotic. This is not an innate
response to the demands of nationalism but rather a modish exploitation of a
characteristic flavour. Stanford provides prime example of this approach. He
was the pre-eminent Irish-born composer not only of his generation but of
the century. Only John Field in the previous century occupies such an undisputed position of honour. And yet Stanford, who was one of those who
attacked Moore for his tampering, was himself to become a target not for the
same offence but for one closely related. Arthur Bax, for one, was later to
comment that he 'never penetrated to within a thousand miles of the Hidden
Ireland'.[10] Stanford's willingness to adopt an Irish mode, notably in the six
Irish rhapsodies and in the Third Symphony, attracted criticism both for
being musically ungainly and more particularly for approaching Irish music
from the outside. There is much that is similar in the approaches of Moore
and Stanford; both men, at different ends of the nineteenth century, essentially interpreted the native tradition for a foreign audience receptive to its
picturesque qualities. Irishness was not central to Stanford's artistic sensibility; his compositional style was more in debt to Brahms than to Ireland. This
ability to assume a musical accent was earlier a feature of Sullivan's work and
particularly of his Irish Symphony in E completed in 1866. Sullivan was later
much perturbed when his ethnic essay was displaced in public affection by
Stanford's work. Another to essay an Irish Symphony, Hamilton Harty, stands
as principal successor to Stanford in the unfolding commitment to the creation of a national style. Harty's embrace of his native traditions proved
more enthusiastic without being innate. His tone-poem *With the Wild Geese*
can be considered the first enduring original composition in an Irish idiom
which succeeds without recourse to folksong. Ultimately, however, Harty's
creative voice was as catholic as was that of his predecessors.

The treatment of autochthonus music as an exotic is one thing, but the
embrace of the spirit of alien nation is another and Ireland, which could
never compare with its neighbour's traffic in immigrant musicians, through
its musical and literary reputation began to attract composers of quality. In
the first half of this century both Bax and Moeran were independently to
don Irish mantles as exotics. With customary passion, Bax moved to Ireland
for periods commencing in 1902 and immersed himself in all things Irish for
over a decade before turning his attentions east. This is not to be critical of
Bax or to dismiss the exotic as ephemeral; he was no musical tourist; his
affection and engagement with Ireland went to the core of his being for his
period here. His production of plays and poems under the successive pseu-
donyms Dermod McDermott and the more enduring Dermot O'Brien and a

succession of works such as the tone poems *Cathleen ni Hoolihan, Into the Twilight, In the Faery Hills*, and *Roscatha* along with the later *In Memoriam*, dedicated to the memory of Padraig Pearse, all evince the degree of Bax's involvement with the life and national sentiment of an adopted country. Moeran's commitment to things Irish emerged more gradually despite his advantage in having an Irish father, the Revd J.J. Moeran having been born in Dublin. Moeran was even more eclectic in his approach to creativity and his Irish mode evident in the Symphony in g minor and in the Violin Concerto was essentially an occasional voice which finds no echo in, for instance, later substantial works such as the Sinfonietta and the Serenade in G major. Despite very different compositional personalities and their individual responses to the influence of nationalism, Bax and Moeran were alike in their openness in an age made inward through the suffusion of heightened ethnic sentience. Their response was consistent with that of many French composers from Auber and Bizet through Chabrier, Debussy, and Ravel who found in Spain and its music similar exotic attraction. Nationalism sponsored diversity and this very diversity was to prove enchanting to those sufficiently confident in their own heritage to enable them occasionally to appropriate the picturesque.

NATIONALISM'S HARVEST

To record that nationalism has had a detrimental impact on the course of music in Ireland is not to claim that the doctrine is invariably adverse to the art. The difficulty, and difficulty there has been judging by the jejune creative harvest of the past two centuries, lies more in the response to the movement than in the movement itself. The unattached histories of the literary renaissance here and of composition in other lands such as Italy attest that nationalism can actually act as an incitement to imaginative endeavour. It is interesting to note that opera, a form ideally suited to a nationalist expression with its referential and visual qualities and more direct appeal to communal emotion, has received relatively little attention from Irish composers. The history of this genre alone demonstrates that whereas in other countries composers utilized the protean nature of nationalism to their advantage, in Ireland, discovering an agreed response to the phenomenon diverted considerable energy for the greater part of two centuries. The unfortunate association of traditions with more expedient practical considerations meant that Ireland experienced difficulties in exploiting nationalism's exceptional ability to adapt to local circumstances. It was not the case that the intelligentsia was indolent but rather that it proposed too great a variety of response. While nationalist movements may start with the committed few they only succeed if they harness popular support; an art without directional consensus would inevitable suffer in an age that valued clear definition. The fractured tradition of music also points the fact that Ireland is not as culturally or ethnically homogenous as was proposed by some nationalist propaganda. A percipient observer might conclude that republicans' enduring celebration of Theobald Wolfe Tone, a Northern Presbyterian and leader of the United Irishmen whose agitation provoked the Act of Union, is as much inspired by the necessity to conceal the underlying divisions within the island's community as it is a parading of a convenient totem to a united nationalist ideal. Unanimity of purpose has ever been an exemplar of the doctrine. It is thus not surprising to find the nationalist movement's leaders concentrating on a coherent issue such as language and to discover it dominating the cultural agenda whence consequently it was afforded the preponderance of resources. The nineteenth century has bequeathed to us the low status afforded music; its practitioners were frustrated by the want of appreciation and the lack of career opportunities and rewards; and crucially the musical community was enervated by the Sisyphean polemic as to the *true* nature of a national expression. Aggravating this situation was the fundamentally weak state of education and structures. The relationship between a colonial history and national self-assurance is the subject for another debate, but there can be little doubt that it took some decades of autonomy to instil the communal confidence necessary for Irish composers to present to audiences at home and abroad original works created free of the shadow of parochial expectation. It equally took time to realise that a living culture must be an emanation and its character and constitution must needs evolve and cannot be decided on by decree. Similarly it has taken some years to overcome the dominant notion of exclusivity and to arrive at a realization that discrepant traditions could fructify each other. The lessons of cultural insularity in the 1920s and economic protectionism in the following decade teach that Ireland could not cut itself off in an age of increasing communication; nor, if the nation is to take its place in the wider community, would such a course be advisable.

This paper has concerned itself with the failure to realize a consistent response to the phenomenon of nationalism. In part this was due to the general fractured retort that can be traced back to Tone and the subsequent emergence of two disparate nationalist paths. Debilitated by division and unable to fashion a consistent expression, music moved to the cultural fringe in the nineteenth century. An extreme age demanded a clear response and music was eclipsed by literature. But there is promise in this century despite the fact that the synthesis of traditions has not been achieved. The division remains but has today become outmoded. There is more tolerance of artistic freedom and an abatement of dogmatic insistence on a set mode of expression.

This is doubtless a result of the greater assurance that an ethnic sensibility can survive exposure to alien influence and can even be enriched through dialogue. The power of the media and ease of communication and transport along with the increasing integration of Europe have also contributed to the more open and pluralist disposition. Practical circumstances have improved: concert halls in Dublin and Limerick and a greater availability of educational opportunity although most in the profession must harbour profound reservations about the consistency and accessibility of music in the crucial state sector. There remains the truism that as a people we will not sponsor a thriving musical life without a broad systematic scheme of training focused on appreciation and the development of some level of technical skill. The general trend, however, remains positive. The more secure infrastructure, the increasing industry of native composers, the establishment by the Arts Council in 1986 of the Contemporary Music Centre as both an archive and advocate for new Irish composition, and the unfailing support afforded by the national broadcasting service all attest the burgeoning vigour of music in Ireland.

NOTES

1. D. Donoghue, 'The Future of Irish Music', *Studies*, XLIV (Spring, 1955), 109–114.
2. M.A.G. Ó Tuathaigh, 'Ireland and Britain under the Union, 1800–1921: an overview', in P.J. Drudy ed., *Ireland and Britain since 1922* (Cambridge, 1986), 8.
3. See N. Kelly, 'Music in Irish Primary Education, 1831–1922', *Proceedings of the Educational Studies Association of Ireland Conference, Dublin 1979* (Galway, 1979), 48–56.
4. T. MacDonagh, *Literature in Ireland* (Dublin, 1916), 209.
5. Quoted in B. King, *Mazzini* (London, 1902), 106–7.
6. G. Russell, 'The Gaelic and the Anglo-Irish Cultures', *Irish Statesman*, III (Dublin, 17 Jan. 1925), 586–7.
7. Correspondence Moore with Stephenson, 1807, collected in Lord J. Russell ed., *Memoirs, Journal and Correspondence of Thomas Moore*, 8 vols (London, 1853); also cited in A.P. Graves, *The Celtic Song Book* (London, 1928), 28.
8. A. Cronin, *Heritage Now* (Dingle, 1982), 31.
9. E. Ó Gallchobhair, 'Ativism', *Ireland To-day*, I (Dublin, Sept. 1936), 57–8.
10. A. Bax, foreword to A. Fleischmann ed., *Music in Ireland* (Cork, 1952), iii.

Music and Religion in Ireland

PATRICK O'DONOGHUE

Dá mbéadh mileoidean agamsa
Ní bhéadh Críost gan cheol anocht
Is é ag teacht ó áras bán a fhlaitheasa
Chuig an mainséar bocht,
Do shéinnfinn ceol do chuirfeadh gliondar ar a chroí
Ceol nar chualthas riamh ag píobaire sí
Ceol chuirfeadh na realtaí ag rince i spéartha na hoích.
(If I had a melodeon
Christ would not be without music tonight
when he was coming from his white heavenly house
to the poor stable,
I would play music which would gladden his heart
Music never heard from the fairy piper
Music that would put the stars dancing in the night sky.)[1]

One wonders, however, what style of music would the old man in the poem provide to celebrate the Incarnation of the Lord today. Would Charpentier's *Messe de Minuit* be beyond the capabilities of his *bosca ceoil* or would Honneger's *Christmas Cantata* or 'Glory to God' from Handel's *Messiah* come to his mind as a suitable tribute to the Saviour of the world? Perhaps he would play *Adeste Fideles*, *Le Coinnle na nAingeal* or some contemporary popular Christmas song. This wide range of musical possibilities pertains to the Catholic liturgy as it is celebrated in Ireland in the 1990s. Such a rich diversity is the result of many factors which have shaped liturgical music today.

This consideration of the topic 'Music and Religion in Ireland' will begin with the early Christian era and the period from the evangelisation of the Irish in the fifth century. An overview of subsequent developments will follow with a consideration of the position immediately prior to the Second Vatican Council's renewal of the liturgy.

The response of Irish composers to the challenge of providing contemporary music for the liturgy in the vernacular languages of this country will then be treated. The significance of the call to inculturation contained in

Sacrosanctum Concilium (Constitution on the Liturgy, 1963) will also be addressed at that time with some observations on the importance of developing a musical ethos for the liturgy which would express both the unity and the diversity of musical expression in the Irish Catholic church at the end of the twentieth century.

MUSIC IN CHRISTIAN ANTIQUITY

It is clear from a study of early Christian literature that the new religion and its rituals did not easily cohabit with either Jewish Temple worship or the musical and ritual practices of the pagan rites of Greece and Rome. Instrumental music met with disapproval from the beginnings of the Christian church. Even the prophets were invoked to criticise the use of musical instruments by the Jewish people: 'Away from me with the noises of your songs; / the playing of your harps I do not wish to hear' (Amos 5: 23). Theodoret (*c*.393–466) asserted that instrumental music was introduced into Jewish worship during the sojourn in Egypt in an attempt to entice the people away from the attractions of sacrificing to Egyptian deities:

> God had not allowed musical instruments because he enjoyed their sound but rather as a gradual replacement for the foolishness of idol worship.[2]

At the end of the second century Clement of Alexandria (140–220) also stated his objection to instrumental music and what he perceived as its unfortunate results. In the *Paidagogos* he writes:

> When a man occupies his time with flutes, stringed instruments, choirs, dancing, Egyptian krotala and other such improper frivolities, he will find that indecency and rudeness are the consequences.[3]

Heterophony and polyphony were also rejected by the early Christian church since these styles seemed to contradict the spirit of *koinonia* and the sense of unity which communal singing in unison represented. Cyril of Jerusalem (315–387) went so far as to assert that: 'it was only so that we might sing in unison with them that the triple Sanctus of the seraphim was revealed to us'.[4]

The emerging tradition of Christian hymnody which had been anticipated in the New Testament (Colossians 3:16) is illustrated in the letter (*c*.112) of Pliny the Younger (governor of the province of Pontus and Bithynia) to the Emperor Trajan: 'They were accustomed to meet on a fixed day before dawn and sing alternately among themselves a hymn to Christ as to a god'.[5]

These hymns served to teach the faith to the people and allowed them to express that faith in worship. It is evident from both textual and musical perspectives that these early examples of Christian hymnody were new poetic compositions quite different from previous biblical works of a prosaic nature.

> The texts are shaped into stanzas of two or more lines. Each stanza employs the same meter, rhyme scheme and number of lines. Music is composed for the first stanza, and each succeeding stanza is sung to the same music.[6]

The early Christian church therefore adopted a fresh approach to music in ritual and by banning what it considered unsuitable it marginalised the offending rites and highlighted the Christian ideals of community and worship of the true God.

The role played by women in worship, with particular reference to their participation in religious music at this time is clearly outlined in many sources. Since the singing of women played a significant part in pagan ritual their vocal participation in the Christian liturgy came to be regarded as suspect. The *Didascalia* (a third century anonymous document written in Greek and also known as the *Catholic Teaching of the Twelve Apostles*) contains the following admonition: 'Women are ordered not to speak in church, not even softly, nor may they sing along or take part in the responses, but they should only be silent and pray to God'.[7]

Isidore of Pelusium (d. 440) writes of the changed attitude towards women's involvement in the liturgy:

> Perhaps women were originally permitted by the Apostles and presbyters to join in singing so as to prevent them from gossiping in church. But later this permission was withdrawn since it was learned that they did not gain any salutory fruits of penance from divine song, but used the sweetness of melody for disturbances of every kind, since they looked on it in exactly the same way as theatre music.[8]

This is perhaps the background which precluded women from singing in the sanctuary area even as recently as 1967.

MUSIC IN THE EARLY IRISH CHURCH

When Christianity was brought to Ireland in the fifth century by St Patrick a similar though non-violent struggle ensued between the imported religion and the local pagan customs.

What is surprising, something due in large measure to the genius and zeal of St Patrick, is that so many were drawn to believe in the gospel, and that the Church continued to thrive without violent opposition or persecution.[9]

This gentle and remarkably rapid transition from a pagan to a Christian way of life and liturgy provides an early example of inculturation which was consonant with a similar spirit of tolerance and accommodation which had finally emerged in the broader European church with an acceptance of certain elements of pagan worship which were considered 'good and noble'.[10]

The development of monasteries about one hundred years after the arrival of Patrick contributed to the growth of a distinctly Irish church which tolerated the local culture. The monastic schools facilitated the study of both Latin and Irish literature:

> The traditional learning of the 'filidh', which was transmitted in the Irish language, often in the medium of verse and poetry, was not despised but actively promoted and finally written down for posterity by the monastic scribes. The Irish and Latin traditions flourished side by side and influenced one another in a number of ways.[11]

An example of such a meeting of cultures is provided by the *Antiphonary of Bangor* – a manuscript composed between 680 and 691 – which is a storehouse of native compositions of prayers and hymnody. In this respect it has been noted that

> What surprises one most is the fluency and depth displayed by the Irish in the composition of hymns and versified prayers in Latin as early as the second half of the sixth century about a hundred years after the initial conversion of the country.[12]

The initiative of the Irish monks in composing their own hymns demonstrates not only their mastery of the Latin metres but also their desire to create a particularly Irish tradition of sacred music which would reflect the genius of the developing native church. In this respect one commentator notes:

> The author of 'Hymnum dicat', the most popular of all the hymns of the early Irish Church, was well acquainted with the works of Prudentius and Fortunatus, but decided to write a hymn which, even in classical metre, would be more congenial to the Irish spirit of prayer than anything produced by either of them.[13]

This blending of two traditions is further demonstrated in the hymn to the martyrs *Sacratissimi martyres* whose metre is clearly not one of Latin origin:

> The hymn has nine stanzas, with four lines of irregular length in each stanza, and four accentual beats in each line. . . . The literary background for this new metrical development is found in ancient Irish verse-form, which, before the coming of Christianity, consisted of similar accentual or strictly rhythmical patterns.[14]

Irish monks travelling mainland Europe absorbed some of the traditions and practices of the great religious houses and on their return they incorporated them into the native Irish liturgy:

> Clearly, they had no intention of creating a new liturgy, but they felt free to combine elements from various sources. The Celtic [liturgy] was indeed a melange of foreign elements, Roman, Gallican, Mozarabic, and Oriental patterns, together with . . . indigenous liturgical compositions.[15]

Unlike the experience of the early Christian community, instrumental accompaniment to liturgical chants was not eschewed by the Irish church:

> Since Irish annals from the ninth century record the destruction of church organs, it may be assumed that the singing was accompanied, or that instrumental music was utilized in at least some locations in Ireland.[16]

Additionally with regard to our topic it has been observed that the use of the eight-stringed harp – hung from the girdle – is recounted by Giraldus Cambrensis in the twelfth century.[17]

THE EARLY REFORM OF THE CHURCH

Reform of Irish monastic life began with the Céili Dé movement in the eighth century. Their spirituality is reflected in the Stowe Missal, a priest's private mass book, which includes some Irish texts. The monastery of St Mael Ruain in Tallaght – from whence the Stowe Missal originated – was an important centre for this renewal movement. Mael Ruain, its saintly abbot, was one of the leading advocates of reform. This churchman was a complex individual who, ascetic in personal practice, imposed a strict rule on his monks while also managing to display a refreshing measure of common sense.[18] A reference to music in one particular source would seem to indicate that Mael Ruain was however, in this respect, somewhat puritanical:

Cornan of the Glen was a holy anchorite as well as an excellent piper. Mael Ruain often sent him presents: He said once to Mael Ruain's monks: 'I would like to play a tune for the cleric.' Mael Ruain gave his answer; 'Tell Cornan that these ears are denied being offered to earthly music that they may be offered to the music of heaven.'[19]

Yet the sacred and the secular were compatible components of the poetry of the Céili Dé which, particularly in the hermit poetry tradition, dealt with nature: 'The distinction between religious and secular or natural seems not to exist here'.[20]

The organisational reform of the dioceses of Ireland was effected by the Synods of Cashel, Rathbreasail and Kells (1152) whose changes in structures at a diocesan and parochial level permeated all aspects of ecclesial life by bringing about a general alignment with the universal church thereby demonstrating the influence of the Gregorian renaissance.[21] About this time the Irish church was further influenced by the conquest of the Anglo-Normans and by its contact with the religious orders of Europe. This resulted in a beneficial absorption of these foreign influences into the native spirituality:

> Ireland came into closer contact with the rich Marian literature in Latin and other languages, and it was readily accepted, translated and given an unmistakable Irish dress.[22]

An important example of this genre of Marian spirituality is discussed by Diarmuid Ó Laoghaire who poses the question:

> Could anything be more truly Irish than the medieval 'Caoineadh na dTrí Muire' (The Lament of the Three Marys) still sung, not least in Cnoc Mhuire (Knock), with its heartfelt 'Och ochón' and its typically direct and intimate language?[23]

I speak of an 'absorption of foreign influences' as not all the elements of the native Celtic liturgy were lost at this time despite the best efforts of the Anglo-Normans to impose the Sarum rite. Patrick Brannon in his study *The Search for the Celtic Rite* states:

> The survival of the Celtic hymn *Ecce fulget clarissima*, concordant with a text in the Irish *Liber Hymnorum*, indicates that not all elements of the Celtic use were eliminated or forgotten in late fifteenth-century Anglo-Norman Ireland.[24]

SACRED MUSIC AND THE FOLK INFLUENCE

The earliest medieval polyphonic settings of the Mass demonstrated a variety of compositional styles.[25] The employment of secular song style – largely the achievement of Guillaume de Machaut in the first half of the fourteenth century – may have paved the way for the use of popular folk tunes as the musical bases for polyphonic Mass settings. This is exemplified during the early Renaissance period by the works of such composers as Dufay, Ockeghem and Josquin as well as in the parody Masses of the later part of that era. This influence can also be seen in the devotional music of many countries. The Italian *laude spirituale* (contained in thirteenth- and fourteenth-century manuscripts), for example, comprise a collection of 150 vernacular songs some of which are quite simple and folk-like:

> Melodically, the laude spirituale reveal the influence of Gregorian Chant, of the troubadours, perhaps also folksong. A popular element is evident too in the obvious derivation of formal characteristics from the round dance with refrain.[26]

A closer link with folksong is demonstrated by the German *Geisserlieder*[27] of the same period. These short melodic pieces – many with a folk structure incorporating rhyming couplets for the leaders and refrains for all – were sung by the bands of flagellants, groups of pious penitents, who travelled Germany in the middle of the fourteenth century during the time of the Black Plague. Similar links with folk tradition can be seen in the Spanish and Galician-Portuguese *Cantigas*,[28] which record miraculous interventions by the Virgin Mary and which were written in the vernacular in a popular and often dance-like style.

In Ireland the fourteenth-century *Red Book of Ossory* contains eight *Cantilenae* which bear the popular tune titles to which they were sung, six of which are in English and two in French. These were written in Latin by Bishop Ledrede who had been appointed to the diocese of Ossory from London in 1317.[29] A much later example of this tradition can be found in 1684 and Bishop Luke Wadding with his collection of English religious texts fitted to Irish and English folk tunes. These were also non-liturgical pieces designed 'for the Solace of his FRIENDS and NEIGHBOURS in their affliction'.[30] We also find one Fr William Devereux (1698–1771) who, inspired by Bishop Wadding, compiled carols in his collection *The New Garland*, some of which are sung to this day in the parish of Kilmore, County Wexford.[31]

This widespread composition of religious songs, many of them rhythmic and folk-like, point to the extra-liturgical emphasis of the sacred music of these centuries at a time when the people were removed from full participation in the chants of the Mass by the elaborate music of the liturgy.

A TIME OF PERSECUTION

While the church authorities at the Council of Trent grappled with the details of the Counter-Reformation the Irish people were dealing with the vital preservation of their faith under a reign of religious persecution which prohibited the worship of the Catholic populace. The sumptuous church music of the Baroque era with its air of triumph 'celebrating her victory over the chaos of the Middle Ages and the crisis of the Reformation'[32] was a luxury which the Irish people could not afford. The cry of the Irish people in that time of their distress is not unlike the plea of the psalmist in the *De Profundis* (*Psalm* 129) appealing to God to listen to his cause:

> Out of the depths I cry to you you, O Lord!
> Lord, hear my voice!
> Let your ears be attentive
> to the voice of my pleading!

This cry may have provided the inspiration for the setting of this psalm written by Giolla-Bhride Ó hEoghusa (d.1614) from Donegal who entered the Franciscans and spent some time at Douai before becoming head-professor at Louvain (1607–1614). The music in this example is from George Petrie, the nineteenth-century collector.

ⴳiolla-Ḃriġde Ó h-Eoġusa—ob : 1608.

O áite ḃoiṁne ḃéic mé   D'iomċair, le fíor-ġlór Do ḃéil,
Cuġaḋ, a Rí-ḟlaiṫ neiṁe,   M'anam-sa na n-olc n-aicḃéil ;
Éisc mo ġuṫ, a Rí na rann,   Do ċuir m'anam uile a ḃóiġ
Anois ó táim a n-aċrann.   Aḋ maiṫ, a Ċriaṫ 's a Ċrionóiṫ.

Bíoḋ Do ċluasa ġo h-aireaċ   Ó ṁaroin ṁoċ ġo neol-neoin
Aġ éisceaċc le m'aġallṁa ;   (a)A Rí na ġlóire ḃrioċc-ḃuain,
Cuirse ná ḃéan lem' ġuiḋe,   'Cuir Israel a ndóiġ ġo léir,
A Ċriaṫ na sé soċaiḋe.   's tú cárrcaiġ iaḋ ó ain-ṁéin.

Má cuirir ġaċ peacaḋ a suim   Óir maille leis an Rí ṁór
A Ḋia, nó a (b)móḋ coṁcruim,   Atá an cróċaire an-ṁór,
Cia lé'r féiḋir seasaṁ leaṫ   's as líonṁar n-a ḟocair 'tá
A Rí niṁe na mór-ḟearc ?   Fuasġlaḋ ḋaoine tré ró-ġráḋ.

Óir aḋ' ḟóċair tá ġo buan   Saorfaiḋ Sé Israel ġo léir
Cróċaire aġus siot an-ṁuar ;   Ó uile olc is ain-ṁéin,
D'iomċras ġo foiġiḋeaċ leaṫ   Mar sin ġo saora inn uile
Críḋ ḋliġṫiḃ, a Rí ró-ċearc.   Príoṁ-ṫobar na cróċaire.

(a)=1 Rí.   (b)=meaḋ.?

The Penal days are reflected over the years in other religious poems and songs. One notes the Advent hymn *Díon na ndóigheach* taken from a larger poem *Aithrighe agus Brón Banbha* by Tadhg Ó Neachtain (d.1742), a writer and renowned scholar who lived variously in Connacht and County Meath. This poem was written during a time of great persecution in Ireland (referred to as *Banbha* in the original text). The music is again from Petrie:

"An Colm"   ó Ṗécri

n.ḋ. (a) Seinncear na ḋá nóca seo ġo h-an-éadcrom, ġearr; óir níl aċc siollái ġearra ann.

As Aiꞇriże aġus bròn banḃa.

Taḋġ Ó Neaċtain.

Díon na n'óoiġeaċ Dia na n'óúl
 Do'n té a ṡireas a ṡearc-rún ;
Dóċas a n'Dia is maiꞇe,
 's fuireaċ do ṡíor a ꞇróċaire.

Is maiꞇ caras cuinġ ḋil Dé,
 A n-óiġe is a ḃforóne ;
Ġíḋ do'n ḃéal do luaiꞇreaḋ lán,
 Is oleaċt ḋóiġ san Tiġearna.

Póġann is smaċtann Sé sinn,
 Mar sin sinn-ne ní tréiġinn ; (a)
Do'n deoraċ ḋaor ḋáileann Sé
 Tróċ're maraon is cruaiġe.

Níl 'n a Croiḋe inn do ċráḋ
 Nó sinn ġo bráꞇ do ḃloġaḋ,
Nó as cuiṁne inn do ċur
 Leis ġo ḋeiṁin is ḋeacair.

An Dara Cuid.

Sinn-ne do tuill ḋiombuaiḋ Dé
 'Casaḋ cúl le ár ġCoiṁḋe ;
Inn féin fáꞇ a. tréiġean tráċ,
 Ár marḃaḋ is ár maslaḋ.

Oċ !seo fáꞇ o'ḟill uainn a ḋearc
 'Cuir ár n-aṁġar as aṁarc,
Cluas boḋar do beir Sé ḋúinn
 Tré mar tuill sinn a ḋiombuaiḋ.

The religious and secular works of Tadhg Gaelach Ó Súilleabháin (1750–1799) and Pádraig Denn (1765–1828) have been extensively treated by Nóirín Ní Riain in the second volume of *Irish Musical Studies*. Here I will refer only to the use of the folk tune *Sean Ó Duibhir a' ghleanna* to accompany their religious poems; Tadhg Gaelach's *A Íosa Mhic Mhuire, a Rígh ghil na Righthe* and Pádraig Denn's *Aréir is mé ag macnamh ar Iosa mac m'Athar*.[33]

The trend noted in other countries of using popular native tunes of a secular origin combined with the expression of religious sentiment is clearly a widespread demonstration of the closeness of the people both to their faith and to their indigenous tradition. In the Irish context this was despite the persecutions and the attempts of the English to suppress Catholicism and nationalism. Once again here, the distinction between the sacred and the secular is often blurred, yet the authentic religious sentiment of the people cannot be questioned. The Irish, their religion driven underground, responded by making their spirituality an integral part of their daily living.[34]

The influence of the Baroque era Italianate style on the liturgy can be seen in the work of the Irish harpist and composer Toirdhealbhach Ó Cearbhallain (b.1670) who is better known in English as 'Carolan'.[35] Carolan's *Elevation* would seem to replicate *The Elevation Toccata* of that time[36] and demonstrates the emphasis on the Elevation of the sacred species which was almost universal:

The Mass was consequently a celebration whose festivity was heightened by orchestra and polyphonic music, while the consecration was hailed by band music, jubilant ringing of bells and in the Philippines, also firecrackers.[37]

Nonetheless the prevailing style of art music which was so evident in contemporaneous liturgies was notably absent from the celebrations of the Catholic Irish people. 'Put plainly, the impoverished condition of Roman Catholics in Ireland between 1500 and 1800 excluded the possibility of a high culture of sacred music'.[38]

This lack of a more elaborate form of ritual and music did not go unrecorded by the poets such as Eoghan Rua Ó Súilleabháin who looked forward to better days:

> I mainistir naomh beidh céir ar lasadh acu
> in Eaglais Dé go salmach fós
> ag canadh Té Deum gan bhaol gan eagla

(In holy monasteries candles will be alight and God's Church again echoing to psalms and the singing of the Te Deum without danger or fear.)[39]

REFORM AND THE DUBLIN CHURCH

The days looked forward to by Ó Súilleabháin arrived with the advent of Lord North's Relief Bill in the 1780s which allowed the full celebration of the Catholic liturgy with all its embellishments. The styles were generally imported, as were many of the musicians:

> In April 1789 Giordani composed a Te Deum which was sung at the conclusion of High Mass in the Archepiscopal Chapel in Francis Street, Dublin, to celebrate the recovery to health of King George III.[40]

There were several noted appointments of foreign musicians to the Catholic churches in Ireland in the nineteenth century such as Haydn Corri (St Mary's Pro-Cathedral, Dublin), Alois Volkmer (St Andrew's, Westland Row, Dublin) and Alessandro Cellini (Whitefriar Street).[41] There were native musicians too in similar positions:

> such as John Glynn (Dominick Street, Dublin), Joseph Goodman (St Peter's Church, Phibsboro) and J. J. Johnson (St Catherine's, Meath Street), all of whom were enthusiastic composers and were imbued with what were known as 'Cecilian' ideals.[42]

The Cecilian Movement[43] was well established and operative in Ireland by the mid 1870s. The Irish organ of the movement, *Lyra Ecclesiastica*, was first published in 1878 wherein the Cecilian objectives were clearly presented. In this publication those churches who were found wanting in what was considered musical orthodoxy were highlighted and strongly censured:

> We have heard with great regret that the latest addition to the repertoire of the choir of the Church of the Three Patrons, Rathgar, is an adaptation of 'chi mi frena' from Donizetti's Lucia di Lammermoor . . . it is a satisfaction to know that, thanks to the initiative of his Grace, the Archbishop, the recurrence of such scandal will be rendered impossible before long.[44]

The reform of church music in Ireland, however, had begun some time earlier. Paul Cullen, Archbishop of Armagh, was translated to Dublin in 1852 where he strongly supported the campaign to purge profane music from the liturgy and agreed with the objective of introducing the restored Gregorian chant to the Irish church. The Synod of Thurles was convened in 1850 when Cullen was Archbishop of Armagh and addressed itself to liturgical music in articles 38 and 39:

> 38. Nullus cantus nisi gravis, et ecclesiasticus in Ecclesiis adhibeatur. Rectores Seminariorum curent, præpositis etiam præmiis, ut alumni in cantu gravi et ecclesiastico bene instituantur, utque sacras cæremonias probe ediscant.

> 39. Intra Missarum Solemnia nihil nisi Latine cantetur, nec extra Missam in Ecclesiis nisi quod in Ecclesiasticis Libris probatis inveniatur, vel ab Ordinario fuerit probatum.[45]

These decrees indicate the increased predilection of the Irish hierarchy, under Cullen's influence, for a Latin liturgy modelled on the Roman tradition. The Synod of Maynooth in 1875 quoted the decrees of the the 1850 Synod[46] and copperfastened them by restating its preferences for Gregorian chant and the pure Roman Rite (as ordained by Pius IX) and by its insistence on the usage of the correct ecclesiastical books.[47]

Father Nicholas Donnelly (later auxiliary bishop of Dublin and titular bishop of Canea) enjoyed Cardinal Cullen's support in his translation and promulgation of Haberl's *Magister Choralis*. He was a leading light in the Cecilian Movement and was a tireless worker for liturgical music reform. Cullen's successor was Edward Cardinal McCabe who convened the Dublin Diocesan Synod at Holy Cross College, Clonliffe, in 1879. This Synod –

having quoted with opprobrium the earlier Synod which had been held in Maynooth – issued guidelines which were to be implemented by the establishment of a commission which would oversee liturgical music in the diocese.[48] Its directives sought to remove theatrical and profane influences from the music of the church and promoted the use of music which did not distort the sense of the words.[49] Prolonged vocal solos, the playing of the organ in imitation of a profane style was forbidden. The use of instruments other than the organ was also considered and harsh instruments such as drums or cymbals were prohibited. In this regard also, any playing of instruments which would by virtue of excessive volume obscure the words or any similar usage of military effects was to be avoided.[50] The directives end by insisting that 'profane' music should also be excluded from devotions and by admonishing the rectors of churches to ensure that only sincere believers are admitted to the ranks of the choirs.[51] Archbishop McCabe in his address to the Synod pointed out the virtues of music but did not neglect its vices in a style which was reminiscent of Clement of Alexandria: 'but it can also most effectually degrade man to the lowest depths of voluptuous sensuality'.[52] He contended that the theatrical origins of some of the music used in the churches at this time did not follow the exhortation of the Psalmist David, *Psallite Sapienter.*

> If music is to lead to heaven, it must not take its inspiration from the theatre, which unfortunately, as we know from sad experience, is too frequently a nursery, not for heaven, but rather a hotbed where the seeds of vice, planted by original sin, are nursed into precocious depravity.[53]

Dr William Walsh, appointed to succeed McCabe in 1885, was himself, as it happened, a member of the Cecilian Society and was thus concerned with musical reform before his appointment as Archbishop of Dublin. His work *Grammar of Gregorian Music*[54] indicates the particular expertise of the prelate. He continued his active interest in the music of the liturgy during his term in Dublin. In his address to a meeting assembled in the Church of St. James on 10 January 1886 he welcomed the proposal that an organ be procured for the parish. In particular, he showed great interest in the indication that such an instrument would be made in Ireland:

> One remark by Canon Kennedy I heard with special gratification. He has told us – and I take it that his promise is binding not only on himself but on you – that the organ that is to be built here will be an organ of Irish manufacture.[55]

Archbishop Walsh took a particular interest in music at the Pro-Cathedral. Haydn Corri's successor as organist and choir director, Professor Glover, did not meet with Walsh's approval because of his preference for music of the classic era and his apparent neglect of Gregorian chant:

> The professor had a predilection for the Novello editions of the Masses of Haydn and Mozart and the choir had never acquired more than six vocalists – ladies as well as men.[56]

Thomas McDermot succeeded Professor Glover and an improvement in repertoire was noted though 'the choir still remained mixed and limited to six singers'.[57]

The suggestion of Edward Martyn, a wealthy young Galway landowner, to Archbishop Walsh that the Palestrina Choir, founded by Vincent O'Brien and himself would be ideal as the resident choir of the Pro-Cathedral was readily welcomed by the Archbishop. By way of incentive Martyn offered an endowment of £10,000 in this regard though with certain stipulations:

> It was to be a male voice choir and the music sung should be Gregorian or works of Palestrina and the Palestrina school; no music after 1700 was to be sung.[58]

Thus, with one stroke, both the traditional repertoire and the composition of the Pro-Cathedral choir were altered drastically. An interesting anecdote recorded by Mary Purcell indicates the reaction of the public to these changes:

> George Moore, a friend of Dr O'Brien's, took a gloomy view of the conditions and said that the poor were being driven from Marlborough Street to Westland Row, because of the changed repertory, while Merrion Square Catholics, parishioners of Westland Row, were leaving Westland Row, the proximity of poorer, unwashed worshippers proving unbearable to them.[59]

The installation of the Palestrina Choir in Marlborough Street in January 1903 narrowly preceded the reforming *Motu Proprio* of Pope Pius X, *Tra Le Sollicitudini* of 22 November 1903 (Feast of Saint Cecilia).

The records of the cathedral choir committee demonstrate that the transition from the mixed choir to the all male choir proved somewhat difficult. The two female members could not be accommodated under the new arrangement and Archbishop Walsh suggested some kind of compensation while the organist who would have less to do thereafter should not, he opined, suffer any pecuniary loss. Mr Brendan Rogers, the organist in question, was a supporter of the Cecilian ideals yet his music selection was subject to review by the committee (which for the most part was chaired by Edward

Martyn but was headed in this instance by Bishop Donnelly): 'The list of organ music for January was examined and approved of, one item, "March in G, Smart," having been struck out'.[60] The Committee even prohibited the use of two stops *Vox Humana* and *Voix Celeste* during sacred services. Mr Rogers appeared not to comply on several matters with the directives set forth by the committee. In 1904 his accompaniments to the chant were discussed and it was decided that Vincent O'Brien would in future provide same. This was to be followed later by a restriction in the use of the organ at High Mass and Vespers which resulted in Mr Roger's salary being reduced by a third. The perceived need for further restriction on his impro-visations and a vigorous correspondence with him provoked the following minute:

> Opportunity was also taken to express regret that the whole tone of his [Roger's] letter was not calculated to improve mutual relations & was such as no Committee with any feeling of self-respect could continue to tolerate from any person in its employment.[61]

The clergy of the Pro-Cathedral requested the committee in 1909 to sanction the occasional use of the music of modern masters during the year. This was refused as was a request for an increase in salary by the organist whose behaviour was still considered unsatisfactory. The strong tone of these meet-ings and the unrelenting resistance of the Committee to widening the scope of the music repertoire indicates an unfortunate rigidity which tainted some enthusiastic members of the Cecilian movement.

The conservative Irish church was a fertile ground for such strictures and therefore the Romanisation of the liturgy received further impetus from the reforming *Motu Proprio* of Pope Pius X, *Tra Le Sollicitudini*.

> It being our most eager wish that the true Christian spirit may flower again in every way and be upheld by all the faithful, before anything else it is necessary to see that holiness and dignity of the temple, where the faithful gather to gain that spirit from its first and indispensable source; the active participation in the sacred mysteries and the public and solemn prayer of the church.[62]

Thus the phrase *active participation* became the catchword of the twentieth century liturgical reform movement. Pope Pius X linked the renewal of the liturgy to the restoration of plainchant by which means he considered active participation would be achieved:

Special efforts must be made to restore the use of Gregorian chant by the people, so that the faithful may again assume a more active role in worship, as they did in ancient times.[63]

One wonders how the Irish church coped with this call for active participation. After centuries of repression, the silent Mass – necessary during the time of persecution – had left its imprint on the ritual psyche of the Irish people. Thomas Day, in his work *Why Catholics Can't Sing* attributes the dearth of communal church singing in the United States to the influence of the Irish:

> From the sixteenth century to the nineteenth, whenever they heard a bell, it was coming from a Protestant church. Church bells were something they associated with Protestants. And also when they heard hymns, pipe organs, and choral anthems, they heard them coming from behind the doors of Protestant churches. What must have sustained the Catholic Irish through these years of persecution was the knowledge that they did not need these things (bells, hymns, etc). Their faith was precisely that – faith, unadulterated by amusements. In their opinion, the courageous and the strong kept the faith, while the weak, lured away by music and other niceties, became apostates.[64]

In *Ulysses* Joyce provides us with an interesting account of church music in Dublin in his time which verifies this distrust of the Protestant style:

> He infinitely preferred the sacred music of the Catholic Church to anything the opposite shop could offer in that line such as Moody and Sankey hymns or 'Bid me to live and I will live thy protestant to be'.[65]

While one might not agree with many of the conclusions Day comes to in his study, his insight into the possible reluctance of Irish Catholics to respond to a call for full and active participation in the liturgy is certainly interesting. The traditional Irish sing-song is legendary and those who remain mute in church often prove very vocal in the more relaxed setting of the local public house. In Ireland the singing of hymns, and in particular the practice of singing every verse, is associated with the Protestant churches. Popular Catholic hymnody of the twentieth century, contrasting with the religious song of the Reformed churches, consists of works of fewer verses and of less strident and more sentimental tones. Day detects this influence in American Catholic hymns which in his view have strong Irish overtones:

> There is a little bit of Galway Bay and My Wild Irish Rose in all the mawkish, drippy, sentimental songs that were once considered examples of 'real American Catholic hymns'.[66]

In Ireland the response to the Papal admonition was demonstrated for example in the ongoing administration of music in the Pro-Cathedral in Dublin and by the foundation of the Guild of Choristers (under the Patronage of St Cecilia) in St Mary's Church, Haddington Road, in the fashionable Ballsbridge suburb of the city in 1905.

> The Object of the Guild is to provide trained singers for the Liturgical Services in St Mary's Church, and to afford to the Boys attending St Mary's National School, who may happen to possess the necessary voice and capabilities, an opportunity of taking an active part in the several functions of the Sacred Liturgy of the Church.[67]

Saint Mary's Church,
Haddington Road.

Guild of Choristers
Under the Protection of St. Cecilia.

Music List

Latin Sung Mass

SUNDAY 28TH JUNE 1992 9.30 a.m.

ENTRANCE HYMN	TU ES PETRUS	
INTROIT	OMNES GENTES	CHANT
KYRIE ELEISON	MISSA BREVIS	PALESTRINA
GLORIA IN EXCELSIS DEO	MISSA BREVIS	PALESTRINA
CREDO	No 3	CHANT
OFFERTORY MOTET	JUBILATE DEO	AIBLINGER
SANCTUS	MISSA ST. HENRI	KAIM
BENEDICTUS	MISSA ST. HENRI	KAIM
AGNUS DEI	MISSA ST. HENRI	KAIM
COMMUNIO	INCLINA AUREM	CHANT
COMMUNION MOTET	AVE MARIA	ARCEDELT
	SALVE REGINA COELITUM	ROSSINI

The officers of the Guild were to be elected from among the ranks of the boys and the election was to take place each year on St Cecilia's Day (22 November). Gentlemen of the choir were accounted as honorary members of the Guild.[68] We can only conjecture about the reaction of the ladies of the choir in Haddington Road to this all-male establishment on the basis of a remark contained in James Joyce's *Dubliners*. Aunt Kate was not impressed by the commitment of her niece to the choir loft, considering the papal attitude to female singers in the liturgy:

> No, continued Aunt Kate, she wouldn't be said or led by anyone, slaving there in that choir night and day . . . Six o'clock on Christmas morning. And all for what?[69]

The male choir continues to the present to sing the Latin liturgy in Haddington Road and remains faithful to the Cecilian ethos of their charter as one can observe in their music programme for 28 June 1992.

REFORM AND THE TWENTIETH CENTURY

The twentieth century was heralded in church music by the call of *Tra le Sollicitudini* to return to what was seen as a Golden Age, when the plainsong of the Medieval period was at its height. However, the new century saw composers of church music (like composers of secular music) experiment with melody, harmony and rhythm in a manner that compelled the Church to come to terms with contemporary musical expression. Musical boundaries were expanding as exemplified by developments in the new 'science' of ethnomusicology and the emergence of new forms such as *Gebrauchsmusik*. The *Harvard Dictionary of Music* describes the latter as follows:

> Characteristic traits of Gebrauchsmusik are forms of moderate length, simplicity and clarity of style; small ensembles; avoidance of technical difficulties; parts of equal interest and so designed that they can be played on what instruments are available; soberness and moderation of expression; emphasis on 'good workmanship'.[70]

Ethnomusicology is the name given to the study of the music of different cultures and its relationship to particular societies and their rituals:

> In contrast to proponents of Gebrauchsmusik, who wanted to create music with an identifiable use, ethnomusicologists were coming to understand that all music has a function in society.[71]

The functional approach and the rediscovery of native ritual and tradition laid the foundations for a new musical style which would only be possible in the field of liturgical music when the call to reform was issued in the Sacred Constitution of the Liturgy *(Sacrosanctum Concilium)* in 1963.

The invitation to full and active participation in the liturgy extended by Pope Pius X had been accompanied by the exhortation to achieve this goal through the restoration of the Latin chant. As one can see, the promotion of this particular genre of music contrasted with the emerging concerns of the more practical *Gebrauchsmusik* and the ethnomusicological move towards indigenisation with all its respect for native language and culture:

> His [Pius X's] attempt to reintegrate the song of the assembly into the liturgy while prohibiting the use of the vernacular meant that congregations were expected to sing music written for specialists. In most places, this was possible only by accompanying chant on the organ, which drastically changed the nature of the music.[72]

It is clear from the above that the attempts made to achieve Pius' goal were executed in what proved to be an uneven fashion.

A brief consideration of popular Irish hymnals of the twentieth century will indicate the state of hymnody from the 1920s to 1963. The *Redemptorist Hymnal* (first published in 1947) includes such pieces as *God bless our Pope, O Mother I could weep for mirth* and *To Jesus Heart All Burning*, all of which would have been used exclusively in such devotions as holy hours, novenas, sodalities, retreats, processions (May and *Corpus Christi*) along with the popular Latin Benediction chants, *O Salutaris Hostia, Tantum Ergo* and *Adoremus in Aeternum*.[73]

The Holy Ghost Hymnal of 1954 (compiled by Father Joseph Corless CSSp) includes a large corpus of plainsong in addition to a small body of congregational hymns. Apart from such simple pieces the musical participation of the congregation in the Mass (what should have been their central act of worship) was greatly overshadowed in the popular experience by their opportunity to proclaim the praises of God in song through the singing of vernacular hymns during devotions.

The richness of Una Ní Ogáin's collection of vernacular Irish hymnody, *Dánta Dé*, points to the possibilities displayed in the emerging nation state for developing a distinctive native liturgy which could dialogue effectively with the culture of a certain section of the people.[74] As we shall see that traditional element was included in later post-Vatican Two compilations thereby ensuring that the Irish hymn tradition was not lost in the the rush to embrace the new liturgical music.

SACROSANCTUM CONCILIUM AND AFTER

Sacrosanctum Concilium was promulgated on 4 December 1963 and was the painstaking result of the discussions of those who attended the Second Vatican Council (1962–1965). In the introduction to this document we read that the implementation of the Council aims 'to adapt more suitably to the needs of our own times those institutions that are subject to change'.[75] In liturgical music a spirit of change had already taken root in Europe. This was a result of many factors, the most noteworthy of which was the encyclical of Pope Pius XII *Mediator Dei* (issued in 1947) which 'was hailed by liturgists as the Magna Charta [*sic*] of the liturgical movement'.[76] Other significant precursors of this major liturgical reform included the introduction in 1947 of a bilingual rite which was initially approved for use in France and which was subsequently extended to other national groups. In 1955 the Encyclical *Musica Sacrae Disciplina* of Pius XII laid down norms for sacred music which were implemented in the 1958 Instruction *De Sacra Musica* issued from the Sacred Congregation of Rites. This allowed the use of vernacular hymn singing in the *Missa Lecta* (Mass that was read as opposed to the Solemn High Mass or *Missa Cantata*) in order 'to encourage fuller participation of the faithful in the Mass' and 'to prevent the faithful from attending as "dumb and idle spectators".'[77] It should be noted however that plainchant was restored as the norm by this Instruction.

At this time there was a scarcity of vernacular music even though some European countries had had singing in their own languages in their liturgies for decades. However, pioneers such as Joseph Gelineau in France had to some extent, through their compositions, prepared the ground for emerging developments. Gelineau had researched the early religious and folk music of several cultures (including Irish) in an attempt to create a 'universal' sound for his settings of the new translation of the French Psalter (published in 1950) which could be used internationally. In the course of his studies he discovered that the common link in these early pieces was the use of the pentatonic scale and as a result

> he wrote melodies of the utmost simplicity, consisting of a change of note on each accented syllable while the unaccented syllables are just fitted into whatever time there is to elapse before the next accent'.[78]

These psalm settings proved very popular in France and this unique style was used for the singing of psalms in English (the Grail version of the English Psalter having been produced in 1963) with antiphons composed by various musicians on both sides of the Atlantic. The texts used were taken from the lectionary of the International Commission on English in the Liturgy (ICEL). In this way Gelineau influenced the liturgical music of many nations and 'helped to restore the Psalter as the Christian hymnal par excellence'.[79] He was not without his critics though, including Richard J. Schuler who, in the 1965 Fall edition of *Sacred Music*, gave a particularly negative review of Gelineau's *Voices and Instruments in Christian Worship* criticising him for approaching music as a theologian rather than as a musicologist and calling into question the veracity of some of his historical facts.[80] The importance of sacred music as a constituent element in any liturgy is reflected in the fact that Chapter VI of *Sacrosanctum Concilium* is given over entirely to the consideration of this topic. The now familiar catchphrase of 'active participation' appears in art. 113 and in art. 114 which stresses that bishops and other pastors of souls should ensure that

> whenever a liturgical service is to be celebrated with song, the whole assembly of the faithful is enabled to contribute the active participation that rightly belongs to it.[81]

At the same time the preservation of the treasury of sacred music is strongly encouraged. Gregorian chant is highlighted as 'distinctive of the Roman liturgy; therefore, other things being equal, it should be given pride of place in liturgical services'.[82]

The inclusion of the phrase 'other things being equal' introduces a significant nuancing which modified the 1958 Instruction (which, as we have seen, regarded chant as the norm) by allowing for the introduction of newly composed mass settings. The highlighting of the active participation of the people by the 1955, 1958 and finally by the 1963 documents entailed this essentially pastoral concern becoming an important factor in the selection of music for the liturgy, and indeed it was to be the perspective from which the other exhortations with regard to the preservation of chant and polyphony would be viewed. To this end, as well as providing for the development of vernacular mass settings, the tradition of devotional music was also encouraged by the Council document.[83] In addition the indigenous music of particular peoples was, for the first time, accorded its due respect and dignity:

> In certain parts of the world, especially mission lands, people have their own musical traditions and these play a great part in their religious and social life. Thus, in keeping with art. 39 and 40, due importance is to be attached to their music and a suitable place given to it, not only in forming their attitude toward religion, but also in adapting worship to their native genius.[84]

This reference to music and its encouraging link to the principles of liturgical adaptation were crucial factors in the development of the national liturgical music of many countries, including of course Ireland.

Composers were exhorted to 'develop sacred music and to increase its store of treasures' and were given a mandate to provide not only for large choirs, but also for the needs of more modest musical groups and for the facilitation of 'the active participation of the entire assembly of the faithful'.[85] It must be said that these changes were not welcomed by all the faithful, some of whom were happier in 'the old dispensation'. Such people even went so far as to translate the *actuosus* of *Sacrosanctum Concilium* (rendered by most commentators and by official translations as 'active') with their preferred term, 'hyperactive'![86]

These comprehensive changes in the approach to music in the liturgy seemed to reverse the previously negative attitude of church authorities to music other than chant. These changes also heralded an openness in attitude to music of different cultures coupled with the already conceded promotion of the liturgical use of the vernacular. This latter development can be seen as echoing the account of Pentecost in the Acts of the Apostles where people of every nationality heard the Twelve preaching in their own native languages (Acts 2: 1–11). The new openness in these matters was further highlighted and advanced in the Instruction *Musicam Sacram* on music in the liturgy, issued by the Sacred Congregation of Rites in 1967:

> The Church does not exclude any type of sacred music from liturgical services as long as the music matches the spirit of the service itself and the character of the individual parts and is not a hindrance to the required active participation of the people.[87]

Musicam Sacram also considered the constituency of the choir. It allows for the participation of women in mixed groups and it grudgingly accepts the possibility of an all female choir.[88]

With regard to the treasury of sacred music and its preservation the Instruction offers some interesting ideas:

> Those parts of the traditional treasury of music that best meet the requirements of the reformed liturgy are to receive attention first. Then experts are to study the possibility of adapting other parts to the same requirements. Finally, parts that are incompatible with the nature of liturgical service or with its proper pastoral celebration are to be transferred to an appropriate place in popular devotions particularly in celebrations of the word of God.[89]

Concerning new compositions, composers are urged to respect the tradition of the past while noting the new liturgical requirements.

The objective is that 'any new form adopted should in some way grow organically from forms already existing' and that new works will become a truly worthy part of the Church's musical heritage.[90]

MUSICAL INSTRUMENTS

While stating the esteem in which the pipe organ is to be held in the Latin Church, *Sacrosanctum Concilium* gives permission for the use of other suitable instruments in keeping with 'the dignity of the place of worship'.[91]

The use of such instruments has, as we have seen, been treated very cautiously over the centuries. *Sacrosanctum Concilium* (later quoted by *Musicam Sacram* art. 62) paved the way for the introduction of many different instrumental styles in the liturgy. This was not without controversy, however, particularly with the introduction of the 'folk mass' and the appearance of guitars. Father Tom Egan – concerned that the guitar was somewhat incongrous in the context of Irish liturgical music – thought back to Carolan and suggested that 'if we really want stringed instruments in church, why not the Irish Harps?'[92]

Further evidence of the difficulties involved in the transition from the exclusive usage of the pipe organ is to be found in the 1969 directive of Archbishop John Charles McQuaid of Dublin. This stated that 'the use of any musical instrument, other than the organ, in any Church service is forbidden'.[93] However, by this time the usage of other instruments had alredy captured the popular imagination and newspapers of the day indicate the adverse reaction to this stricture while subsequent practice demonstrated the ineffectiveness of the measure after the archbishop had relinquished his office in 1972. That same year the National Commission for Sacred Music issued a statement which gave broad permission in this area:

> In churches which do not have the means of procuring a pipe organ, and at special Group Masses, permission could be given to use the violin or fiddle, the harp, the flute, or the feadóg (tin whistle). These instruments have a well-established place in the culture and traditions of our people (cf. Instruction, 1967, n.63) and, in the hands of skilled musicians, they can be adapted for use in divine worship, (cf. Liturgy Constitution, Art. 120).[94]

HYMN SINGING AND HYMNALS

It is true to say that the Irish church in common with other national churches was unprepared for the emerging agenda in liturgical music. The singing of hymns for the entrance, offertory, communion and recessional processions became the regular practice in most churches. This phenomenon, later dubbed the 'four hymn syndrome' illustrated the paucity of suitable hymnody as the people's vernacular repertoire comprised only of devotional music. Some borrowing from the Anglican tradition ensued and so *Abide with Me, The Lord's my Shepherd* (Crimond), *Praise to the Lord the Almighty*, and *Nearer my God to Thee* were (and in some cases are still) heard in Catholic churches throughout the country. The publication of the *College Hymnal* by Seamus O'Byrne in 1964 was the first post-Vatican Two compilation in Ireland. The compilation included some plainchant settings, twelve hymns in Irish and twenty-six in English. The *New Liturgy Handbook* was published by the Irish Hierarchy's Commission for Sacred Music in 1966 and this contained forty hymns in both Irish and English. In 1970 Monsignor John Moloney, then Administrator of St Mary's Pro-Cathedral in Dublin, compiled a small hymnal entitled *God's People Sing* under the auspices of the Dublin Diocesan Commission for Sacred Music. The response to this hymnal on the part of the Pro-Cathedral congregation serves as an example of the pioneering work which was undertaken in this regard in certain churches throughout the country. The success of the initiatives in congregational singing are recorded by Oliver O'Brien, then choral director at the Pro-Cathedral, and a son of the first director of the Palestrina Choir:

> Copies of the Hymnal 'God's People Sing', are distributed to the congregation. The people readily avail of the hymnal and as a result are already singing with greater confidence . . . The response by the people to all this persevering effort has been remarkably good, and it has not been found necessary to have 'ginger groups' strategically placed in various parts of the Church.[95]

The emphasis on hymn singing continued for many years and in 1973 another hymnal, the *Veritas Hymnal*, was produced. This has stood the test of time and is still widely in use today. Its publication was commissioned by the National Commission on Sacred Music and was assembled in collaboration with the Irish Church Music Association (which had been founded in 1969). It contains 146 hymns many of which are in Irish or in English with Gaelic melodies while it also contains some other material comprising of standard traditional hymns and newer compositions.

The institution of the National Commission on Sacred Music, the Irish Church Music Association and the *Schola Cantorum* (an episcopally-funded music element attached to the boys' secondary school at St Finian's College in Mullingar) contributed enormously to the work of renewing liturgical music in this country. The early emphasis on hymn singing was replaced in many places by an attempt to meet the needs of the requirements of the call to full participation in the liturgy. The parts of the Mass which rightly belonged to the people received some attention. The singing of the Responsorial Psalm was highlighted and this sometimes resulted in the use of the Gelineau settings. Due to a lack of vernacular Mass settings this part of the renewal took longer to initiate. The monks of Glenstal contributed three settings of the ordinary of the Mass in 1966, 1972 and 1973 respectively, and these assisted the enlightened in their zeal for singing Mass parts. The first liturgical music seminar held in Dublin in May 1969 used the *Mass in G Minor* by Leighton Lucas which had been approved by the National Commission for Catholic Music in England. Dublin organist and composer, Daniel McNulty, produced the *Mass in honour of the Precious Blood* in 1969, one of the first Masses by an Irish composer to be accepted for use in this country.

MASS SETTINGS IN IRISH

Sean Ó Riada, before his untimely death in 1971, composed three masses using Irish texts. The best known of these, published in 1971 as *Ceol an Aifrinn mar a chantar i nGaeltacht Chúil Aodha* (Music for the Mass as sung in the Gaeltacht of Cul Aodha), is enthuiastically performed inside and outside of the Gaeltacht (the Irish speaking areas of Ireland). The Mass parts include the *Kyrie Eleison, An Ghlóir* (*Gloria*), the Preface Dialogue, the *Sanctus, An Phaidir* (Our Father) and the *Agnus Dei*. Apart from the absence of the Creed and the inclusion of the Prefatory Dialogue this setting takes on the form of the classic Mass compositions of earlier eras. The missing parts are a psalm setting, a Gospel acclamation, a memorial acclamation and the great Amen, all of which are quite significant elements of the reformed liturgy. The second Mass (published posthumously in 1979) is thoroughly modern in its form, however, incorporating the parts missing from the earlier work. This setting, less well known outside Irish speaking congregations, is nonetheless a worthwhile contribution to the native Irish repertoire. Sean Ó Riada's religious work is an example of one response to the challenge of inculturation in the liturgy. This is evident in his compositions 'in which the idiom and syntax of the ethnic repertory are "recomposed" so as to provide a musical vocabulary answerable to the text of the mass ordinary in Irish'.[96] Father Tom Egan in 1969 had supported this kind of initiative in an article in the *Furrow*:

> If we are searching for a new sound in our music for Mass, we ought to seek it in the light of article 119 of the Constitution on the Sacred Liturgy which refers to 'nations which have their own musical traditions', and directs us to give suitable place to this music not only in forming attitudes

towards religion but also in adapting worship to native genius. A new sound in our liturgical music, then, would most suitably be a distinctively Irish sound.[97]

Ó Riada's seminal works in this area were followed by Irish Mass Settings from Sean Og Ó Tuama (*Aifreann i nGaeilge*, approved by the Dublin Sacred Music Commission for use in that diocese), Siúr Colmcille Ní Chonáin (who wrote many masses for the community of Mary Immaculate College of Education, Limerick), Máire Ní Dhuibhir, Fiontán Ó Cearbhaill, Tomás Cardinal Ó Fiaich, Micheál Ó Ceallacháin, Pádraig Ó hEaráin, Pat Ahern, Tomás Ó Canainn and Liam Lawton. Father Pat Ahern's four-part *Aifreann Phádraig Naofa* blends traditional style with harmony while retaining appropriate liturgical functionality and accessibility. It is possibly the second mass in Irish to find extensive usage outside exclusively Irish Mass celebrations. The traditional Irish Group, *Siamsa Tíre*, founded by Father Ahern, gave the first performance of this Mass in Saint Mary's Pro-Cathedral, Dublin on Saint Patrick's Day 1984. The setting of *Rian Phádraig* (used in the Mass as a recessional hymn) is a worthy tribute to our national patron both in its original Irish text by Father Oliver Crilly and in its English translation by Father Dermod McCarthy.

Father Liam Lawton's 1993 *Aifreann Laserian Naofa* (*Molaise*) is the most recent popular Irish setting to be composed. Inspired by the history of St Lazerian, the man who came to be known as 'Molaise' (My Light), this setting is a lively and refreshing meeting of Irish folk music with deliberate liturgical pragmatism which is enhanced by its minimal harmonic interest. As the composer has put it:

> The pieces are arranged in this edition for piano and organ and I have kept the arrangements quite basic and simple to be accessible to all.[98]

The Irish speaking community has been well served by composers of liturgical music particularly when we remember the limited size of the population who worship regularly in that particular language. There is an increasing trend however towards the use of such music in liturgies outside of the Gaeltacht and this represents a welcome adoption of our native language and distinctive musical style.

COMMISSIONED MASSES

The Music Panel of the Irish Commission for Liturgy commissioned four masses for the Irish Church in the 1970s. Seoirse Bodley's *Mass of Peace* and Thomas C. Kelly's *Mass for Peace* were published in 1976. Both works have a distinctively Irish air about them and were hailed as the first masses of the new dispensation to be written specifically for Irish congregations. In his introduction to the Mass, Bodley calls attention to his two versions of the *Gloria* one of which is sung throughout by all those present while the other only involves the congregation in singing the refrain and the Amen.

> The Alternative Version is thus a means by which the congregation could become familiar with the music of the entire Gloria before they attempt to sing the Gloria straight through, without the use of the refrain.[99]

This openness to the needs of the congregation and the acceptance of their rightful role in liturgical singing also finds expression in the structure of T. C. Kelly's Mass. There are frequent references to 'All' and 'Choir' demonstrating the possibilities of the two sharing the ministry of music as partners rather than as opponents. The main difference between these two settings lies in the choral configuration of the Kelly Mass which contrasts with the simplicity of Bodley's. This initiative was followed in 1977 by the publication of another two masses. The *Mass of the Immaculate Conception* by Fintan O'Carroll displays the same openness to congregational participation while still managing to provide scope for the choir to enhance its text with harmony. In his introduction the composer states that 'it is designed to be sung by cantor (or celebrant or choir or all three) with congregation.'[100] All three mass settings are in regular use throughout the country and they have served to shift the emphasis from the rendition of hymns to the singing of the parts of the mass which are proper to the people.

By contrast with the popularity of the above mentioned masses Gerard Victory's *Mass of Resurrection* (also published by the Irish Commission for Liturgy in 1977) never achieved widespread usage (perhaps due to the abundance of Masses then available) despite the fact that it is a fine setting with a very appealing version of the Our Father in the manner of a *berceuse*.

MASSES FOR SPECIAL OCCASIONS

The composition of Mass settings in Ireland has continued to flourish over the years. The commissioning of Masses for special occasions has proved to be a rich source of inspiration and encouragement. Unfortunately, many of these compositions do not survive beyond the memory of the occasion for which they were written. An example of this is Seoirse Bodley's *Mass of Joy* (composed in 1979 in honour of St John of God) which is, unfortunately, rarely used today, despite its distinctively Irish style and the lilting melodic interest of the work.

Sister Aideen O'Sullivan, a member of the religious order of the Medical Missionaries of Mary and a prolific composer, dedicated a Mass in 1987 to her foundress Mother Mary Martin on the occasion of the Golden Jubilee of the foundation of her Order. The Communion Hymn *The Promise* inspired by quotations from the Gospel of Luke, the prophet Isaiah and the *Book of Revelation* encapsulates the charism of that order and follows the directive that religious music should be based in holy Scripture.[101]

Father Tom Egan provided a setting of Eucharistic Prayer II for a national celebration of European Music Year (1985) which took place in Mullingar. He used a *laoi fiannaíochta* which had been recorded in Donegal in the early part of this century as the musical base for this work. The setting of the prayer is punctuated with fourteen acclamations (in place of the three normally used) which allows the regular participation of the congregation (along the lines of the Eucharistic Prayer for Children). This combination of an ancient Irish tune with the modern liturgical application of the principal of active participation demonstrates the possibilities of a healthy integration of native tradition with dignified innovation.

Margaret Daly's *Kainos Mass* was composed in 1986 to mark the tenth anniversary of the foundation of the Irish Institute of Pastoral Liturgy. This setting is based on a fragment of an old Gregorian *Gloria* which was renewed in this modern work. Such composition resonates with the call of *Sacrosanctum Concilium* (art. 23) to forge links with the past and grow from the rich musical heritage of the Church.

Peadar Ó Riada composed a mass, *Aifreann Eoin na Croise*, in honour of St John of the Cross to mark the occasion of the quater centenary of the saint's death in 1991. The setting of the Irish text of the Mass written for the Cúl Aodh male voice choir is haunting and reflective in style by express intention of the composer.

> This Mass originated out of a desire to draw people into a more meditative worship. The music, prayers and chants of the liturgy prepare us to become attentive and receptive to the word of God. The opening chant chosen here is "An Marnabh" the oldest prayer in Muscraighe Uí Fhloinn.[102]

In this instance we observe an effective wedding of native spirituality, text and music along with the desire of the composer to create a timeless liturgy. The opening chant with its atmosphere of attentive seeking of God's presence leads to the ideal of true communion with God:

The five short prayers sung simultaneously with the opening chant are meant to awaken in us that which we have inherited from our people – the linking of past and future – the present. Time is transformed in the House of God. Thus we hope to find the 'Cosán Draíochacht' (The Secret Ladder) to the presence of God.[103]

The same occasion was marked by the English *Centenary Mass* of Ronan McDonagh which captures the spirit of Ireland in its music, in the texts of the accompanying hymns and in its haunting instrumental *Súile an Choilm*:

The music of the Mass echoes the prayers and aspirations of our people. It is a living music because it is rooted in our native soil. It therefore calls forth in us a response that is native, communal and religious.[104]

Michael McGlynn, Director of *Anúna*, a Dublin-based folk-chamber choir, was requested to write a mass for the thirty-ninth O'Malley Clan Rally which was held in Trinity College in 1991. This is a choral setting which is imbued with a medieval polyphonic sense and which also strikes some Irish chords. One of the pieces from this work *Maria Matrem Virginem* is a typical example of this curious blend of the ancient and the modern in both universal and national styles. The interesting harmonies are complemented by the distinctive solo material which rises in a mannered fashion above the sustained choral underlay.

The Beatification of the Seventeen Irish Martyrs in Rome on 27 September 1992 was the occasion for the composition of an anthem (*The Seed of Martyrs*) and a mass in their honour by Mary McAuliffe (who had studied with Sean Ó Riada in University College Cork). Once again a distinctive Irish quality permeates these compositions. In the performance of the anthem (by Our Lady's Choral Society, Dublin) in Saint Peter's Square during the Beatification ceremony it could be said that (on that symbolic spot from where so much liturgical uniformity had previously emanated) the normative usage of native music in the liturgy was firmly established.

LATER HYMNALS

In 1978 the Irish Institute of Pastoral Liturgy published *Alleluia! Amen!* (a supplement to which was produced in 1981), a compilation of some of the worship music used at the Institute. This hymnal contains contemporary compositions which are seen as complementing the pieces of traditional hymnody to be found in other compilations. Contained in the hymnal are a mixture of native productions (works by composers such as Joseph Walshe,

Kevin Healy, Aideen O'Sullivan, Tom Egan and Margaret Daly, music director of the Institute) and internationally produced material (from people like Lucien Deiss, Joseph Gelineau, Paul Décha, Jean Paul Lécot and John Foley). The hymnal places a strong emphasis in its style of presentation on the particular role of music in liturgies, a fact noted in his introduction by Bishop Dermot O'Mahony of Dublin:

> Not only are the priorities for music in the Liturgy clearly indicated, but the notes which accompany each section provide the priest, the organist and the congregation with a kind of 'teach yourself' kit for understanding the role of music and song and its appropriate application to any specific celebration.[105]

A third national hymnal *Hosanna* – A National Liturgical Songbook For Ireland – published in 1987 was the fruit of the work of the Advisory Committee on Church Music of the Irish Episcopal Commission for Liturgy. The pew edition contains the words of the most frequently used hymns from *Alleluia! Amen!* and the *Veritas Hymnal*. The three music supplements produced for this hymnal contain material from a variety of sources both national and international. This demonstrates once again the multilateral interface between the native and the universal Church. The third supplement to *Hosanna* is noteworthy for its provision of an appropriate repertoire for funeral and marriage liturgies, thus presenting more suitable alternatives to an increasing trend of using secular songs whose lyrics quite often do not match the integrity of the Christian celebration.

LITURGICAL MUSIC IN POPULAR IDIOM

The Carmelite Centre at Gort Muire in Dublin was the most noteworthy institution which offered initial support to folk or popular-style liturgical music in the 1970s and 1980s, using a repertoire which was mainly of American origin. Fiontán Ó Murchú, a Dominican priest based in Cork, has cultivated the folk music style in many ways, particularly by his annual sessions at Knockadoon which gave rise many new compositions. Emerging from this school of liturgical music is Feargal King, a prolific composer whose works (which include his popular *Mass of Christ the King*) are becoming more widely used throughout the country.

The Charismatic movement in Ireland introduced a measure of 'Spirit' music into their prayer groups and their liturgies. Much of the movement's eclectic repertoire is now contained in the hymnal *Hail Christ Our King* in which devotional music is set alongside new compositions.[106]

Other Irish composers have composed American-style folk music over the years. The repertoire of the group *Shekinah* (some of which is composed by Father Paul Healy, a past pupil of the *Schola Cantorum* in Mullingar) combines modern popular music trends with renewal spirituality to create an authentic liturgical music which is both in tune with contemporary culture and profoundly in touch with sacred texts. *To You I Pray* (edited by Brian Foley) is the title of a collection of liturgical music in the folk style compiled by Solas Music in Northern Ireland in 1993. This hymnal represents a unique collection of folk-style music exclusively written by Irish composers.

PSALMODY

The singing of the Responsorial Psalm at the Sunday Liturgy (which is strongly recommended in the new rite) was greatly enhanced by Fintan O'Carroll's collection *Psalms for Sundays and Major Feast Days*.[107] For almost two decades the Irish church rejoiced in the use of this very helpful compilation. Margaret Daly's three volume series of cantor-friendly psalms, *Cantate* (1991) is another welcome addition in this respect. Sister Veronica Kennedy published *Salm Caintic Cruit* (1992) a collection of psalms and canticles written in Irish for harp or guitar accompaniment which can be readily used in the Mass and for the Office. In addition other composers have put music to particular psalms such as Sue Furlong's setting of Psalm 62 ('O God you are my God') and Tomás Ó Canainn's setting of Psalm 95 ('Canaigí amhrán nua don Tiarna').

PAST, PRESENT AND FUTURE

It is interesting to note how an almost puritanical attitude towards music and musicians is echoed in various eras. In the past, when a spirit of renewal with regard to music in the liturgy pervaded the Western church, it seems invariably to have been accompanied by a movement which sought to cleanse the rites from anything considered unsuitable or 'profane'. This was especially evident when the process of confirming the Latin rite as the universal mode of worship was in train. Regrettably, the attitudes of such movements persist to this day and are characterised by the dogmatism of those who attempt to stifle the natural evolution of a type of worship music which acknowledges and expresses the Church's rich tradition and which at the same time incorporates contemporary styles with a native underlay.

Rediscovering our native Irish tradition is certainly the challenge of the times. It is undeniable that much liturgical music was imported from other countries in the 1960s and '70s and that this openness to other styles of music is in keeping with a spirit of sharing the mission of Christ with peoples throughout the world. This borrowing from other traditions also has an unhealthy aspect however which was once to be seen in the mission lands where native culture was often supplanted by the colonising influences of the missionaries. This led to the kind of cultural schizophrenia described by Frank Senn:

> The sounds of African or Asian instruments, the rhythms of native tunes and dances, and the sight of colorful apparel is juxtaposed with German or English hymnody and with clergy dressed in black gowns or cassocks and surplices.[108]

In the same way the Irish Church is called to rediscover the riches of our Celtic heritage and claim for ourselves a liturgy and a music that is distinctively Irish, yet linked to the Universal Church.

In this regard the problem does arise with how precisely we can determine what exactly comprises Irish culture in our time. The cultural differences between urban and rural communities are still quite considerable and even from parish to parish cultural elements appear to be remarkably variable. The 'Rock' Mass in the working-class suburb of Neilstown in Dublin (where *Sweet Caroline* is reportedly the recessional 'hymn') is, after all, a far cry from the Latin Mass in Haddington Road! In the past thirty years Irish liturgical composers have demonstrated their talent in providing a native music for our worship. From the overview of the repertoire covered in this article we can see the richness of what has been composed so far and we can look forward with some measure of confidence to future compositions of this calibre. The challenge is now to own this music and use it regularly in worship along with the riches that we have inherited from the Irish and from the universal Church.

Though one can concur with Cathal Cardinal Daly in his observation that 'there is an immense amount of work still to be done in the field of liturgical music in Ireland'.[109] It must still be admitted that the raw material for progress is clearly present. The conviction and the will to create a liturgy which expresses the faith of the Irish people at the end of the second millenium is the key to success in this vital area of the life of the Church and the way towards experiencing the kind of renewal which is clearly the wish of the Fathers of the Second Vatican Council.[110]

EPILOGUE

The Eurovision Mass for the Feast of Pentecost 1994 came from Duisce Abbey in Graignamanagh, Co. Kilkenny. This highly acclaimed liturgy featured traditional and contemporary Irish music and gave to liturgical musicians a sense of native pride to equal that which was witnessed after the performance of the *River Dance*, the contemporary choreographical treatment of traditional Irish step-dancing which accompanied a modern choral/instrumental piece composed for the 1994 Eurovision Song Contest hosted in Ireland. The enthusiastic reaction of people in other European countries to the liturgy was also on a par with their response to the music and choreography of the Eurovision feature. At a time when busy executives are enjoying the quiet and calm of the Gregorian chant, recorded by the monks of Santo Domingo de Silos, as they negotiate the traffic on the M 25 or the Champs Elysées and the Irish church is rediscovering its native musical roots one's mind comes to the oft quoted lines of T.S. Eliot:

> We shall not cease from exploration
> And the end of all our exploring
> Will be to arrive where we started
> And know the place for the first time.[111]

NOTES

1. Eoghan O Tuairisc, 'Oiche Nollag' in Máire Ní Dhuibhir (ed.): *Tús* (Dublin: Foilseacháin Abhair Spioradálta, 1989), 8. Author's translation.
2. Theodoret, *Graecorum affectionum curatio* 7, 16 quoted in Johannes Quasten, *Music in Pagan and Christian Antiquity* trans. Boniface Ramsey O.P., (Washington DC: National Association of Pastoral Musicians, 1983), 64.
3. Clement of Alexandria *Paidagogos* 2, 4 in Quasten (as n.2), 61.
4. Cyril of Jerusalem *Catechesis Mystagog* 5, 6 in Quasten (as n.2), 69.
5. Quoted in Edward Foley: *From Age to Age* (Archdiocese of Chicago: Liturgy Training Publications, 1991), 31.
6. Foley (as n.5), 32.
7. Quoted in Quasten (as n.2), 81.
8. Quasten (as n.2), 81.
9. Michael Curran, 'Early Irish Monasticism' in Michael Maher (ed.), *Irish Spirituality* (Dublin: Veritas Publications, 1981), 10.
10. Anscar J. Chupungco, *Cultural Adaptation of the Liturgy* (New York: Paulist Press, 1982), 8 q.v.
11. Chupungco (as n.10), 12.
12. Chupungco (as n.10), 15.
13. Curran (as n.9), 16.
14. Curran (as n.9), 16.

15. D.M. Hope, *The Medieval Western Rites* in P. Brannon, 'The Search for the Celtic Rite', *Irish Musical Studies* ii (1993), Gerard Gillen & Harry White eds. (Dublin: Irish Academic Press, 1993), 15.

16. Brannon (as n.15), 15.

17. Nóirín Ní Riain, 'The Nature and Classification of Traditional Religious Songs in Irish', in Gerard Gillen & Harry White eds. (as n.15), 191.

18. The story is told of an anchorite of Cluain Ua Duban whose genuflections during the various canonical hours of any day would number seven hundred. Of him Mael Ruain remarked: 'Upon my word . . . a time will come before he dies when he shall not perform a single genuflection.' So it was: his feet were afflicted so that he was unable to perform a vigil for a long while before death, because he had done too much in other days.
    from the *Monastery of Tallaght* text cited by Pádraig Ó Fiannachta, 'The Spirituality of Céili Dé' in Michael Maher ed. (as n.9), 26–7.

19. Ó Fiannachta (as n.18), 27. Quotation from the *Monastery of Tallaght* text.

20. Ó Fiannachta (as n.18), 23.

21. See Peter O'Dwyer, *Irish Medieval Spirituality* in Michael Maher ed. (as n.9), 57.

22. Diarmuid Ó Laoghaire, *Mary in Irish Spirituality* in Michael Maher ed. (as n.9), 51.

23. Ó Laoghaire (as n.22), 51.

24. Brannon (as n.15), 35.

25. See Richard H. Hoppin, *Medieval Music* (New York: W. W. Norton & Co. Inc., 1978), 382.

26. Hoppin (as n.25), 314.

27. Hoppin (as n.25), 315f.

28. Hoppin (as n.25), 318f.

29. Ní Riain (as n.17), 191.

30. Luke Wadding, *A Pious Garland* in Ní Riain (as n.17), 191.

31. Ní Riain (as n.17), 192.

32. Chupungco (as n.10), 34.

33. Ní Riain (as n.17), 195.

34. See Ní Riain (as n.17), 192–3.

35. Charles Acton, *Irish Music and Musicians* (Norwich: Eason & Sons Ltd., 1978).

36. Ní Riain (as n.17), 205 q.v.

37. Chupungco (as n.10), 34.

38. Harry White, 'Church Music and Musicology in Ireland', in Gillen & White eds. (as n.15), 333.

39. Diarmuid Ó Laoghaire, *Irish Spirituality in Modern Times* in Michael Maher ed. (as n.9), 126.

40. Gerard Gillen, 'Church Music in Dublin, 1500–1900' in Brian Boydell (ed.), *Four Centuries in Ireland* (London: BBC, 1979), 26.

41. Gillen (as n.40), 26.

42. Gillen (as n.40), 26.

43. For further treatment of the Cecelian Movement see Harry White and Nicholas Lawrence, 'Towards a history of the Cecilian Movement in Ireland', in Gillen and White eds. (as n.15), 78–107.

44. Gillen (as n.40), 26–7.

45. Bishops of Ireland, *Decreta Synodi Plenariæ Episcoporum Hiberniæ apud Thurles* MDCCCL (Dublin: James Duffy, 1851), 25.
I have translated the quoted excerpts as follows:

> 38. No singing is allowed in Churches, unless it is solemn and Ecclesiastical. The rectors of seminaries must take care as a primary responsibility that the students are instructed well in the chant so that they may properly learn the sacred ceremonies.
> 39. Nothing but Latin may be sung during Solemn Masses, nor outside of Mass in churches is anything to be found, unless it is contained in the approved Ecclesiastical books, or is approved by the Ordinary.

46. *Acta et Decreta Synodi Plenariæ Episcoporum Hiberniæ (Habaitæ apud Maynutiam) MDCCCLXXV* (Dublin: Browne & Nolan, 1877), paragraph 72.
47. *Acta et Decreta Synodi Plenariæ Episcoporum Hiberniæ* (as n.46), paragraph 73.
48. *Synodus Diœcesana Dublinensis* (Dublin: Joseph Dollard, 1879), 32.
49. 'Quapropter praxim, quæ alicubi obtinet, adhibendi in divinis officiis non solum cantum levem et profanum set etiam musicam ex theatro mutuatam et sordes scenicas redolentem vehementur improbamus et penitus interdicimus' from *Synodus Diœcesana Dublinensis* (as n.48), 23.
50. *Synodus Diœcesana Dublinensis* (as n.48), 34.
51. *Synodus Diœcesana Dublinensis* (as n.48), 34.
52. *Synodus Diœcesana Dublinensis* (as n.48), 42.
53. *Synodus Diœcesana Dublinensis* (as n.48), 43.
54. William J. Walsh, *A Grammar of Gregorian Music with Numerous Exercises and Examples* (Dublin: M.H. Gill & Son, 1885)
55. William J. Walsh, *Addresses by the Most Rev. Dr. Walsh, Archbishop of Dublin* (Dublin: M. H. Gill & Son,1886), 379.
56. Mary Purcell, *Dublin's Pro-Cathedral* (Dublin: Pro-Cathedral, 1975), no page numbers.
57. Purcell (as n.56).
58. Purcell (as n.56).
59. Purcell (as n.56). The Pro-Cathedral is situated in the north city-centre at Marlborough Street while St Andrew's Church, Westland Row is south of the River Liffey.
60. *Minutes of the Cathedral Choir Committee of St Mary's Pro-Cathedral, Dublin* (Nov. 1902–June 1926). Minute book held in the Pro-Cathedral. Minutes of the meeting of 23 December 1902.
61. *Minutes of the Cathedral Choir Committee* (as n. 60), 7 January 1905
62. Norita Lanners, *American Essays in Liturgy* vol. ii 'Chant: From Gueranger to Gelineau', (Washington D.C.: The Pastoral Press, 1984), 6.
63. Robert F. Hayburn, *Papal Legislation on Sacred Music 95 A.D. to 1977 A.D.* (Collegeville: The Liturgical Press, 1979)
64. Thomas Day, *Why Catholics Can't Sing* (New York: Crossroads, 1991), 20.
65. James Joyce, *Ulysses* (London: Penguin Books, 1986), 540.
66. Day (as n.64), 27.
67. Charter of Guild of Choristers, St Mary's Church, Haddington Road 1905 (in the keeping of the Church).

68. Charter of Guild (as n.67), q.v.
69. James Joyce, *Dubliners* (New York: Bantam Classics, 1990), 158.
70. Quoted in Foley (as n.5), 153.
71. Foley (as n.5), 153.
72. Foley (as n.5), 154.
73. Leo O'Halloran (ed.), *Redemptorist Hymn Book with Music Accompaniments* (Dublin: Cahill & Co., 1963).
74. Una Ní Ogáin, *Dánta Dé* (Dublin: Fallons Ltd., 1928).
75. *Sacrosanctum Concilium* (1) in T.C. O'Brien (ed.), *Documents on the Liturgy, 1963–1979: Conciliar, Papal and Curial Texts* (Collegeville: The Liturgical Press, 1982), 4
76. Lanners (as n. 62), 8
77. Lanners (as n. 62), 14
78. Clifford Howell: 'A new approach to Vernacular Psalm Singing', *Worship* xxx (December 1955), (Collegeville, 1955), 27
79. T. M. Gannon quoted in Lanners (as n.62), 14
80. Richard J. Schuler: 'Review of Voices and Instruments', *Sacred Music* xcii (Fall 1965), 83–88.
81. *Sacrosanctum Concilium* (114) in T.C. O'Brien (ed.) (as n.75), 24.
82. *Sacrosanctum Concilium* (116) in T.C. O'Brien (ed.) (as n.75), 24.
83. *Sacrosanctum Concilium* (118) in T.C. O'Brien (ed.) (as n.75), 24.
84. *Sacrosanctum Concilium* (119) in T.C. O'Brien (ed.) (as n.75), 24.
85. *Sacrosanctum Concilium* (121) in T.C. O'Brien (ed.) (as n.75), 25.
86. Editorial 'Time Bombs at the Vatican Council', *New Jersey Catholic News* xxxiii (Spring 1993).
87. *Musicam Sacram* (9) in T.C. O'Brien (ed.) (as n.75), 1295.
88. *Musicam Sacram* (22) in T.C. O'Brien (ed.) (as n.75), 1297.
89. *Musicam Sacram* (53) in T.C. O'Brien (ed.) (as n.75), 1303.
90. *Musicam Sacram* (59) in T.C. O'Brien (ed.) (as n.75), 1304.
91. *Sacrosanctum Concilium* (120) in T.C. O'Brien (ed.) (as n.75), 25.
92. Thomas Egan, 'Church Music in Ireland since the Council', *Music* (a supplement to *The Furrow*) iii (Summer 1969), ed. P. McDonnell (Naas: Leinster Leader Ltd., 1969), 11.
93. Letter of John Charles McQuaid, 19 March 1969, for the clergy only (in the possession of this author).
94. 'Statement on the use of musical instruments in the Sacred Liturgy', Irish National Commission for Sacred Music, March 1972 (Paper in the possession of this author).
95. Oliver O'Brien, 'The Pro-Cathedral', *The Bulletin* iv (April 1970), private circulation (Dublin: Dublin Diocesan Press Office, 1970), 2.
96. White (as n.38), 335.
97. Egan (as n.92), 10.
98. Liam Lawton, *Aifreann Lazerian Naofa* (no publication details, 1992), Introduction.
99. Seoirse Bodley, *Mass of Peace* (Dún Laoghaire: Irish Commission for Liturgy, 1977), Introduction.

100. Fintan O'Carroll, *Mass of the Immaculate Conception* (Duń Laoghaire: Irish Commission for Liturgy, 1977), Introductory Note.
101. *Sacrosanctum Concilium* (121) in T.C. O'Brien (ed.) (as n.75), 25.
102. Peadar Ó Riada, *Aifreann Eoin na Croise* (no publishing details, 1991), 5.
103. Ó Riada (as n.94), 5.
104. Ronan Mc Donagh, *St. John of the Cross: Centenary Mass* (Dublin: Carmelite Publications, 1991), Introduction.
105. Margaret Daly (ed.), *Alleluia! Amen!* (Dublin: Veritas Publications, 1978), 6.
106. Jim Sherlock (ed.), *Hail Christ our King.* (Dublin: Cedar Media & Communications Ltd., 1993).
107. General Instruction of the Roman Missal (36) in T.C. O'Brien (ed.), (as n.75), 478.
108. Frank Senn, *Christian Worship and its Cultural Setting* (USA, Fortress Press, 1983), vii.
109. Cardinal Cathal Daly, homily on the occasion of the Mass for the Quatercentenary of Palestrina, Maynooth College, 2 February 1994.
110. R. Kevin Seasoltz, *New Liturgy, New Laws* (Collegeville, 1980), 201.
111. *Little Gidding* in M. H. Abrams et al. (eds.), *The Norton Anthology of English Literature: The Major Authors* 5th edition (New York: W. W. Norton & Co. 1962), 2535.

Music in Irish Education

FRANK HENEGHAN

MUSIC EDUCATION DEFENDED

It has been claimed that the health of a civilization can be measured by the status of the arts within it. This is to beg many thorny questions, not least those demanding a definition of art itself and of the other parameters by which a civilization may be constrained. We live in an age where the quality of life is undoubtedly dominated by the interaction between technology and the economy, which in turn can conveniently, though erroneously, be construed as synonymous with the civilization of which it is merely an outcrop. Technology has benefited the arts too, few more than music, but the sheer splendour of its achievements has tended to blunt our consciousness that it is after all, in this context and as it should be, merely ancillary to the processes of art itself. The partially dehumanizing and unequal battle for the more overt creature comforts, in which technology is an easy victor, and particularly so in the critical field of education, constantly deprioritizes the refining powers of the humanities while, with guile, it becomes a facile seduction by which we are enticed away from a true evaluation of the contribution to life of the arts and of those who uphold them; indeed what is owed to them is often devalued and taken too much for granted in our materialistic society. So it is in Ireland, and so too is the all-too-familiar summons, to a dignified and self-justifying survival strategy, being sounded.

There is a moral dimension to the enjoyment of the arts which must be made to touch the conscience of those, surely the vast majority, who feel their sense of the commonality of humanness stimulated and celebrated by that participation. This moral responsibility is one of promoting comprehensively and effectively the processes by which the arts become the property of those for whom they are intended. This benign campaign should then, *inter alia*, take the form of an initiative to promote active participation in music. Commitment to the agency of music education, by which alone music can become a real refining force in the community, must be inculcated in or exacted from those who have themselves benefited from the process, sometimes without realizing the attendant debt they owe; this, too, is the particular aim and the unashamed thrust of this chapter. It is one of the

153

enigmas of our contemporary civilization that such advocacy should be necessary, but the fabric of communication in art is complex, and sometimes
esoteric to a frustrating degree; it presupposes education and, above all,
effort, albeit richly rewarded, if it is to reach its most effective manifestations. This is to suggest a spectrum of astonishing variability, for there is
within any normal sample of humanity an unpredictable range of interest in,
propensity and talent for, participation in artistic endeavour, even without
stressing unduly its inherent aesthetic. There is a generally accepted correlation too between art and human feeling; inversely, all human beings must
surely feel invited potentially by the artistic vehicle to harness, for expression,
and to savour the intrinsic qualities of human sentience. But it is a characteristic human weakness to seek enjoyment with minimal effort, nowhere more
than in music because of its saturating presence and accessibility. Regardless,
therefore, of the level at which this encounter takes place, some knowledge of
its conventions and style must be acquired and internalized if it is to function
satisfactorily. Aesthetic response may be a secret event, and so it should be,
for it would be an immoral intrusion on the sensibility of fellow humans to
suggest that their modes of feeling can be controlled or that this is the hidden agenda of artistic education. But it is possible to influence the purely
objective sequences by which perception in art is transformed into understanding, self awareness, and that inner consciousness of pleasure which we
can all feel and attest to, simply because it is such a familiar experience. It is a
function of formal education, the assault by one man's skill on the sensibilities
of another, to enrich the scope of this transmutation, as it is a responsibility to
ensure that its benefits are administered wisely and democratically, that targets are appropriately set and aims understood as achievable. The music
education context in Ireland is a classic and, indeed, a unique case for consideration in this connection.

It is my view that, in an Irish sense, if the response to music is to reach
the generally self-fulfilling level that is its ultimate goal, music itself must
be treated more seriously in relation to the national education provision, as it
arguably is, to a greater extent, elsewhere. It is not my intention here to
overstate the philosophical advocacy which is so copiously and freely available to vindicate the place of music in the educational curriculum. But the
most telling rationales must be constantly plied in educational circles to
ensure that the basic decision as to levels of investment, both intellectual
and financial, in the promotion of music in the system is the outcome of
conviction of its value in humanistic terms. At those who are likely to ask
the question '*why* music education?' – and they are all too numerous in
these days of economic astringency – a peremptory fist must be shaken in a
reply which as validly asks 'and why *not* music education?'; but the stance
must be defended.

THE DILEMMA OF ÉLITISM

To claim that we are human because we are musical is surely a challenging assertion, stressing as it does an unexpected relationship, an ownership and a responsibility. The universal attachment to music in its protean forms is a fact of human discourse which is verifiable by simple observation. It is virtually undeniable that music as an artistic pursuit – as aesthetic experience – is given only to man, and is the product of his demiurgic power. This is nevertheless to hint at an élitist and educationally problematic aspect of music which probably relegates the vast majority of listeners to an arm's length relationship with it. Schoenberg succinctly defined the dilemma when he observed that 'if it is art it is not for all, and if it is for all it is not art.'[1] Is this to suggest that the net of music in caring education must be of finer mesh and be less selectively or more tolerantly cast; what are the compromises involved, what the price to be paid if the universality of musical experience is to be validated (for that is the goal, and a fundamental consideration, if enlightened educational policies are to be vindicated)? Music has too much to offer to be allowed to become the property only of an élite. Failure to realize that the aim of music education should be not to consolidate but to dismantle barriers of artistic communication is a danger which, in dramatic statement, is believed by some to be effectively forcing music out of the school educational experience in Ireland. This is simply because a significant cohort of the population, which might decide otherwise, is choosing not to participate in it for reasons of straitened educational timetables, in which the attractions of music as a plausible subject option are dwindling; this reported development merits the most searching analysis and is not to be dismissed lightly as mere scare-mongering.

Music has other functions less intrinsic than the controlled expression of the workings of man's spirituality and inner self: this is a widely held view. Its pleasures can be overtly cerebral; it can be simply cathartic; it can, *inter alia*, be used to stimulate the imagination, or the emotions arising from a search for cultural identity. Regardless of any attempt to impose a limit on its scope, a promise to go no further should not be exacted from those who would champion the cause of music or extol its more utilitarian contributions to human affairs. In historical, economic, political and social terms a study of musical pursuits in a society can be a revealing microcosm of life as lived in that society. As a vehicle for influencing human behaviour music has long been recognized as a potent enabler. Powerful statements of its value in the process of education were vibrant in Plato more than two millenia ago, and have been reiterated ever since, no more forcibly than in this century. Music in its most inspired utterances is a glorious culmination, but its less pretentious forms should not be disparaged so long as they can be functionally justified on their own terms; this is a germane consideration in educational matters.

The familiar rôle-definitions of composer, performer and listener (and, perhaps, teacher) might suggest exclusivity but, of course, they largely coalesce. There is no monopoly on creativity, given the relationship of interpretation to composition and, likewise, the connection between reception and performance. Aristotle asserts that in the mimetic processes of music in performance we advance the frontiers of knowledge; we learn something, and therefore the exchange becomes definitively a pedagogic, and indeed also a pleasurable one.[2] Kodaly tells us that 'there is no such thing as tone deafness; there is only trained and untrained hearing',[3] an assertion which again stresses the rôle of the teacher. Music need not be confrontational and dichotomous, suggesting merely performer(s) and audience, and reflecting certain norms of Western art music; it can and should be more democratically and invitingly considered as procreative and participative. It is arguable that music-making is a universal faculty as much as it is a universally shared experience. Its agent is education, its beneficiary the whole of humanity, but

> there are relatively few people who are capable of understanding, purely musically, what music has to say. Such trained listeners have probably never been numerous, but that does not prevent the artist from creating only for them. Great art presupposes the alert mind of the educated listener.[4]

The chasm that can exist between giver and receiver is as evident in music as in any other branch of the human sharing symbolisms. The difference between a simple folk-song and the scale of the enduring masterpieces of celebrated musical genius may almost suggest discrete genres, while the pleasure they give when aptly targeted need not, as far as we can tell, differ very much at all; this is a crucial consideration in the varied spectra of educational provision, where materials must have the flexibility, but not necessarily always the ultimate quality, to reach their target. But let it be understood that the criterion of quality and aesthetic value may always be insisted upon without its being seen to militate against certain genres of audience-friendly music; quality judged by standards of craft and feeling, rather than by decibels and the vulgarity of indiscriminate emotional discharge, can be an impartial leveller.

The twentieth century has finally banished the romantic notion that music is a universal language, in the sense of its being immediately accessible to all as if by some magic. Like verbal discourse its processes and its powers of communication must be inculcated and enhanced by reiteration and reinforcement; without education the refinement to its most effective utterances is seriously inhibited. The concepts of standard, value and judgement are essential to the cultivation and maximization of music's power to communicate and achieve its more sophisticated and subtle aims. The educational challenge is daunting. Let us continue, therefore, to address it in an Irish context, for already a wider spectrum of germane concern has been sketched; but let us also ask ourselves whether the true artist can 'stand aloof from life and confine his art within the narrow bounds of subjective emotion? Or should he be where he is needed most, where his words, his music, his chisel can help people live a better, finer life'?[5]

This liberated view of music education, sensitively, responsibly and professionally plied, offers a key to the solution of what for many of us is a familiar problem, one which I propose to define and address in the uniqueness of Ireland's experience.

THE UNIQUENESS OF THE IRISH MUSIC EDUCATION DILEMMA

In commenting on the characteristics of music education as it currently operates in Ireland, it is essential that the move from the general to the specific should isolate those features which together outline its truly distinctive profile. These should invite mature reflection as to their level of dissonance and the potential for amelioration by generally agreed educational principles and other forces of reform; they should also define a unique challenge to the ingenuity of those who recognize and are prepared to tackle the problems exposed. It is axiomatic that no system is wholly resistant to improvement; it is paradoxically euphemistic to pronounce the Irish system as neither satisfactory nor unsatisfactory. Ours is altogether more depressing, for it has also been and still is demographically ineffective, in ministering unequally to the needs of the population; apart from its arbitrariness, it is additionally vulnerable in failing to address such fundamentals as astute analysis of what its internal pedagogic needs are. The fact that Ireland has been reliably judged to be trailing the European provision – where comparisons are apposite and painfully telling – is an indictment of a nation which would proudly claim to value culture, but whose provision in relation to music falls far short of the power of fine words to disguise. But it is not just the levels of provision that are inadequate; the difficulty is compounded by the lack of a comprehensive national policy to underpin and optimize that provision, to act as a yardstick to register embarrassment at its current paucity and its inevitable reproach, and to accept responsibility both for its neglect and for its improvement.

At social and cultural levels education may lay claim to attempting the perpetuation for posterity of that which society values: there should be no decree against its being also a form of human pleasure when skilfully and caringly plied. Art may be a characteristic expression of the collective psyche of a community but it comprises the myriad personal engagements, valuations and judgements of beauty by every individual within that community; these experiences must be cherished too for their precious intrinsicality.[6] Where then does the responsibility for the essential choices lie when the preservation of the monuments of human experience, particularly those of art, is a desideratum? This is an ethical question and a critical one where art is concerned. The appropriation of the processes of judgement, evaluation and eventual choices in art must be rationalized and should aspire to the criterion of universal validity; otherwise their value is compromised and open to question. The social responsibility to envelop all the nation's children in meaningful musical experience, at whatever level, is being unambiguously proposed here. Music is not for the few; it should be for all.

Music as art, as pseudo-art and as craft offers as fascinating a spectrum of human endeavour as it is possible to provide from the potential variety of a single topic; its content is too extensive and the progressive mastery of its method too crucial to the formidable demands of the art form itself, to its peak levels of enjoyment (but to all the intermediate phases too) and to the expectations of contemporary society, to be left to the devices of desultory provision. Here again we have a statement of an Irish problem which has recently exploded into a chorus of frustration and concern.[7] There is also the vexed question of the democracy whereby the nation can collectively decide on its own attitudes to music and to the advocacy of its importance in schooling; if educationalists in music dare to subscribe to the validity of that democracy (bearing in mind the false comfort that it is not universally accepted in pedagogical circles) a plethora of questions may invite an abundance of disconcerting and disturbing answers. As a nation are we content with the passive imbibing of just music (of a variety that, for the majority, can be conveniently controlled by the flick of a switch or by a whimsical decision to indulge in the anaesthesia of a disco) or do we crave the discrimination, the education, really to distinguish between what is good and what is better? Have we a clear idea of the range of available music and the ability to choose with fastidious perception? Are our children conditioned to the educational propriety and desirability of music, in whatever form, as a curriculum subject, and is their experience of it a positive and natural one, or indeed an experience at all, in school? Here again I want to argue that if music is not vibrant in the school ambience, all other strategies to promote it are seriously compromised. Is the subject user-friendly, while preserving impeccable standards of genuine educational choice? If we as teachers dare to test the nation's mood or judgement with honesty, we should not be too surprised to find that a sophisticated taste may not always be shared by our students or by their parents. The security of an imposed canon may offer a comfortable continuity with our own education, but it can lead to complacency and to pedagogic mediocrity if not plied with skill, flexibility, imagination and a real sense of communication. What, then, are the choices? For the dedicated, for the enthusiast and certainly for those who wish to influence educational provision in artistic terms, their choices must be driven by a constant search for strategies aimed at meeting the students half-way; only then can the more subtle tactic of refinement be addressed. And as to the curriculum itself, there must be mature deliberation, to seal its relevance to conditions as we find them, not as we imagine them, and sensibly to delimit its realistic scope.

In formal education, as an agent of preservation, consideration of materials and method naturally raises this ethical question to the level of a challenge to educational decision-makers, even as to the question of choice of philosophical approach. Do we subscribe to the aesthetic, to the blandly urbane or to the purely cathartic; what are to be our criteria and how arrived at? It is unacceptable merely to make the facile claim that it is less important as to *why* we enjoy music – as Absolutists, as Expressionists or as Referentialists – than that we *do* enjoy it and that we have copious opportunity to indulge that propensity. This may not be substantiating a uniquely Irish quandary but it is certainly defining a relevant one. The comfortable awareness of the universality of musical experience may be reassuring, but its uniqueness in national contexts should sound caution. We should not be deceived into believing that the methodology of its life enrichment through formal education can be plucked indiscriminately from ambiences alien to our own. Can we break loose from the stultifying stranglehold of an educational cycle which is perniciously self-generating in all the illogical sequence of its flawed evolution, however benign its stated intention as it proceeded? Having broken with our colonial past, are we sufficiently secure in our cultural identity, as expressible in musical terms, not to regard our birth to Europe, and our future, as embodying new threats to the distinctive plurality of our cultural inheritance? And who can weave the strands of that inheritance into a wholly natural and plausible educational programme which is both consistent and distinctive? But let us now attempt to articulate at least one Irish music education dilemma.

In considering the deeply interdependent social and educational implications of music as a human resource, Christopher Small, in *Music – Society – Education* (1980), has come close to crystallizing the root causes of some of our concerns in relation to Irish music education. In his introduction he refers to the inherent arrogance of the European musical tradition and the 'inbuilt certainty of the superiority of European culture to all others that has given Europeans . . . the confidence to undertake the cultural colonization of the world and the imposition of European values and habits of thought on the whole human race . . . and to view all other musical cultures as at best exotic and odd.'⁸ Small is undoubtedly referring to the tradition of *central* European high culture and its offshoots, which incidentally include the sub-cultures of jazz and pop; it is arguable that the ethnic elements are subconsciously being relegated, but not by him, to the company of the 'exotic and odd'. Ireland, though musically European by bilateral adoption, has a fabulously rich treasury of traditional music; but it is as fabulously mismanaged, in terms of its undeniably half-hearted adoption by that sector of the population which, through questionable educational processes, has been conditioned to an exclusive predilection for the musical culture of Europe. This socially influential group, largely of urban and Anglo-Irish origin, is and has been potential prey to the inroads of this astonishing, highly desirable and therefore self-inflicted invasion. But the cultivation of this imported music, alien in the sense of its comparatively latter-day adoption, is itself open to severe criticism as to rationale and method, as will become apparent. It is not necessary to subscribe to Small's cynical carping at the élitists being 'bewitched by the idea of music as product' (to the point of obsession with standards and even with virtuosity) to be sympathetic to his analysis of certain current misguided attitudes to music education. He refers to

> the evil effects of the excessive professionalization of music, [which] might be tolerable if applied only to the training of the professional musician, but the training of professionals is unfortunately taken to a very large extent as the model for music in education generally, including that of the vast majority who have no intention of making music a career . . . thus completing the vicious circle which excludes the majority from any significant musical experience in school.⁹

In Ireland we have, even still, musically speaking, a relatively unsophisticated population which has been historically conditioned to a certain diffidence about valuing its own culture (except in overtly nationalistic outbursts) while being progressively exposed, through the media, to the supremacy of the so-called classical tradition. History has also left a legacy of undiscriminating respect for the quasi-academic in music, very often shorn of the aural, practical and creative elements which are its lifeblood; there is a homogeneity, too, in attempts to apply this unnecessarily unrelieved monotony to a school-going population whose musical involvement, investment and contributory experiences define a whole spectrum of widely diverging expectation. There is no need to abandon an idealistic pursuit of excellence in order to participate meaningfully in music-making without aspiring to professionalism. But here the real lacuna is being highlighted, for what is needed in Ireland is the efficient inculcation of the skills of modest but artistically effective music-making, and this presupposes a more widespread, sophisticated and relevant teaching resource than can currently be called upon. Even more importantly, the social respect and recognition accorded to the relatively small cohort of professionals who can successfully develop those skills must be capable of attracting the musically talented into their own profession to guarantee a healthy process of regeneration. Again the interpenetration of the social and educational dimensions is pervasive.

THE EVOLUTION OF MUSIC EDUCATION IN IRELAND[10]

To suggest that music education in Ireland is in crisis is to imply a lamentable degeneration from a hitherto happier state; this latter, of course, has not been the case. Two fairly recent pronouncements on the subject throw down the gauntlet to providers of education. In 1985 (ironically termed the European Year of Music) Donald Herron in *Deaf Ears?* stated succinctly that 'the young Irish person has the worst of all European "musical worlds".'[11] Ciarán Benson, more peremptorily, isolated a root cause of the plight, in his seminal challenge.

> By any standards the state of music education is not a happy one in Ireland. If there is a defence of the present situation to be made on educational grounds then it should be heard. We need to distinguish explanations that have to do with an inability to finance a comprehensive national programme of music education from explanations that have to do with an inability to establish the importance of music education. Inactivity and failure of commitment which are rooted in the latter are most damaging in the long term.[12]

The stark reality encapsulated in these statements begs many questions and invites us to analyse past practices which have yielded so bleak a harvest and augur so depressingly, albeit still unpredictably. The ghost of Samuel Johnson stands guard over this enquiry, for he admonishes that

> to judge rightly of the present we must oppose it to the past; for all judgment is comparative, and of the future nothing can be known. . . . The present state of things is the consequence of the former, and it is natural to inquire what are the sources . . . of the evil we suffer. . . . There is no part of history so generally useful as that which relates . . . the extinction and resuscitation of arts, . . . the useful or elegant arts are not to be neglected.[13]

Historical evidence can illumine the conditions which obtain in the field of music education in Ireland today as to their underlying causal relationships with the past. Although current concerns and feelings of crisis are centred, and rightly so, on the crucial area of secondary education, it was a far different story when the architects of artistic education essayed their tentative philanthropy in the years following Lord Stanley's introduction of the National School System initiated in 1831. In the interim Ireland has gone through a fascinating metamorphosis defined periodically by colonialism and politico/ nationalist unrest, self-determination, and Euro-membership, each with a significance in terms of the progress of music education. It is not proposed here to do more than give a flavour of that development by relating it to a choice of relevant key concepts in a very personal interpretation of the evolution of the present profile.

As the colonial phase developed from the beginning of the nineteenth century, education, that potent enabler in moulding the mind of the people, was recognized as of critical importance. The hedge schools, feared by the conqueror in terms of their capability to foment, were formidable agents of propaganda where they were invoked or merely sampled, but it must be remembered that education and literacy were not generally advanced; nevertheless there was vested interest in arresting the equivocal nature of this approach to scholarship.[14] 'The government authorities were suspicious of these schools, fearing their potential for political subversion and alleging immoral content in books used in hedge schools.'[15] The nation was, typically, divided in a sharply etched dichotomy in socio-economic, religious and political terms. It is no great exaggeration to claim that on one side of the divide were Catholics,[16] deprived by the ravages of the penal laws, poorly literate, nationalist and fiercely loyal to and dependent for leadership on their Church; on the other were Protestants who enjoyed that sense of independence which their closer affinity with the ruling powers made possible. (The dissenting majority in the 'six counties' of Northern Ireland is a special case, which is outside the general scope of this paper.) But these groups were polarized and problematic for educationalists seeking to unite them in a single educational endeavour. It might seem to have been an unlikely scenario in which communal music might have flourished; it is all the more laudable that the attempt was made, as much as it is still a source of some conjecture as to why.

There was a convincing rationale in favour of a national education scheme which favoured the state action of 1831; it was humanitarian and magnanimous but it was also utilitarian. On the one hand access to the three Rs could lead to emigration and a better life for some through that means; on the other, access to rudimentary schooling in an ambience of marketed impartiality could, ideally, result in a more loyal workforce at home. The introduction of music was seen as a liberalizing force, but documented contemporaneous commentary does little more than establish a certain naïve aestheticism; the extrinsic benefits of mellowing the recalcitrance and suspicion of a so-called barbarous and quasi-conquered race were, however, stronger than the aesthetic incentives, the idea of refining and homogenizing the nation into colonized contentment, even domestic bliss, an attractive prospect. The basic decision to have music, when introduced to the curriculum within a decade of the enactment, was nonetheless as epochal as the 1831 Establishment of the Irish National School System;[17] the strategies were potentially even more complex than the protagonists themselves could have realized. One simple but inspired maxim prevailed, however, and from it grew a promise which as to its final delivery is still relevant but largely unfulfilled. To determine the disposition of a people a national network of persuasion would have to operate. In the case of an educational objective this could only be achieved through the mass schooling system; private enterprise and community input could be helpful on the periphery but they were no substitute. 'In the context of post-Union politics the government felt that the schools could serve politicising and socialising goals, cultivating attitudes of political loyalty and cultural assimilation. The danger of separate school systems operating without official supervision needed to be countered.'[18] The phenomenon of a solution in search of problems was amply defined by this largely Victorian initiative.

A multiplicity of forces interacted to yield a configuration for music education which eventually established itself and persisted well into the twentieth century before the forces realigned themselves in different contexts and potency. It is essential to appreciate that in the early part of the nineteenth century and for most of the 1800s, the percentage of the population in receipt of schooling of any sophistication was minimal. Primary education as we now understand it would have been the limit of expectation for the vast majority; the uptake at secondary level was as minuscule as its quality was questionable.[19] The Catholic Church, representing the religion of the majority, was predictably and inevitably to exercise its considerable power in the educational arena; its attitude to music and its place within the curriculum, although somewhat peripheral to the main thrusts of its own deeper strategies, was none the less of paramount importance to the promotion of the subject in its delimited potential. The Church was the traditional seat of native learning and popular trust; the clergy and those in training for orders were the receivers, the holders and the wielders of pedagogic strengths which owed little if anything to the political power of the land in terms of their acquisition. In these circumstances the Church, with its cerebral capabilities and inbuilt tactical philosophies, emerged as a force to be reckoned with in political and socio-economic terms. It championed the cause of its flock. It laboured and even vacillated, under pressure from divisions within its own ranks (recruited largely from a peasantry hungry for possession of the land and hostile to the descendants of the planter), between a restrained nationalism and its own disciplinarian attitude to certain establishment values. Politically astute, it used its influence to achieve its own ends; suspicion and fear of proselytization were to be key elements in its campaign and decisions, affecting majority music education in the process.

Ultimately the churches succeeded effectively in (re)establishing denominational segregation in the wider structures of the schooling system. This increased their influence, not only in religious affairs but in other subject areas, which could then be expected to reflect prevailing internal values; this was significant, and in the case of the Catholic Church was to favour the classical and academic norms which coincided with its particular ecclesiastical needs and experience. A notable by-product of this rationale, possibly born of the Church's perception of every male as potentially a candidate for holy orders (defining a cult to which a large number of Catholic parents subscribed in relation to their aspirations for at least one of their sons) was the subsequent absence of music as a serious subject in boys' schools; this ostracism of artistic pursuits in the academically overcrowded educational process was secondary only to another socio-economic pattern in Irish education, which type-cast young men as bread-winners, for whom the liberal arts were deemed superfluous as far as their education was concerned. The perception of music as relevant mainly to the female population, and that very selectively in a class-conscious society, has wrought untold damage and dies hard even in these days of more enlightened educational opportunity.[20]

An overriding consideration in the promotion of a practical subject such as music was in choice of educational method and materials and their relevance to prevailing circumstances; these restraints should not be underestimated from the comfortable perspective of the twentieth century, with its enhanced resources. The mobility of professional performing musicians was restricted by the limited possibilities for travel; in the case of a country, such as Ireland, on the extreme Western European seaboard, the opportunities for the people to hear music at first hand were marginalized as far as music of the Western high-culture tradition was concerned, and no other had respectability. The colonizer's base was dubbed 'the land without music'[21] an unpromising source of inspired method. Happily for Britain this is no longer the case, but in nineteenth-century Ireland educational strategy succeeded in ignoring, and even in effectively outlawing, the native music of Ireland as a valid possibility to fertilize the school experience, which suffered a twofold deprivation in consequence. First, there was potentially no exposure to live music, particularly in the instrumental mode; secondly, of course, the teachers themselves had no tradition or skill base from which to draw. Furthermore, confidence in the real political intentions of the system was slow to develop and school attendance patterns were unpredictable and generally poor, particularly in rural areas; thus the ideal of a generally availed of national school dispensation did not at first obtain.[22] The only feasible response to these characteristic conditions was an approach to music exclusively through singing; even in more propitious circumstances this would still have been eminently defensible because of its inherent excellence and its natural and normally simple base. Thus the first essential decision narrowed itself to a choice of method; the promotion of instrumental skills was deferred to a later stage. Insistence on the vocal strand yielded to fashion in grafting on to the need the prevailing method, namely an academically oriented system of interval training named after its author John Hullah.[23] The system had its detractors from the beginning; their criticisms were directed at its over-academic and inflexible approach (which seemed out of place with the capability of the teaching force and of the pupils) and against the unimaginative nature of the materials. This latter view would be endorsed by twentieth-century analysts, who would additionally give unreserved support to the pressures, exerted with questionable success at the time, to have indigenous materials inserted into the syllabus.

The attitude to native elements is a phenomenon in itself which demands comment, since it is an aspect of music education in Ireland which is still far from coming to terms with the complexity of achieving a balanced curriculum based on a genuine awareness of plurality (certainly duality) of tradition; but in the nineteenth century conditions were considerably more polarized. The norms of Western culture, the complete spectrum of which must be stated to have been foreign even to the colonial powers, found the native Irish well beyond the pale. Conversely the traditional music of Ireland was unknown to and devalued by the reigning powers, if indeed it even merited consideration or evaluation. Such was the chasm between the social strata which reproduced itself too in educational practices, that native culture, either in language or in music, was so inexorably conditioned to its own inferiority that it existed only as a discrete subculture which was extra-mural to the established educational system. There was thus a lethal dichotomy which militated against the system being a popular movement; this was quite in phase with the established exclusivist and unchallengeable position of Western European high art. On the one hand, the interplay of language (Irish and English) with the history and music of Ireland could breed cultural nationalism, erecting an impenetrable barrier which the establishment could not or would not bridge; on the other hand, the remoteness, esotericism and inaccessibility of European culture, in the anti-aesthetic school experience of children typified by the Hullah method, was to become a psychological *pons asinorum* which the schoolgoing population had little opportunity to

negotiate. As a result of this equivocal policy it is doubtful whether the population at large had any more than a whimsical tolerance or an imperfect
understanding of the presence of music as a liberating force in their schools;
nor indeed would there have been or was there any great passion for its survival except amongst a few committed contemporaneous commentators. It
is arguable that, in the late twentieth century, although both traditions have
consolidated and strengthened their positions, they are still far from finding
common educational ground which advances beyond a position of an
apartheid which is, withal, not lacking in mutual respect. This situation may
very well be an accurate reflection of the characteristic parameters of and
educational intractability between the two traditions (aural/oral and notational/
reflective), to which the insatiable scholarship which has fed on Western art
music alone can amply attest. And world music educationalists are now
proposing new standards which demand protection (from contamination)
and preservation of ethnic traditions without undue interference with the
freshness of their primal origins and characteristics. There are provoking
educational challenges in these intentions, for current concerns about
the conservation of authenticity in the performance of community-based
traditional music may well tend to inhibit its insinuation into the formal
educational experience of children.[24]

The promotion of singing as the vehicle of musical instruction in primary
schools was not, then, an inspired choice in the nineteenth century; it was a
pragmatic one, as it was indeed the only possible one, and it was not invul-
nerable as to method. It is bemusing and prophetic to find both practitioners
and theorists in the nineteenth century attacking the Hullah system almost
before it had time to establish itself in Irish schools; it was criticized in Britain
also as 'overlaid with the technical pedantries of the science, abounding in difficulties insuperable to children'.[25] The champions of 'fixed' and 'movable'
doh were locked in unyielding battle as much in the nineteenth century as
now. Hullah's highly mechanical system, which related to the 'fixed' doh,
was rejected on many scores. It was inimical to native culture and its tunes
'"belong to no country . . . [and] are sung in no home". . . . It was culturally
discontinuous with and alien to the population it sought to educate';[26] furthermore it could not cope, except under great difficulty, with the demands of
modulation, thereby limiting its suitability in more complex applications.
The use of Hullah was, indeed, on the decline from 1860 onwards. A pitched
battle was arranged in 1893 under the guise of a Public Schools Competition,
with suggestions of a conspiracy, in which the Tonic Sol-fa system of
Curwen prevailed, after which it quickly completed the superannuation of
the earlier method. Concessions were made to demands for a native dimension, based on the quality of some of the material available; the Anglo-Irish
ballad, laced with the drawing room elegance and anæmic[27] nationalism of

Moore's melodies, began to have its day in an inexorable progress towards a norm as we currently view it. The Tonic Sol-fa system is a relatively unsung precursor to the implementation of the celebrated Kodaly concept, which has become one of the wonders of twentieth-century achievement in mass music education and is currently highly organized, effective and fashionable as a vocally-intensive and aurally-aware system.

Such success as the Tonic Sol-fa system enjoyed confirmed, in principle, a vocal tradition with the promise of choral development; whether it reliably laid the foundations of a performing mode of any depth and breadth is somewhat more questionable, and it was not equipped to deal with the norms of instrumental music, which demanded the transition to staff notation. In relative terms there was room for some complacency in this rudimentary form of music education, inculcated by teachers who were themselves the products (or the victims) of deprivation. It was modest in its demands on the abilities of teachers; as implemented, it eventually embodied monetary incentives for those with superior skills, which were thereby stressed as non-mandatory. The attractive virtuosity (mostly instrumental) of Western and of native art was only arbitrarily accessible and it was outside the school ambience or consciously extra-curricular; in nineteenth-century Ireland it did not transmute itself into an expectation that the general education system should contribute to and be responsible for its development, however rudimentary. The immeasurable advances of the twentieth century, the result of improved resources and access to the media, point anew and uncomfortably to the widening chasm between naïve music-making and virtuosity. It is therefore arguable that the simple method of the nineteenth-century, grounded only in the vocal mode, effectively emphasized the discrete modes of amateur and professional musicianship; it may have painlessly but realistically relegated the majority unequivocally to the listening periphery, but it did not tempt educational policy-makers into misguided curricula based on professional norms and aspirations, without backup. Sooner or later it must be admitted that a popular education movement, such as a national system purports to be, cannot simultaneously accommodate mere cultural exposure and professional standards within a single syllabus. In the interests of the majority who are to be served (and cajoled into the rôle of enthusistic audience) it is critical to recognize that two streams of music education exist; they must be separately ministerd to, but the professional strand is ill-at-ease in general education without special advocacy.

The observations of Christopher Small (referred to earlier) are, after all, searingly pertinent, and it is nowhere more evident than in the 1992–94 Irish debate surrounding the Leaving Certificate syllabus. This is not an exercise of ephemeral significance; it is, rather, a core contemporary issue, the solution to which, if tackled in depth, holds the key to a new general realization of how equitable music education should function, simply because all the critical factors are embodied in its brief.

The deprofessionalization of music education, and its retention within a generally accessible and effective mode, have been greatly assisted in Ireland by an approach through singing, surely the most natural and primeval form of music-making. But, as documented evidence of its effects amply prove, it is susceptible to the implementation of a hidden agenda through its insepa-rability from words and their persuasive power. The example of the coexis-tence of such a diverse and astonishing range of incognate themes as *The English Child*, *Sweet Heart of Jesus* and the rebellious *Boolavogue* in the repertoire of a typical Catholic child in the nineteenth century is sufficient to illustrate how loyalty, piety and patriotism (or sedition) could be stimulated, depending on the underlying force.[28] It also, of course, emphasizes the partly questionable nature of song as a purely musical experience. On the other hand, no force has been more effective than the evolution of Western art music in asserting the supremacy of instrumental forms and in conditioning attitudes to the acceptance of this ascendancy. No doubt this has been assisted also by Absolutist philosophical arguments which have found their way into education, so much so that it has not been unusual for instrumental music to be regarded by some as alone defining real musical experience in the education of the young.[29] Yet this perception, indefensible as it is, has infiltrated the system and has proved to be problematic in an Irish context. Pressures to introduce instrumental music into Irish schools made them-selves felt long before the turn of the century, but it is difficult to establish a satisfactory pattern of success in implementation; the reasons are obvious because they are still so pertinent a century later. Ireland did not have a clas-sical tradition in music; furthermore, in an ostensibly child-centred educa-tion system (primary school education being the only kind in question) teachers just were not equipped to provide this professionally-orientated and skill-based service. The psychomotor dimension in music-making merits separate comment; it will be explored presently. It is significant that such instrumental music tuition as succeeded, though weakly, in establishing any presence within the school system did so from the dawn of the new century only as an outcrop of private enterprise; in other words, it had to be paid for separately, outside school provision, or gratuitously donated. The collective method of teaching vocal music is based on a natural instrument (the voice) and does not become technique-intensive until a voice of quality is identi-fied and singled out for special solo training. In the case of instrumental teaching it is treated as overtly skill-oriented from the very beginning; because it responds best to the one-to-one mode it is heavily cost-laden and has come to be regarded as an economic embarrassment in most popular education contexts. There is thus a sharp dissonance in the working out of strategies which demand the inclusion of instrumental music in the school experience, without the professional and financial outlay for its enjoyment at an acceptable standard. The twentieth century has not yet found a satisfactory solution to this dilemma beyond the unworthy subterfuge of borrowings from the private domain; the issue is at white heat within the Leaving Certificate syllabus revision.

ASSESSMENT

The three criteria of economy, efficiency and effectiveness are ineluctable in educational terms, as elsewhere, and inevitably bring into focus the tool of assessment. There has been an arguably unrealistic and romantic notion (and not only in Ireland) that in a pleasure-intensive and humanistic pursuit such as music-making, particularly within the activities of children, the need for comparative, even indirect, evaluation should be played down. In this context two further aspects of late nineteenth-century Irish music education merit consideration as having had a profound effect in setting a scene which has persisted in remaining controversial. The related mechanisms of *Payment by Results*[30] and competitive music-making[31] are interesting examples of control, standard-setting and incentive which are as old as the education process itself; they can be demonstrated as having had both fructifying and debilitating effects in education, rather more in terms of being considered notorious disincentives for some. The whole question of the competitive in music education, in the writer's view and in consequence of its survival as a necessary yardstick of progress (absolute and relative), has benefited from mature reappraisal. It was inevitable in the child-centred system of the time, where teachers had to offer a spectrum of stipulated instruction, that subjects would be played off one against another in financial terms, bearing in mind that the threefold perspective of the central education authority, of the agent (being the teacher) and of the consumer, or pupil, might not have been at one. Many teachers came to regard the acquisition of the necessary skills, through personal investment of time and effort beyond their *ab initio* training, too work-intensive in relation to the potential monetary gains from the system.

> The principal grievance was not that music was devalued in the curriculum but rather that teachers who had spent time and money obtaining certificates of competency in music were no longer paid for them. . . . Not only was music as an art form stripped of its dignity but those who practised it were also, due to the conditions under which it was taught and the potential destructive criticism which was likely to ensue. These events instilled anxiety in the teachers and fear in the pupils. . . .[32]

Consequently teachers could not be blamed unduly for having made pragmatic choices in relation to worthwhile subjects in terms of attainable
rewards, particularly as failure in the three Rs blocked the financial returns
from 'secondary' subjects. In the case of music, however modest the targets
by twentieth-century standards, the natural reaction of teachers in the late
nineteenth-century was to distrust their own capabilities, understandably so,
given the mismatch between teacher training provision and the demands of
the incentive system. It is a generally accepted fact the overall quality and
continuity of school music education in Ireland therefore suffered a severe
setback in the period when *Payment by Results* was in operation. This is significant mainly in its replication a century later when, in a different context
– that of student/parent evaluative criteria and decisions, and their reflection
in school curricular choices by management – it has had the same effect in
deprioritizing music at the consumer level, or so we are led to believe. We
seem not to have learned from the mistakes of the past.

Although *Payment by Results* was not in itself a method of assessment it
nevertheless brought into focus the inevitable correlations between value
judgements and success in professional contexts. It is unrealistic to attempt
the isolation of music (and by implication, music education) from the
healthy challenge of competitive evaluation, if indeed the term is not in
itself tautological. In the ruthless world of high-powered commercial propaganda, even the very young are beguiled into undiscriminating rank ordering
of the idols of the pop scene; in this respect twentieth-century marketing
strategies exploit the malleability, as much as they abuse the fragility, of
children's sensibilities. This however does not invalidate the dictum that,
regardless of the undisputed powers of organized promotion, the pursuit of
excellence and of quality in performance, and the related ability to discriminate artistically, are part of the congenital inheritance of the human condition and should be nurtured. It is therefore not wholly surprising to find that
the gradual progression from the milder form of competition, as exemplified
in *Payment by Results*, to the more confrontational public and semi-public
versions of the same principle, as practised in school-based mass performance and at feiseanna, beginning from the late nineteenth century, should
have been embraced, in Ireland as indeed elsewhere; it is largely a phenomenon of the twentieth century which, in music, is hotly debated as to its precise effects and relevance in an overall educational context. Fundamentally,
there is an irresistible excitement in competition which seems to fascinate
the human psyche; that it is intimately related to educational procedures is a
simple deduction from its nature – in music as skill-based display and as a
means of somewhat aggressive assessment. Its capability, albeit subjectively,
to establish the generalized dichotomy between ascendency and mediocrity
is cited as having proved eventually to have been a disincentive at the levels

of the less talented, of the less committed and therefore, by implication, at the average and supremely critical interface where the teaching function felt the need to concentrate its efforts. It may be provocative to call into question the naïvete of the educational psychology which seeks to remove assessment from the experience of children and older students in musical contexts; there are three reasons advanced for this point of view. First, the idea is ill-at-ease with the intrinsicality of technical and artistic skills in the presentation of Western and, indeed, much other music at virtually all levels, amateur or professional; confrontational performance implicitly invites evaluation, judgement and approbation, without which its basic aspiration to quality is at risk. Second, the flight from assessment does not hold with the norms of other school subjects and of subsequent post-educational realities. Third, formal evaluation is seriously to be reappraised for retention in the context of current attitudes to educational priorities based on results, which threaten the uptake of music in the critical senior cycle of second-level education. Regardless of any analytical scepticism based on nineteenth-century statistics, showing causal diminishing involvement and disenchantment with intra-musical competition, the stark reality is that the twentieth century has unequivocally adopted and reasserted the general principle of competition with all that it entails; this is nowhere more in evidence than in overt instances of prioritization by which music has been externally threatened in this century, though not without a certain compensation that should be acknowledged. The two germane issues which most obtrude, and have defined the growing dilemma for music education in Ireland, are the Irish language and, latterly, the technological explosion, in which Ireland has to survive as a player. As to assessment itself, which is always by implication a competitive tool, we have happily accepted the examination system as an unexceptionable norm within the life of children; only the egotistically sensitive and the naturally diffident are seen to suffer unduly from it and imaginative ways of dealing with this problem, when it arises, have had to be invoked.

LANGUAGE AND TECHNOLOGY – COMPETITION WITHOUT CHOICE

It has often been suggested that the twin events of the disestablishment of the Church of Ireland in 1869, and the fall of Parnell in 1891, had a profound effect on the attitudes of the Protestant ascendancy in Ireland to their Irishness.[33]

> Their language was being appropriated by the peasants in a frantic effort to free themselves, by emigration, from the poverty of their existence. Paradoxically and simultaneously the thinkers amongst the ruling

classes, to whom a sense of identity would obviously have been crucial, turned to the Irish language for that new identity.[34]

Feis Ceoil, though sincerely non-sectarian, is an outstanding instance of the
ascendancy's attempt to be involved in the adoption of a new cultural image
which at first identified with a revival of the ancient customs of Ireland. The
generally preferential access of this group to the benefits of higher education
produced a cultural intelligentsia in which they were influential far beyond
their numerical strength, if indeed they did not dominate the movement.
One of the effects of this was the linking of traditional music, and by extension music itself, with the native language of Ireland, creating an educational context which was to endure and to influence the educationalists of
post-Treaty Ireland, however controversial the thrust with which the campaign was eventually to be implemented. When political self-determination
came in 1921 the seeds which had been sown were to burst into extravagant
growth as a language revival to which all things cultural were to be clearly
subservient. However, this crusade had recourse to music as a facilitator in a
way similar to the method adopted by the nineteenth-century educators. It is
perhaps wishful thinking to ponder on whether music as an intrinsic benefit
in education would have been included or retained in the curriculum with a
higher profile if the language issue had not been such a commanding preoccupation. On balance the survival of music in an enhanced vocal tradition
owes something to its usefulness to the language strategists; it was exploited
in this context to its advantage. On the other hand the obsession with the
language revival defocused concerns about the potential cultural contribution that music could make. In the event the imposition, over a period of
more than fifty years, of a draconian school-based language programme was
destined to overburden the curriculum, however benign its intentions, to the
detriment of fragile subjects such as music, which was perceived to be
peripheral in the *sui generis* context of its educational value. Of course
music of the Western culture received no official boost. It was left to the
musicians to champion their subject in schools and to effect progress within
the crippling constraints of available time. A companion difficulty was the
non-instrumental bias inherited from the historical circumstances of the
nineteenth century.

It is not the concern of this paper to pass judgement on the success of the
language campaign. It is sufficient to record that, as it waned before the
advancing waves of European identity, it was replaced by new concerns
which were far from flattering to the prospects of music education. The dis-
mal findings of the 1985 Arts Council Report, *Deaf Ears*? must be viewed
against the pressing need seriously to adopt European citizenship with its
attendant economic responsibilities. It must also be considered against the

promotion of continental languages and, more recently in the aftermath of the Green Paper, *Education for a Changing World*,[35] against the need to concentrate on technological training. Neither of these latter concerns has a cultural base in spite of a collective potential to facilitate cultural activities; however, each is educationally significant and therefore poses a threat to music. Each, *per se*, consumes the scarce resource of time, but is an important contender for student (and parental) subject preference in employment contexts. Secondly collectively they force music to vindicate itself as a viable option in resourceful time management by the school-going population.

A NEW *'FIN DE SIÈCLE'* PERSPECTIVE ON MUSIC EDUCATION IN IRELAND

It is now possible to attempt the definition of a profile for the current state of music education in Ireland in relation to its evolution. For the population at large we are dependent (and we should openly promulgate that dependency) on the school system for the development of capabilities in musicianship, taken to mean listening and literacy skills. Although schools of music have operated in the larger towns for more than a century and are becoming also more numerous and influential, they belong to a movement which, however unflattering to the rationale of their coming into being in the first place, belongs to the élitist concept of music education. They provide a fine but generally unavailable opportunity, and only to the favoured few; the élitism taunt arises, not from any artistic snobbery, but from the socio-economic reality that the service they provide is denied the school system, simply because it is available only on payment of a fee, albeit modest and heavily subsidized in most cases. Stubborn insistence on the general schooling dispensation as being the appropriate vehicle for the inculcation of basic musical skills may very well yet prove to be a rallying cry to establish music with its rightful rôle in Irish education.

Our primary school music programme understandably relates most recognizably to its historic roots in the nineteenth century. It may be harsh to observe that it seems not to have progressed appreciably in basic concepts beyond the main features of the last century. Singing is still the mainstay of the curriculum, but the practice of instrumental music is quite outside the primary school experience of most children. The teaching process itself is hampered, more than it is aided, by the intrinsic nature of the training rationale for child-centred nonspecialist education, which demands that each teacher should take all subjects; thus, although specialization in music is practised in colleges of education, it is not complemented with a commitment to the appointment of ex-quota staff, or to the allocation of time, to serve the special needs of subjects such as music. Although informal arrangements may show dramatic successes in isolated cases of enterprise, the staple provision of teaching resources is mercilessly restricted at source, so that most young teachers emerging from college are ill-equipped to undertake imaginative teaching of the subject, simply because their own acquired skills are necessarily so rudimentary.

It is generally held that the introduction of the 'creativity' phase with An Curaclam Nua (The New Curriculum of 1971) seriously destabilized the teaching of music in primary schools, causing withdrawal or, in some cases, virtual collapse. Marie Mc Carthy has succinctly commented on the post-1971 situation:

> As in the initial years of the twentieth century when a new curriculum was introduced, music education was initially borne on the wings of idealism and teachers' enthusiasm. Later it was pitched back into the reality of having no support system or resources to assist the implementation of the 'ideal' curriculum.[36]

An analysis of this predicament is offered below. It should be observed that if the Irish had clung to a hubris which eschewed the partial and undiscriminating adoption of imported ideas, this crisis might never have arisen. The promotion of creativity in Britain, a fashion that was established and which prevailed there from the nineteen sixties onwards, was amply supported by peripatetic teaching of instrumental music, which had an efflorescence which is only now showing signs of suffering from the fairly recent financial cutbacks in that system; for the relatively impoverished conditions prevailing in Ireland a decade later its failure was predestined and should have been predictable. The most profound effect of the uncertainty of provision in primary schools has been that it destabilized the music education context in secondary schools owing to the fracture of the continuum; this phenomenon occurs in the case of many children who enter second-level with so little music from their experiences in primary schools that the music programme at the higher level must be undertaken afresh from fundamentals.[37]

The commanding dilemma in secondary music education therefore has become the crisis in relation to the standards attainable at Leaving Certificate; it is also separately dealt with herein. The bone of contention is, however, itself merely the tip of an iceberg. But the realities of the evolution of secondary education in Ireland demonstrate that it never has been in phase with enlightened views on the promotion of music as a genuine school-based option generally available; the rush in geographically privileged larger towns which house a specialized school of music to partake of private tuition in classical music is proof of that. And then there has been the tragedy of those who have progressed from primary to vocational schools only to be utterly disenfranchised. Secondary schools developed slowly from the middle of the nineteenth century; but they could not boast of general accessibility until more than a century later. They were fee-paying, financially straitened, and virtually controlled, for the majority, by the religious orders of the Catholic Church which, as already stated, worked to an agenda of its own which was unenthusiastic about the accommodation of music in a vibrant programme. It must be said in relation to some of the convent schools, and to their eternal credit, that a belief in the refining influence of music acted as a stimulus to offer it to girls, mainly by way of non-mainstream instrumental training. At the same time the academically driven music programmes favoured by secondary schools, when they did offer them, were redolent of the aurally-deprived nineteenth-century British 'Oxbridge' models so scathingly attacked by Stanford for their scholarly aloofness from music-making as a social aspiration:

> Fifty years ago music was there but it was dormant. The volcano was occasionally in eruption but only fitfully. . . . The University [Cambridge] itself did little for the art. . . . What work was done was the result of individual effort, which far outstripped the academic. . . . Scores are interesting to those who can read them. The vast majority cannot do so; but they are not tone-deaf – they must hear, or music is a closed book to them.[38]

This barrenness of approach can perhaps best be summarized in another comment, made early in the twentieth century, about the programme in girls' schools in Ireland 'that could be fulfilled by a deaf mute';[39] the situation in boys' schools was even worse, if that could be considered possible. Finally there is the supremely critical question as to what is the real function of music education in schools – whether, in fact, secondary education in music is capable of ministering to the needs of the whole spectrum of demand from a variously committed population. The fractured continuum to third-level education is a case in point. And the confusion surrounding the widely differing demands of education for performers, as against that for listeners, has exploded, in the context of secondary education, into a *cause célèbre* in recent years, and is the single most urgent question in contemporary music education in Ireland. Furthermore, the secondary schools are in the throes of a transition in curricular reform, precariously caught between a Junior (Intermediate) Certificate syllabus which, in spite of protestations as to its pedagogic excellences, is as yet unproved, and a Leaving Certificate Syllabus which aspires, at this interim stage, to the doubtful goal of providing a continuity which simultaneously serves both popular and pre-professional standards. Caution in making any but the most tentatively modest claims for this strategy 'on the wing' is manifesting itself in ministerial intervention as this paper goes to press.

The unsatisfactory status of music in the preparatory phases can hardly be expected to favour stability at the higher levels. Nevertheless, it is my belief that specialists in music education who have been able to avail of travel and cross-fertilization from the wealth of ideas, philosophical and pedagogical, flowing from global sources, now have the capability to influence Irish music education in a top-down strategy which is long overdue; they are also well represented at the decision table. But this should not be allowed to remove the problems of third-level education itself from focus. These are the difficulties of recruitment, with a suspicion, in the short term, of over-provision in relation to the quality of the material available (itself a true reflection of the starved situation at second level); the need to promote the self-esteem, the social acceptance and the employment prospects of its graduates; the ongoing dilemma of the disparity between the standards of school-based music, currently under investigation, and university entry criteria; finally, the progress of its noble attempt to come to terms with the growing perception that the 'centrality of performance' must be a critical criterion and an ineluctable element of music education policies. The last of these considerations calls for fundamental reappraisal of the attitudes of third-level music educationalists to performance as a degree-earning pursuit. The recent (1993) establishment of a forum for the Heads of Third Level Music Departments shows a healthy willingness to work towards disen-gagement, for the common good, from unilateral practices rooted in vested interest; this initiative is matched by a mutual tolerance of the academic drift of the practically-based institutions and the promotion of performance options in hitherto academically-intensive schemata.

A thematically important *codetta* is merited here so as to comment on the contribution to the national profile of other agencies of music education, acting outside the school ambience. The all-too-few schools of music (having their origins mainly in the nineteenth century and then in humble aspiration) have proudly succeeded in setting and maintaining standards in performance which, at their finest and across the spectrum, have earned respect within the most discriminating international education forums. Because of their virtually exclusive adherence to classical European traditions and the eventual pursuit of excellence, they have tended to be regarded, on the one hand as élitist to the point of setting uncomfortable or impossible standards outside the capability of the majority, on the other as a salve to the public conscience in demonstrat-ing that quality music education is available, even if it has to be paid for. They have been joined more recently by a network of fee-paying schools coming close to establishing a satisfactory geographical spread; they have between them absorbed the best of the professional teaching talent, leaving the private sector largely bereft and, apart from some notable exceptions, pop-ulated with teachers of modest attainment, limited potential and professional isolation. Community effort has also flowered in orchestral and choral activities, the former relying to a great extent on borrowed instrumental skills inculcated institutionally. I have no competence to comment on the traditional scene beyond observing that it seems less fraught in catering admirably for the development and pleasures of its devotees, and in having a highly significant if discrete presence in Irish musical life; but because its evolution harks back to community-based activity, its profile is understandably not so obvious in the demand for reform in formal music education contexts.

THE CRITERION OF RELEVANCE IN THE TRAINING OF PERFORMERS AND LISTENERS

There are two overriding quandaries which apply across the whole spectrum of music education and they are closely interrelated. The first quandary is ethical and it concerns the relevance of music education as a species of public property which nevertheless is addressed to the cultivation of music as an art form. It is a classical quandary of educational practice to establish and agree on the level at which the receivers of education may dictate their own requirements; the concepts of value and judgement, and the related ability (together with the necessary timespan) to bring them into play, will always remain controversial. But in Ireland we need to encourage a relaxed attitude in seeking to remove the siege instinct which keeps so much of music education narrow in focus, often to the detriment of those whom it is intended to serve. Current world thinking, in philosophical terms, is at last progressing beyond the hitherto claustrophobic high-mindedness of a purely aesthetic approach to the teaching and to the experience of music as based almost exclusively on the norms of the European classical tradition. It is now being more carefully couched in terms which embrace all *genres*. The relevance of the whole corpus of music (to life and to education) is now being appraised more meaningfully with reference to the objective criterion of its 'craft content' and the subjective one of its expressive powers. This process is a potent leveller which can value democratically; no music is excluded nor is any inviolable. Schoenberg, perhaps unintentionally, and Prokofiev (as quoted earlier) alert us to the fact that music may have functions other than the purely aesthetic, and that it should not be outlawed in these extrinsically beneficial modes. The pragmatic and utilitarian approach to the fertile presence of music in the human experience cries out for such a dispensation and must assuredly modify or superannuate many of the cherished assertions of the traditionalists. In this respect there is an air of expectancy as David Elliott, the latest star to mount the philosophical firmament, prepares to launch his book,[40] which attempts a quantum leap in the way we might view the music education of the future. Certainly in Ireland we have not yet succeeded in making music a real experiential presence in the life of the majority as influenced by formal educational processes. Where we recognize that we have failed as music educationalists, it might be productive not to tarry over our acknowledgement of omissions, but equally to economize in the apportionment of blame elsewhere; above all we must search for more effective strategies to bring about the corrective changes we identify as being necessary. The sentient involvement in the pleasures of music may frequently be pre-aesthetic, but this is the raw stuff of which ecstasy is born. The educational process, intrusive by nature, should seek to vindicate itself by a flexible and tolerant approach to the promotion of insight into the human condition; it is not diminished in the purity of its intention if, at times and as appropriate, it applies subtle processes of refinement which aspire to raising all experience to higher levels of artistic fulfilment.

MUSIC OF THE WORLD CULTURES

Current world concerns in music education are concentrated on the adoption of 'music of the world cultures' into education – an ambitious venture of almost incalculable complexity, considering that the criterion of 'authenticity' has been opened up for discussion and definition; the themes of two recent world conferences – 'Sharing Musics of the World' (Seoul 1992) and 'Tradition and Change' (Tampa, Florida 1994)[41] – show the seriousness with which this campaign is being promoted. Ireland is, so far, beyond the pale of these concerns in a multi-cultural sense, but we have the pressing need to address our own bi-cultural circumstances and to bridge the gap which separates native and classical traditions. Here is another educational failure which can no longer be attributed to the callousness and insensitivity of a foreign power (this has been a typical world attitude to ethnic music where the Western tradition has held sway) but to our own incompetence in failing to project the dignity, distinctiveness and indispensability of each subset without making comparisons which have little relevance.

THE TWO STREAMS OF MUSIC EDUCATION

A second quandary facing Irish music educationalists is the productive and palpable disentanglement of the pedagogical elements which constitute appropriate training for listening and performing. The latter, which invaginates the former, is normally the more complex and time-consuming, since it usually applies to those who have taken a decision to invest time and concentration in the effort. Conversely, and perhaps more relevantly to current thinking, the methodology of the deprofessionalization of performance to admit larger numbers to its joys in the school experience, however modest the encounter, demands mature planning and implementation. Until this is achieved without undue artistic compromise, the curriculum and syllabus revision for secondary schools will continue to be little more than an amateurish travesty.

The seminal statements of Herron and Benson,[42] dating from 1985, invited an updated profile of music education in Ireland and an analysis of the evolution which has proceeded from historical developments; the need arose from a certainty that the state of the art in educational terms was 'not a happy one'. Let this further enquiry be prefaced by a pungent commentary from Bennett Reimer on a profession rent by self-doubt and, in Ireland's case, showing in its provision an imperfect empathy within its own membership and with the population it is endeavouring to serve.

> What the profession seems to need at the moment is not persuasion about any particular philosophy, but articulation, refinement, and careful application of the commonly held but largely unarticulated, unrefined, and imperfectly applied beliefs now current. . . . It would be difficult to find a field so active, so apparently healthy, so venerable in age and widespread in practice, which is at the same time so worried about its inherent value.[43]

The pervasive confusion in Ireland arises from a failure to recognize in practice the sharp distinctions between discrete categories of music students and to discriminate meaningfully between them as to their educational requirements. Apart from the well-known triumvirate already referred to – composer, performer and listener – there is the closely related division between academics and practitioners and, by no means synonymously, there are performers and listeners. The functions of all these groups may overlap and interpenetrate, but essentially they define different educational approaches and methodologies. There is even the danger that, within any of these groups, excessive isolation from cross-fertilization by another germane group may occur with deleterious effect. In defining this daunting educational mission I have claimed elsewhere that 'in the field of human endeavour, there could scarcely be a more comprehensive array of faculties simultaneously demanded for exercise than those which musical performance calls into play. . . . The cognitive, affective and psychomotor domains can be exploited to their limit by the masterpieces of musical literature.'[44] Along the axis of the psycho-motor dimension in music-making the most significant divide occurs. The purely athletic and muscular demands on the performer in music highlight the dramatic differences between knowledge and skill in music; they also draw the crucial distinction which defines two worlds of methodological difference, a distinction which additionally and unquestionably defines the rôles of performer and listener.

In identifying with the 'centrality of performance' slogan as an enlightened realization and aspiration in planning for music into the new millenium, I am conscious of how ill-prepared Ireland is to cope with this new, albeit exciting, task. It is likely to create new crises if suitable provision and teaching support structures are not put in place to meet it; alternatively it will cause the collapse of current curriculum targets or hold them up to ridicule as vapid and unrealistic. Lest the impression be created that there is here a naïve and cheap artifice to patronize the performer as the more eminent in the hierarchy of musicians, let it be asserted that this view is supported by a humanistic theory of democracy in the functioning of music as art, recognizing the validity of the creative contribution of all participants in a musical communication.[45] Should it be necessary to identify one indispensable function without which artistic transmission in music would be inhibited within impossible theoretical constraints it ought to be unexceptionable to claim that music ideally must be physically heard, a claim which seals the rôle of the performer as *primus inter pares*. Performers, according to George Steiner in *Real Presences* (1992) are the 'master intelligencers' of music. The simple reality is that most people are drawn to music because of the desire, not just to create as in composition alone or merely to listen, but actively to participate in performance. It is therefore timely that this deceptively simple solution to the problems of music education should now be coming into currency in Ireland, and we should marvel at it. But, of course, it does not remove one whit from the basic need to proceed simultaneously along the time-honoured pedagogical routes to the acquisition of what is now referred to attractively as musicianship. Fundamentally all who aspire to meaningful participation in the enjoyment of music must be trained to listen; as Roger Sessions so aptly put it, we must all *first* become virtuoso listeners. And so these two distinct but intimately interwoven strands of music education have been identified, but the nerve centre of Irish sensitivities and reproach has been touched,[46] for each demands a teacher specialization that is just not forthcoming at an acceptable standard should the two teaching functions be merged; our current teachers are not specifically trained in sufficient number for this comprehensive double specialism. Are we about to demand more from our school music teachers than their training could ever have envisaged for them?

THE CREATIVITY OF PERFORMANCE

It might be interesting to advance an interpretation of the healthy development, in Ireland as indeed elsewhere, to the current rationale which aligns an emphasis upon performance with the popular perception of music in society. Until 1971 at least, music education in Ireland had been dominated by the historical preeminence of academically-driven programmes; these were perceived as the only ones with an educational respectability worthy of promotion. These programmes began to yield, in the still so-called New Curriculum[47] for primary schools, to a new fashion in the guise of 'creativity' with all its implicit elements of proactive and interactive learning and skills orientation. However, this innovation, being totally out of phase with the capability of cruelly straitened timescales in teacher training courses, was soon found to have caused severe alienation, from sheer panic, amongst non-specialist teachers. It was an innovation which also uncomfortably challenged the regime of an outworn teaching methodology. This panic must undoubtedly have been transmitted to the students; if we are to believe the findings of the Arts Council Report – *Deaf Ears?* – of 1985 the outcome seems to have been little short of a significant withdrawal from the music programme. The reason why the creativity phase failed is twofold. First, it was foreign to the largely circumscribed and objectively-based training the teachers themselves had received. Factually it must be admitted that creativity of the flamboyant and uninhibited kind is rare in the population, the subjective approach seldom being as naturally plied as the objective, which responds more comfortably to pre-learned sequences. The call to creativity was going against the grain; moreover, it was mercilessly unmasking shortcomings at personal levels and at close quarters. More than any other threat to the abilities of teachers, it was giving exposure to the more talented at the expense of the less, and in unacceptable ways, not least in the embarrassing betrayal of innocent incompetence in that most uncomfortable of all forums – the classroom. Second, and even more obviously, creativity is conditioned, in the practice of music, by the prerequisite of physical and, indeed, other skills; without them, or worse still as a substitute for them, the urge to creativity becomes stultified and barren. Creativity belongs in the precious area of aesthetic response; it challenges and tests the truly gifted, eventually separating them from the less talented, and in operation it is a ruthless task master, unflattering to the modest aspirations of the majority. The reality in music, however much we might wish to have it otherwise, is that, in aesthetic terms, it is in the area of refining the potential of perception by subtly objective means that the majority of teachers enable their students to consummate their aesthetic experiences. No wonder, then, that the creativity phase was less than successful. But it had one useful by-product; it eventually heightened awareness of the altogether more potentially fruitful approach through conventional performance, which if imaginatively taught (Ay, there's the rub) can challenge creativity to its ultimate. In real terms, of course, this rediscovered approach raises many artistic questions as to standards attainable in a comprehensive programme of involving all in rudimentary performance, for to aspire to more than that under current circumstances in Ireland would be fatuous. Imperfectly preconditioned to the management of its demon, we stand at the portals of an entrancing world of music-making; to avail fully of its potential a major reappraisal of available resources and the will to build bridges of communication and cooperation between different strands of the teaching community are prerequisites.

TOWARDS A SOLUTION

If we aspire to be taken seriously as a sophisticated and civilized nation, committed to the value and relevance of art to life, our agenda for its promotion must be capable of transcending the finely pointed distinctions in defining its parameters and its scope in élitist terms. Such a pragmatic approach, avoiding the arcane, must minister comfortably to a multiplicity of expectations, even the avowedly modest ones. And in this latter regard Bennett Reimer's wise eclecticism might very well provide a non-contentious starting point, for in asserting that 'music education should be primarily about *music* education; that is, education for the aesthetic, or musical, qualities and values of music as art. There is really no problem in understanding music's functional, non-aesthetic uses and the values of such uses',[48] he also counsels that 'to insist on studying nothing but the monuments of music literature, to rule out that large segment of music which, while well made and genuinely expressive is not of the *crème de la crème*, is to deprive a great many people of any musical satisfaction at all and to expect that all musical experience should be at the deepest level of involvement.'[49]

Does Reimer here expose a root cause of division in contemporary Irish music education? Has anyone sought to understand and to explain the profound unease which oppresses the Irish music teacher in day-to-day encounters in the classroom? But enough has been said about the testing criterion of relevance to inspire and instil confidence anew in the imaginative teaching musician.

We need resources, most of all an inspired and inspiring teaching force in sufficient number to mount the kind of programme which would do justice to the sometimes subconscious levels of thirst for artistic experience which is a normal human condition and no less likely to be the norm in Ireland than elsewhere; there is a widely held and plausible view, too, that historical inheritance must have enriched the Irish psyche with a more vibrant readiness for the expressive possibilities of music to be enjoyed.[50] We must reach *détente* between our Celtic heritage (in its intrinsic forms and as modified by other now indigenous cultures, many of them language-based) and the overpowering genius of Western art which has apparently tended to dominate purely ethnic and native strains. Above all, this ambitious and subtlety-laden educational programme cannot be left to the arbitrary devices of private enterprise; it must permeate the general education system, be embraced by it and become as passionate a cultural pursuit as any other national aspiration. But the complexity of the problems militating against a healthy and thriving musical environment in Ireland, as the product of our educational system, does not end there. Vastly uneven distribution of opportunity throughout the country cannot fail to cause concern to those whose carefully evolved convictions lead them to wish and demand that it might be otherwise. The continuum that should obtain between all levels of the educational process in the subject, particularly as between the conventional subdivisions of primary, second-level and tertiary, is lethally fractured for the majority of students. This is less pernicious in itself than in the frustration and confusion it causes in maintaining stability in the meaningful classification of students, from a variety of backgrounds, in the maximization of educational effectiveness within the formal system. The programme for rationalization of the separate ideologies driving each of these streams of music education urgently needs philosophical clarification, if not redefinition, for they currently encapsulate ambiguities and dissonances which must be faced and removed if music education is to be taken seriously as a stable and fertile component in the total curriculum. The relationship between academic and practical pursuits in music, and their promotion as discrete *or* as inseparable components of the curriculum, have never before been so actively debated as in recent times. The final emergence of the 'centrality of performance' in music education as the shibboleth of the closing decade of this century seems to be based on a consensus that does no real violence to cherished convictions within the whole musical community; if sensitively acted upon in Ireland it holds the key to a dramatic progression towards a truly eclectic dispensation, but let the difficulties not be underestimated. Is it tenable that the diverse musical needs of the community be satisfied by a single-stranded curriculum in the subject? It cannot be so if music is to be accepted as a symbolism which embraces the diverse forms of human feeling. Music in its highest aspirations, when it seeks to transcend the cerebral, the self-indulgent and the purely cathartic, is a key to the understanding of the emotive life; as such it scarcely needs further advocacy in its claim for inclusion in the planning and implementation of liberal educational programmes. Its significance is eloquently celebrated by Susanne Langer:

The tonal structures we call 'music' bear a close logical similarity to the forms of human feeling – forms of growth and attenuation, flowing and stowing, conflict and resolution, speed, arrest, terrific excitement, calm, or subtle activation and dreamy lapses – not joy and sorrow perhaps, but the poignancy of either and both – the greatness and brevity and eternal passing of everything vitally felt. Such is the pattern, or logical form, of sentience; and the pattern of music is that same form worked out in pure, measured sound and silence. Music is a tonal analogue of emotive life.[51]

If Langer's sensuous prose, when pondered, comes somewhere close to a popular perception, or even to a subconscious awareness, of how comprehensively music can mirror the emotive life, then we must take music's potential seriously; we must exploit its educational possibilities in varied schemata which faithfully minister to the various levels at which its benefits may be savoured. A genuine recognition of the existence of these separate layers of receptivity is the single most critical challenge to those who are involved in the fashioning of the music curriculum in Ireland today. Where a healthy, albeit highly variable, willingness to invest time in musical experience and pursuits can be identified, it should be matched by determination to take it realistically into account in educational planning. This should be considered as a highly pertinent and controversial coda to this analysis of contemporary Irish music education; it is therefore suggested that a single core issue be identified which is capable not only of focusing this most urgent of concerns, but of concentrating educational thought as to how the effects of solutions to that particular problem can beneficially infiltrate the whole system. That issue is the current approach to the revision of the Leaving Certificate syllabus. Because it is a school-based dilemma it handsomely serves the thrust of this paper, again insisting that a subject as important as music education cannot satisfactorily play its crucial and liberalizing rôle outside the general education system.

THE LEAVING CERTIFICATE SYLLABUS REVISION AS PARADIGM

The coincidence of the revision of the Leaving Certificate Syllabus, as the natural sequel to a probationary Junior Certificate Syllabus, with a well-orchestrated climax of dissatisfaction over the current technical administration of the examination itself, should not be interpreted as an ephemeral crisis which will patiently endure the promulgation of a new dictum before evaporating. Disenchantment is being attributed to a genuine concern that the subject is under threat as a plausible Senior Cycle option because of flawed methods of assessment and standard-setting as evinced in comparative examination statistics. There is an unmistakable determination abroad to insist that the revision must address fundamental issues; the feeling of a watershed in the history of Irish music education is galvanic, even prophetic. The Leaving Certificate crisis can very easily be demonstrated to embody all the smouldering questions in Irish music education which this paper has attempted to articulate. The writer has already addressed the labyrinthine problems and far-reaching consequences which are likely to proceed from this revision.[52] Without dismissing the gravity of the overt concerns that have in such timely fashion unleashed public opinion to demand retribution for the injustice and outrage at the neglect of music education in Ireland (for that is the real interpretation of the groundswell of dissatisfaction), an attempt to place the correlations in context is here advanced.

Although the terms of reference of the syllabus committee may very well focus its work efficiently and prevent it from straying into prolix discussion of the larger issues, it cannot but tread on the thorny ground of the accumulated grievance which is now in intrusive mode.[53] The fall-out from experience in the classroom will be there in naked reproach; the difficulty in coping with variable standard and aptitude at the level of virtually uninitiated children who enter secondary education only to have their first real exposure to music will be set against the suspicion with which the so-called élitist institutions are regarded for their potential effectively to set impossible standards for these children from their extramural position of perceived influence. The impossibility of dealing with the performance demand of both the Junior and Leaving Certificate syllabi, at the highest levels, without the silent and unacknowledged help of the 'élitists', by definition from outside the school ambience, will have to be addressed; in fact, the laudable call for the 'centrality of performance' in school music programmes must expose the palpable nonsense of a system whose traditional teaching skills have emanated from sources where performance has been played down as an overt policy. The feasibility of the performance-based curriculum must raise questions as to the ideal content of teacher training programmes and, by implication, a large number of third-level options in music will have to be reviewed as to their relevance to the employment that most of the graduates are likely eventually to embrace. The vexed question of the teaching resource in general will have to be faced in its 'in-service' and state investment contexts. Fundamental considerations of curriculum aims – what students want to learn and what teachers want to teach, the canon under siege from branches of music-making with which it would erstwhile have had no truck, and the criteria for their admittance to and fertile expansion of the syllabus – all these issues are potentially about to impose themselves as pressing topics for debate and decision. And the demands, not only for guidance but for action, do not end there.

The difficulties attending the teaching of music in Irish schools in a programme worthy of respect in a national context can and will be articulated
in alternative ways. Surely it is relevant to ask why, in the wake of published
concerns about the workings of the primary school programme (*Deaf Ears?*
of 1985), curriculum reform did not follow the *locus classicus* of a logical
bottom-up approach; the difficulties of grafting on the Leaving Certificate
syllabus are surely less formidable and disruptive then the modification of a
six- to eight-year primary programme by and by. This concern acquires more
urgency from its being seen to derive from and to epitomize the problems at
the lower end of the fractured continuum in music education. But then there
has always been the tendency in Ireland to allow curricular reform in music to
begin arbitrarily and eventually to collapse into mere syllabus revision,
because of the telescoping of time scales; and the network of communication
in the implementation of policies and the provision and uptake of back-up
training have been unpredictable and not always effective.

To make the secondary school experience in music more performance-
intensive, working virtually from a zero base and currently without the
internal teaching skills in place is indeed an ambitious objective. If the stated aim of the syllabus is simultaneously to embody a grand, but unrealistic,
adaptability which caters both to the searching and implacable demands of
entry to third-level music professional courses at under-graduate level, and a
vaguely-stated deprofessionalized excellence in music as a social grace, an
impossible brief is being outlined. There is a need, if a single syllabus is to
be implemented at Senior Cycle, to choose between a dangerously discriminating plan for a genuine continuum to third-level education, and the much
more socially honest strategy of throwing music education's lot in with the
vast majority and identifying this path unambiguously. The profoundly fundamental question has to be confronted, and answered, as to whether music
deserves a place in general education, if so why, and what is to be its curricular paradigm? Or is there still a furtive crisis of conscience about abandoning
the minority who may eventually choose music as a career, thereby commit-
ting them into the hands of the so-called élitist institutions who will claim
the credit for their subsequent achievements. One of the most encouraging
corollaries of the debate so far, and one which seems to have caught the
imagination of many parties to the discussion, is the bold suggestion that
music should demand equal rights with the sciences and other humanities in
school, seen as a preparation for subsequent specialization at third-level.
This is being proposed in the form of a double stream in senior cycle music,
and it is believed that it would relieve the beleaguered syllabus and essay a
much closer and more natural collaboration between the different streams of
music education, inside and outside of school.[54]

Let it be stated, with some concern, that there is a danger that the Leaving Certificate debacle may leave one dichotomy untouched. There is a lobby which advances the case for the inclusion of popular music in school pro-grammes. It is driven variously by the fashionable democracy of meeting the students half-way or by conviction as to its intrinsic value in artistic terms; either way it must be countenanced. It must have its day, however vulnerable to the value judgements of those who define the socio-aesthetic divide and who hold the power in matters of syllabus content. And there is still the mystifying bilateral complacency which effectively keeps the cults of classicism and native tradition apart, to the great loss of both and of children themselves in the school experience. The question should be raised as to whether participation in music should be just passive, comprising components of knowledge-acquisition and listening, or active, in a 'hands-on' sense of music-making; there now seems to be but one answer to that question. Can it be that the intimacy of the transmission of an oral tradition renders it fragile to the imposition of the methodology of formal education? Or is it that a fear exists that authenticity, exposed as to definition in chrono-logical terms, might become victim to the engulfing onslaught of Western ideas? It may be that we are so conditioned to nineteenth-century thinking that we have not thought to put it behind us and embrace a revitalized con-cept of commitment to holistic music education. Whatever the cause for the failure of the native music of Ireland to establish even a plausible foothold in school-based education, it is a matter of cultural importance that its best features should be insinuated realistically into general music education with a more convincing profile.

CURRENT INITIATIVES

Great hopes are obviously being pinned on the capability of the Leaving Certificate syllabus revision to fire enthusiasm for debate over a wide range of topics relevant to music education. Already it has been effective in the seeming stimulus it gave to a joint venture between the *Irish Times* and Radio Telefís Éireann, in which they hosted a one-day seminar on 'Music in the Classroom' at the National Concert Hall in May 1994. A moving key-note address, deceptively simple but poignantly relevant to the 'centrality of performance' slogan, was delivered by the distinguished American violinist, Isaac Stern, and set the scene for a dignified exposé of many of the issues identified here as critical in the campaign for a better music education dispensation in Ireland. The seminar was remarkable in drawing together an audience of some 800 concerned persons; as a forum for the airing of grievances it was useful too. But it did not signal a sequel; and it is too soon to pass judgement on its effectiveness or to detect an after-shock. An informal liaison between the Irish branch of the European Piano Teachers' Association, the Council of Heads of Third-Level Music Departments and, by extension, members of the Post Primary Music Teachers' Association and the National Council for Curriculum and Assessment led to a meeting with the Minister for Education, Niamh Bhreathnach, in May 1994, and to a promising intervention in the form of the setting up of an advisory committeee to the minister on music education, with particular reference to transitional guidelines for the assessment of the Leaving Certificate in music; its work is ongoing.

A fascinating development within the Dublin Institute of Technology (DIT) may yet prove to have the staying powers required to gather together the various forces to project a new and sustained single-mindedness, currently developing into a slogan referred to as 'Consensus of Concern' for the plight of music education in Ireland. The genealogy of the DIT initiative stamps it as having the hidden potential to prevail as an agent of change and amelioration. It is easy to see how the Institute, formerly administered by a sub-committee of the City of Dublin Vocational Education Committee, embodies and epitomizes what to most foreign observers is one of the riddles of the Irish music education scene – the cohabitation of all levels of practical training under a single roof. It is, of course, a historical by-product of an evolution which finds Ireland still without a conservatory, but ready and able to vindicate the uniqueness of its aproach to the training of performers; it is outside the scope of this paper to elaborate on this rationale, which has already earned the admiration of European colleagues frustrated by and deploring another variety of fractured continuum which militates against the effective training of professional performers.[55] The DIT has, since 1987, been working on a response, based on thoughtful analysis, to the 1985 Arts Council Report, *Deaf Ears?*, but was itself overtaken in 1992 by legislation which effectively converted its main thrust to third-level education. This precipitated a crisis of identity, placing its massive primary and second level music education cohort under threat of virtual vivisection; the crisis has been weathered, or at least held in suspension, and in the process a new stimulus to music education is in sight. The symbolic affinity between the Institute's more junior levels and the ideal of what school-based music, with a bias towards performance, ought to be has been recognized. In an effort to come to caring terms with its century-old responsibility in the area of music education, at all levels, a decision to sponsor a nation-wide debate into the global issues of Irish music education has been taken within the Institute; the debate, which began in the Autumn of 1994, is part of a major research project which aspires to having an influence on educationalists and politicians alike. One of the most likely outcomes of this debate, which will extend over two years and in anticipation has already attracted considerable popular support and sponsorship, will be the setting up of a permanent council specifically to debate and promote issues of music education; the simplicity of this idea, which is well tried and effective in other national systems, invites dismay as to why it has not operated before now in Ireland, where the need is so obvious, in a truly representative and national context. Another objective, long overdue for adoption, will be the introduction of independent monitoring of the operation of music education within primary and secondary schools, particularly those likely from their proximity to one another to offer potential experimental ambience to address and overcome some of the worst features of the fractured continuum.

CONCLUSION

This portrait of music education in Ireland should not be interpreted as a statement of unrelieved gloom. Where talent and opportunity have conspired, we have been able to establish a creditable presence in the world of so-called classical music. Our native music is secure in its advocacy; a large and rich corpus of our folk music is happily intact as a result of the inexhaustible and non-sectarian scholarship of two centuries. The notoriously fickle and market-driven world of 'pop' has been resounding significantly for too long to the successes of Irish contributors to be ignored as a potential force in the education of a young public spellbound by its hypnotic catharsis. The materials of music are there in abundance and in variety. What we need is the impartial hand of eclecticism to infuse the school experience with the best that is on offer, for the tragedy of music in Ireland is that there is no unambiguous correlation which demonstrates that the musical achievement of our most celebrated artists originates in or emanates solely from school exposure.

In summary, the dilemma in Irish music education is that we have allowed ourselves to fall prey to the attractions of beguiling philosophies which we have adopted without checking that the resources to implement them were forthcoming; in essence the rule of relevance has been honoured more in the breach than in the observance. The tentacles of a cornered Leaving Certificate syllabus, apparently unprepared for the admission that it is trying to serve two masters, is in danger of reaching out and destabilizing anew those branches of music education that must feed into and from it. In particular, the slow realization that musicians develop in two main strands – as listeners and performers and later as consumers and professionals – and that the marriage of these modes, commendable as it might be, is not simply solved by writing a new syllabus for schools, must force the conviction that here we have the crisis of Irish music education at white heat. The mote of 'music of the world cultures' is swamped by the shaft of unawareness that our native music needs advocacy of a type that is eluding the specialists who should be championing its more vibrant presence in education. The world of microtechnology has scarcely been mentioned but is far from impressively developed in Irish music education; its towering presence and precipitous advances in the developed nations offer nothing but censure for the self-inflicted loss which Ireland, an important commercial contributor to this sphere, is suffering.

Nobody who subscribes to the idea that cultural education is indispensable to the development of a true sense of Irish identity is free from the responsibility to play a part in it. We need philosophers, not only for their thoughts but for the relevance and the humanistic quality of their wisdom; we need the eloquent to add passionate conviction in the delivery of the written word. Composers must exert their demiurgic powers to celebrate the dynamic qualities of the art in new and imaginative expressions; performers are now more secure than ever in the recognition of the promise of that dimension of creativity which they hold out to all who want to join their ranks. Pragmatists and activists are necessary to fashion schemata which will bring relevant musical experience to the masses, primarily and necessarily in the school ambience. High-calibre school-leavers must be attracted into the profession and given training appropriate to their subsequent responsibilities, so that the processes of transmission have the highest priority. This demands a reappraisal of educational programmes to ensure the professionalism of music teachers and a satisfactory correlation between it and the respect with which the community regards them. Ultimately what happens in the classroom encounter will determine the health and intensity of the musical experience of the nation. Finally, we need not just willing, but cultured, listeners to broaden the base of this educational pyramid; and since we are all listeners we must ensure that we are not betrayed in our own expectations.

Music-making is uniquely a human faculty. It is worth repeating that our musicality is one measure of our humanness and it should be comforting for music educationalists to consider this in relation to their indispensability, but it should also be an ethical matter as to how unselfishly they champion their art. Aesthetic experience, taken in its broadest and most liberal sense, is intimate with human sentience, which is barren without thought; the heart as symbolic of our feelings cannot operate without an input of mind. And so the epilogue to these reflections on music education in Ireland will draw, in the name of music, on the fountain of all progress in human affairs by stressing this contribution of mind; this is to stress too the creative rôle of music education.

To be sure, music is a miracle. . . . What miracle wants of us is not that we, as thinking beings, shall capitulate to it, but rather that we shall do justice to it in our thinking. Precisely because music is a miracle, incomprehensible in the framework of the dominant mode of contemporary thinking, impossibile to fit into the current conception of the world – a miracle not only in its greatest and most splendid, its most exceptional, manifestations, but in its plain fundamentals, precisely because of all that it is our duty to think about it. The purpose is not a rationalization, a setting aside of the miraculous. Thought that is true to its subject does not annul miracles. It penetrates the fog around them; it brings them out of the darkness into the light.[56]

NOTES

1. Arnold Schoenberg, quoted in *An Encyclopedia of Quotations about Music*, ed. Nat Shapiro (New York: Da Capo Press, 1978; second paperback printing, 1985), 237.
2. Aristotle, *Rhetoric*, I xi, 137b, trans. Freese, quoted in Monroe Beardsley, *Aesthetics from Classical Greece to the Present* (New York: Macmillan Co., 1966), 57.
3. Maria Feuer, 'Musical Life – the Kodály Method', *New Hungarian Quarterly* (47, 1972), 208.
4. Feuer (as n.3), 26.
5. Sergei Prokofiev, quoted in *An Encyclopedia of Quotations about Music*, 237.
6. These assertions are exhaustively treated in my 'Interpretation in Music: A Study in Perception, Expression and Symbol' (diss., University of Dublin, Trinity College and Dublin Institute of Technology, City of Dublin Vocational Education Committee, 1990). John Dewey's words might be cited as a typical quotation from the treatise: 'Values are derived from the experiences of life . . . Most experiences have an aesthetic side. . . . they possess and yield meanings that people want to preserve. . . . It is the artist and the musician who through their media allow us to contemplate the experiences of overcoming difficulties and tensions. . . . The arts express human experience, and they make life richer because they make us more conscious of its quality' (par. 6.1.04.). The reader is referred to the treatise for a defence of the thesis that 'the system by which a composer reaches his total audience is simply reducible to the unique encounter between his work and an archetypal listener' (see Abstract and Conclusion). The question of *intrinsicality* is treated in pars. 6.1.06 and 6.1.07 of the treatise. See also my article 'The Search for Beauty in Musical Performance: The Aesthetics of Interpretation' (Proceedings of the Twenty-First Bienniel Conference of the International Society for Music Education, Tampa, Florida, USA, July 1994).
7. The central issue of current concern in music may be concentrating on aspects of the standards achievable in the Leaving Certificate, but it is symtomatic of a

deeper malaise which is highlighted in the Arts Council Report of 1985 – *Deaf Ears?* – which claims that 'the young Irish person has the worst of all European musical worlds.' In particular it is felt that the critical educational phases defined by the slogans 'Music in the Classroom', 'The Centrality of Performance' and 'The Fractured Continuum in Irish Music Education' need to be addressed as a matter of urgency.

8. Christopher Small, *Music-Society-Education* (London: John Calder, 1977; second revised edition October 1980), 1.

9. Small (as n.8), 194.

10. I am indebted to Mr W. Noel Kelly, of Mary Immaculate College of Education, University of Limerick, and to Professor Marie McCarthy, University of Maryland at College Park, for much of the factual information here presented. Their treatises are respectively 'Music in Irish Primary Education' (Cork: The National University of Ireland, 1978), and 'Music Education and the Quest for Cultural Identity in Ireland, 1831–1989' (Michigan: University of Michigan, 1990), both unpublished.

11. Donald Herron, *Deaf Ears?* (Dublin: The Arts Council, 1985), 41.

12. Ciarán Benson, in his Foreword to Herron: *Deaf Ears?*, viii.

13. Samuel Johnson, *The History of Rasselas, Prince of Abissinia* (1759) (London: Penguin Books, 1986), 104–105.

14. For a very concise expansion of this controversial claim the reader is directed to Chapter 1 of John Coolahan's *Irish Education: Its History and Structure* (Dublin: Institute of Public Administration, 1981).

15. Coolahan (as n.14), 9.

16. I follow F.S.L. Lyons, *Ireland since the Famine* (London: Fontana, 1989) in the use of 'Catholic' and 'Protestant' as general terms of religious distinction, notwithstanding more complex divisions. See Lyons, 18ff.

17. Coolahan deals admirably with the historical aspects and philosophical advocacy which resulted in the 1831 Establishment of the National School System (see Lord Stanley's Letter to the Duke of Leinster). In Chapter 1 of *Irish Education* he states that 'Ireland had long had an honourable tradition of concern and regard for education. . . . By the year 1824 . . . the government, the churches and many educational commentators had come to realize that the ability to read, write and do basic arithmetic was highly desirable for the general population. A range of motives from altruism to exploitation was behind the new interest in education . . . an investigative commission favoured combined literary instruction for children of different denominations with separate religious instruction. . . . However, in a climate of hostility and suspicion between the churches and with fears of proselytism rife, Ireland presented a difficult arena for the success of multi-denominational schooling. . . . Thus the stage was set for what turned out to be a long-running clash between the state and the churches.' Lord Stanley, Chief Secretary for Ireland, did not seek to establish a new statute, because of an unfavourable political climate; his initiative, in the light of its subsequent fortunes, may therefore be truly regarded as an epochal gamble.

Superimposed on the introduction of the National School System in Ireland, the work of the aesthetically-aware Sir Thomas Wyse (1791–1862) may be regarded as a culminating thrust towards the introduction of music as a subject in primary schools. An Irish Catholic Member of Parliament, he was described as 'one of the most considerable figures in the history of education in the nineteenth century. . . . It is as the architect of Ireland's national system of education that he is ever deserving of remembrance.' Marie McCarthy, in Chapter IV of her treatise *Music Education and the Quest for Cultural Identity in Ireland, 1831–1989*, deals exhaustively with the sequence of events leading to the introduction of music into schools in Ireland and Britain in the 1840s. She claims that 'Britain's musical inferiority complex at the beginning of the nineteenth century caused the Council of Education to look toward the continent for an appropriate music method. . . . Rousseau's radical educational philosophy . . . the idea of popular education for all social classes became dominant during the late eighteenth century. . . . The machine of methodology took precedence over the humanistic values of music education and as a result anchored it to the science of other subject areas such as language and mathematics. A French method of music teaching designed for use in a monitorial system was imported via an English adoption into Ireland. . . . The rationale for the inclusion of music in the Irish National School System was based on the religious, moral, and avocational effects of music . . . the promotion of music to curricular status in the National School System was founded on the democratic principle of music education for members of all social classes.' This complex ideology, with the embodied dissonance between the aesthetic intent of Wyse and the utilitarian focus of the political pragmatists, did bear fruit in its very enactment in Ireland from 1840, but it sowed the earliest seeds of the truceless war (between the devotees of the intrinsic and extrinsic benefits of music education) which still concerns us.

18. Coolahan (as n.14), 4.
19. Whereas statistics for 1860 reveal that 804,000 pupils were on the rolls of the national school system, the number attending 'superior' schools amounted only to 22,000, according to the census of 1871. By 1911 this had increased to 40,840, but this figure still only amounted to 6% of the school-going population. The vast majority of those who went to secondary school dropped out before completing the senior course (see Coolahan: *Irish Education*, 55).
20. Herron (as n.11) provides copious statistical information on the relative numbers of boys and girls taking music in school, confirming the disadvantage to the male school-going population. A single typical example (from approximately equal cohorts of Senior Cycle students in 1983/84) confirms that 3210 girls (still only 6% approximately of the total number of girls) took music, whereas the figure for boys was 507 (just over 1%). Paragraph 2.15 states that 'it is regrettable that what Richards declared in 1976 as he reviewed the state of music education in boys' schools in this country remains today. In those schools and elsewhere, some ten years later, "the neglect of music is an affront to education standards" (Provision for the Arts, p.16)'. McCarthy provides corresponding irrefutable evidence, from contemporary sources at the end of the nineteenth century, of discrimination against boys in the availability of music in education. In summary she says that 'gender bias [*sic*] in music education . . . was a product of Victorian society and reached its zenith in Irish education in

the last two decades of the nineteenth century. . . . While 75% of boys examined failed, only 47.7% of the girls failed. . . . "A class for ladies in violin playing was started in 1878 [in the RIAM] . . . since the Council believed the violin to be admirably adapted to female performance" . . . . the following regulation was passed by the Commissioners on October 31, 1888: "that in and after the years 1890, 1891, and 1892, respectively, Music will cease to be an examination subject for Boys in the Junior, Middle, and Senior grades, respectively." . . . Such was the sorry fate of boys' music education that in 1893 the music examination was qualified with "Girls only'" (see McCarthy, 'Music Education . . . ', 179–180).

21. McCarthy states that 'the early continental image of Britain as *Das Land ohne Musik* (The Land without Music) influenced the initial stages of popular music education in Britain and consequently in Ireland' (see 'Music Education . . . ', 82).

22. Coolahan (see n.14) states that 'the arrival from Rome of Dr Paul Cullen as Archbishop of Armagh in 1849 heralded the start of a strongly-led Catholic attack against the national school system. Attitudes in Rome had hardened against mixed education and the Catholic Church had become more suspicious of the state's involvement in education. . . . in 1870 it was calculated that the percentage of those enrolled who were in daily attendance amounted to only 30 per cent' (see pp. 18–20).

23. Rousseau's educational philosophy influenced music education in France. It surfaced in G.L. Bocquillon Wilhem's *Manuel Musical*, a method of music teaching emphasizing the 'science of music' and identifying with the monitorial system of education, a cornerstone of British method; the pedagogical principle was one of 'simple to complex'. The British Committee of the Council on Education sanctioned the adoption of the French Wilhem method in 1840. John Hullah was commissioned by James Kay, secretary to the Committee, to prepare an English version of Wilhem's *Manuel Musical*. The resulting textbook, Hullah's Manual, was granted government approval for use in British schools in 1841. Without further investigation or modification, this method was adopted by the Commissioners of National Education in Ireland. It is significant, in the light of subsequent developments, that the indigenous work of John Turner and Sarah Glover did not find favour at this time. Eventually the Hullah system went out of fashion in both Britain and Ireland, to be replaced officially from 1884 onwards by John Curwen's Tonic Sol-fa method (see McCarthy: 'Music Education . . . ', Chapters IV–VI).

24. Two World Conferences, organized by the International Society for Music Education, held in Seoul, Korea (1992) and Tampa, Florida (1994), have addressed the now fashionable issue of 'Musics of the World Cultures' (an agreed nomenclature). Conference themes – 'Sharing the Musics of the World' and 'Tradition and Change' respectively – signal a genuine concern to address the educational contexts of importing instinctive music-making into formal settings. Specialists in the area are yet far from crystallizing schemata which will effectively give even a representative experience drawn from the rich and unwieldy treasury at their disposal. I have had consultations on the the application of their ideas to the arguably simpler problem of *détente* between a single

native culture and the Western tradition. This special case is appreciated as of educational significance, but ready solutions have not been forthcoming.

25. William E. Hickson, 'Music, and the Committee of Council for Education', *Westminster Review* 37:1 (January–April 1842), 29, 41.

26. Marie McCarthy, 'Music Education . . . ', 93.

27. The songs were cast in such a mould that they were not seen unduly to arouse nationalistic sentiments. The new rôle of the English language among the native Irish was paralleled by a new definition of Irish music as presented in Moore's Irish Melodies. This definition expressed sentiments of Irish nationalism which were safe from explicit political biases. See McCarthy, 118 & 146.

28. These three examples illustrate the dominant influences in the life of a typical Irish Catholic child in the late nineteenth century. First there was the established political agenda. According to McCarthy (p.105), 'not only was *The English Child* used to illustrate the interval of a fourth but also to reinforce part of the hidden curriculum of the National School System evident in the lines: "and make me in these Christian days,/A happy English child".' The influence of the Catholic Church has already been noted; its power in controlling the religious repertoire in the numerous schools which, by default, were yielded up to its denominational interests is undisputed. The home, depending on its political sympathies, was a third force which could support or undermine prevailing agendas. The significance of the example is the palpable way in which the aesthetic in music education could be devalued by the extrinsic strategy of language.

29. In my thesis,' Interpretation in Music', I have dealt with this claim in the context of Hegelian aesthetics. 'Hegel (1770–1831) raises one of the irreconcilable problems of the nineteenth century and, although overtly Romantic, curiously anticipates the Absolutists; they in turn reacted against the onslaught of the Wagnerian *Gesamtkunstwerk*, where music, poetry, and drama became a momentous synthesis, raising enormous aesthetic questions. For Hegel the ideal musical process seeks independence of concepts (verbal) other than those that can be conveyed by the musical sounds. . . . Only then can it liberate itself from the constraints of verbal precision. He considers that emotion, as a reaction to the inner world of imagined concepts, can and should dispense with a text, finding its own instrumental voice; it is here that music in its narrowest sense may be said to enter into its own domain' (see par. 2.7.03).

30. The *Payment by Results* era in Irish Education lasted from 1872 to 1899. Coolahan observes that 'as a system of accountability for teachers it laid down precise programmes, regular examinations, and encouraged a narrow and mechanical approach to teaching . . . payments on the basis of their pupils' results were in addition to a basic (albeit inadequate) class-salary . . . payments were restricted to those instances where results were clearly demonstrated through individual examination of pupils by inspectors in the three Rs mainly. . . . The system fostered a narrow focus both in content and method – course content became stereotyped with mechanical rote learning being applied . . . it was carried on too long and in too unvaried a manner. The end result was that it caused serious defects in Irish schooling at the time' (see Coolahan, *Irish Education*, 27–30.) Since it embodied a utilitarian concentration on the three Rs, and was alien in concept to the sub-

jective in education, a subject such as music was exposed in unequal combat. The criteria of monetary value and predictable success in relation to native teacher ability dictated pragmatic choices for concentrated effort; statistics reveal that it militated against music, and there were few who lamented the abolition of the system in 1900.

31. Public singing competitions were initiated in Cork and Dublin in 1892 and 1893 respectively. McCarthy, who is overtly critical of the initiative, rightly identifies that the 'motivation to participate came in two forms – first, the prospect of honor and glory and second, substantial monetary prizes'. There was the inevitable exposure of differences in the developed skills of competing groups, in favour of girls; this could have been exploited as a tool for amelioration rather than interpreted as a negative feature. When in 1897 the competitions were changed from inter-group to intra-group 'the tensions of competition were, in theory, obliterated and exposure to humiliation and failure were minimized. . . . In the latter years of the century, the ills of the competitive element – fear, compulsion, humiliation, jealousy – in children's musical performance were realized as part of the greater recognition of the ills of the *Payment by Results* system' (see McCarthy, 161–165.) An educationally rational, realistic and sensitive reapplication of the ineluctable principle of competition is, in the writer's view, a perennial challenge to the ingenuity of pedagogic strategists; it is capable of yielding attractive dividends on the question of standards aspired to and reached.

32. McCarthy (as n.10), 156 & 160.

33. This theme is developed in my paper 'The Founding of Feis Ceoil and its Influence on Music Education in Ireland' (Dublin: City of Dublin Vocational Education Committee, 1988). Much of the historic material in relation to this claim was drawn from F. S. L. Lyons: *Culture and Anarchy in Ireland 1890 –1939* (Oxford: Clarendon Press, 1979). Perhaps the most telling and colourful quotation therein (p. 2) is that from Sir Samuel Ferguson giving a comprehensive perspective on the dilemma of nineteenth-century Protestants in Ireland, 'deserted by the Tories, insulted by the Whigs, threatened by the Radicals, hated by the Papists, and envied by the Dissenters, plundered in [their] country houses, robbed in [their] town houses, driven abroad by violence, called back by humanity, and, after all, told that [they] were neither English nor Irish, fish nor flesh, but a peddling colony, a forlorn advanced guard that [had to] conform to every mutinous movement of the pretorian rabble – all this, too, while [they were] the acknowledged possessors of nine-tenths of the property of a great country, and wielders of the preponderating influence between two parties; on whose relative position depend[ed] the greatest interests in the empire.

34. Heneghan (as n.33), 4.

35. *Education for a Changing World; Green Paper on Education* (Baile Átha Cliath: Oifig an tSoláthair, 1992)

36. McCarthy (as n.10), 373.

37. In his foreword to *Deaf Ears?* Dr Ciarán Benson comments that 'the majority of Irish primary school children leave school musically illiterate. . . . As a consequence they have no worthwhile basis from which to extend their repertoire, or to avail of music at post-primary level, the curriculum for which is anyway quite discontinuous with that at primary level.'

38. Charles V. Stanford, *Interludes* (London: John Murray, 1922), 11–13.

39. *Feis Ceoil Syllabus of Prize Competitions 1904; Report of Executive Committee* (Dublin: Feis Ceoil Association, 1904), 38.

40. Advance publicity and excited anticipation in the profession, particularly in North America, have already endowed this publication with epochal significance. David Elliott, based in the University of Toronto, is a highly respected educationalist in terms of his powers of expression and his participation at the cutting edge of the current debate in music education. His book, *Music Matters – A New Philosophy of Music Education* is now expected in January 1995. From what is currently known the main thrust claims the uniqueness of being 'the first and only alternative to the conventional "aesthetic education" philosophy that has dominated the theory and practice of music education for more than thirty years'. Since Elliott himself comes from the traditional school, of which Bennett Reimer (See n. 43) is perhaps the most distinguished exponent, his challenge to conventional thinking may be accepted in advance, and as predicted, as a closely reasoned departure from accepted thought; he is therefore setting himself a challenge which must lead to provocative statements. 'The result is a groundbreaking philosophy of music education that provides critically reasoned perspectives on the nature and significance of performing, listening, musicianship, multiculturalism, creativity, consciousness, curriculum development, and more. . . . Following an incisive critique of past thinking, this important text develops a multidimensional concept of music that explains why music making and listening are unique forms of thinking and unique sources of the most important kinds of knowing that human beings can gain.' The coined words 'musicing' and 'musicers' and such provocative chapter titles as 'Toward a New Philosophy' and 'Musical Creativity in Context' (to name but two) are sufficient to herald a publication which may relate very well to the current thirst for fundamental rethinking in Ireland and point to some of the solutions. (The material in quotation is taken from Oxford University Press publicity.)

41. See n. 24 for details.

42. Herron (as n.11), 41 and viii.

43. Bennett Reimer, *A Philosophy of Music Education* (Englewood Cliffs, New Jersey: Prentice-Hall, 1970), 3.

44. Heneghan (as n.6), 1.

45. I pursue this line of thought exhaustively in my 'Interpretation in Music', notably as summarized in the Abstract, Introduction and Conclusion.

46. I refer here to the ongoing debate (1992–94) surrounding the revision of the Leaving Certificate Syllabus for Music; it is not unrelated to discontent, in public as well as in educational forums, over statistical data which are claimed by some to indicate disadvantageous discrimination militating against music as a viable option for Senior Cycle schoolgoers. I have contributed to this debate in my monograph *Revision of Leaving Certificate Music Syllabus (1993–1995) for Irish Schools*, which was submitted in May 1994 to the National Council for Curriculum and Assessment. It may be regarded as a provocative challenge to widely circulated expressions of dissatisfaction, on the grounds that they are insufficiently substantiated by analytical findings. The monograph makes definite proposals for a more equitable provision.

47. An Roinn Oideachais, *An Curaclam Nua* – Teacher's Handbook, Parts I and II
    (Dublin: Browne and Nolan, 1971). Again the reader is referred to McCarthy:
    'Music Education . . . '; Dr McCarthy covers the detail of the New Curriculum
    and its cultural implications in Chapter IX.
48. Reimer, (as n.43), 93.
49. Reimer, (as n.43), 104.
50. Our poets and writers, Synge to Heaney, have established a global reputation
    which has transcended the intrisic Irishness of its inspirational sources.
51. Susanne K. Langer, *Feeling and Form* (New York: Charles Scribner's Sons,
    1953), 27.
52. *Revision of Leaving Certificate Music Syllabus* (see n.46). The reader is
    referred to this paper for a comprehensive, albeit personal, view of the prob-
    lems attending this revision.
52. The National Council for Curriculum and Assessment (NCCA) operates
    through the agency of a number of sub-committees who draft new syllabus
    material. The membership of each sub-committee comprises representation
    from school management, teacher representative bodies, the university (third-
    level) interests, and the Department of Education, with an independent chair-
    person and, as in the case of Music, a ministerial special nominee. The terms of
    reference for music are largely dominated by the need to graft onto the Junior
    Certificate syllabus, currently under trial, a manifold and highly adaptable dis-
    pensation which purports to serve the needs of amateurs and budding profes-
    sionals, listeners and performers (and composers) alike. The intention is to
    popularize music as a subject choice for Leaving Certificate candidates
54. I have argued in my paper *Revision of Leaving Certificate Music Syllabus* (see
    note 46) that the scope of music education in the community is too diverse to
    be catered for within the general school system alone. I have claimed that
    music education must make a vital contribution in schools; on the other hand,
    the needs of those who wish to invest more seriously, whether from the stance
    of outstanding talent or of mere propensity, must rely to some extent on the
    advocacy of private enterprise. The providers in this expanded context should
    be seen as being in a fertile collaboration, not as in a unilaterally threatened
    relationship. The two-tiered syllabus would facilitate and celebrate this cooper-
    ative spirit, to the growing advantage of a wide spectrum of needs; such a syl-
    labus would be educationally plausible and democratically encouraging to the
    efforts of the whole profession.
55. At a debate during the European Music for Youth Competitions held in
    Antwerp in 1991, the Spanish and Portuguese delegates bemoaned the fact that
    the conservatories (specifically in Barcelona and Oporto) were hampered in
    their work by the fractured continuum; the lack of a junior school and the inef-
    fectiveness of the general education system are seen as root causes of the poor
    supply, in number, of young talents suitable for professional studies.
56. Victor Zuckerkandl, *Man the Musician: Sound and Symbol*, II, trans. Norbert
    Guterman (Princeton N.J.: Princeton University Press, 1973), 6.

The Honour of Non-Existence

CLASSICAL COMPOSERS IN IRISH SOCIETY

RAYMOND DEANE

The difficulties faced by the arts in Ireland today reflect those they face world-wide in an age in which human values are increasingly defined in terms of the marketplace. Ireland's ambiguous status as a small geographically marginal divided nation partaking simultaneously of first- and third-world characteristics ensures that these difficulties manifest themselves here in a form exacerbated by all kinds of questions of identity and tradition. First, let us deal with the vexed question of terminology. I intend to persist with the phrase 'classical music' despite its patent inadequacy and ambiguity, as its avoidance would constitute a concession to precisely those ideological preconceptions that I wish to query in the course of this essay. I am using the adjective in a generic and not historical sense, and shall use the qualifications 'contemporary' or 'new' only when this is absolutely unavoidable.

None of the arts exist in such a time-warp as classical music. Even in countries with a lively contemporary music scene (Holland, Scandinavia, France) concert programmes are dominated by a shrinking fund of eighteenth- and nineteenth-century works. In the words of Pierre Boulez '. . . if you had a museum like our concert life, you would have ten pictures in the museum and nothing else – ten beautiful pictures, but that's not enough'.[1] Evidently classical music is very much bound up for us with a kind of militant nostalgia, a comforting assertion that our identity was most satisfactorily established in the period during which the bourgeoisie established itself as the dominant social class.[2] In a society like our own, in which the structures – including the class structures – of the modern European state did not have a chance to establish themselves until the twentieth century was well advanced, it is hardly surprising that a particularly reactionary classical music scene should have been established as a mode of celebrating the despised 'middlebrow' and protecting him/her against the inroads of modernism and pluralism. It is left to the other arts to participate – in at least a nominally critical manner – in the reality of Irish life as it is perceived by the media, while rock music ostensibly embodies the values (some of them purportedly rebellious) of the young, the unemployed, the dispossessed. In the process it makes vast profits for all kinds of vested interests, or 'elites' in the true sense, while the word elitist tends to be reserved for those kinds of music from which no such profits maybe gleaned.

While writers, painters and other artists unquestionably have thorny problems of their own to deal with, they at least possess some kind of infrastructure – however inadequate – within which to deal with those problems. There is a venerable National Theatre in receipt of the lion's share of public funding. There is a publishing industry which, while it faces massive obstacles to international distribution, is nonetheless up and fighting. Irish writers are regarded as a good bet by many leading British publishers, as long as they conform to certain preconceptions that are perhaps not free from a colonial bias. In Dublin there are two museums of modern art, with IMMA (the Irish Museum of Modern Art) in particular involving itself in a creative and publicly conducted dialogue on the role of living Irish artists. The Ulster Museum is not unfavourably disposed towards the work of artists from the Republic. Smaller galleries on both sides of the border reflect these concerns and involvement to varying degrees. The cinema, in the doldrums throughout Europe, has had its ups and downs here also, but with the re-establishment of the Film Board, the foundation of the Irish Film Centre, and several prestigious and well-organised film festivals, things are clearly looking up.

A different picture emerges when we look at the infrastructure for classical music. Pre-eminent among those organisations in receipt of (comparatively) considerable public funding is the Dublin Grand Opera Society-Opera Ireland (DGOS), which functions without an opera house, and concentrates in its annual festival on a repertoire consisting almost exclusively of nineteenth-century Italian standards plus Puccini.[3] The Wexford Opera Festival is heavily funded by both the Arts Council and An Bórd Fáilte (the Irish Tourist Board), and may claim to be the only internationally prestigious classical musical event held in this country. It concentrates on eighteenth- and nineteenth-century operas that have (often with very good reason) dropped out of the repertoire and may be expected to disappear again after the Festival. The fact that Wexford thrives despite considerable critical slating of most of its operas and productions suggests that its attractiveness is not a primarily musical one, and may be traced to the beauty of the surrounding countryside and the legendary delights of convivial Irish hospitality. As for the DGOS, few would dispute that its appeal is confined to a particular segment of the affluent Dublin bourgeoisie, who regard it as a major event in the social calendar at which it would be unpardonable not to be seen. Naturally enough neither of these institutions has ever betrayed much interest in presenting operas by living Irish composers, although one might feel that Wexford would be an ideal venue at which to indulge with regularity in such a luxury. One can only hope that at some future date some dynamic, imaginative (and possibly patriotic) impresario will seize on the Festival's potential as an international shop window for home-grown work.

The scandalous absence of a concert-hall in the capital city was belatedly rectified in 1981 with the opening of the National Concert Hall. Previously, symphony concerts had taken place in two grossly inadequate venues, the Gaiety Theatre and the St Francis Xavier Hall, The latter venue, in the despised north of the city, presented free concerts with often daring programmes to large and enthusiastic audiences under tremendously uncomfortable circumstances. The move south of the river Liffey to the NCH saw an end to free full-length concerts, a shift to ever more conservative programming, and a progressive decline in attendance figures. Nonetheless, the stodgy programming – full of so-called 'gala' events prominently featuring the words 'best-loved' or 'your favourite' over the list of a shrinking number of popular classics – continues to be justified as a response to 'public demand', a chimera frequently instanced as an alibi for the exclusion of contemporary music.

The resident orchestras in the NCH and the only full-time professional orchestras in the Republic are the National Symphony Orchestra and the Concert Orchestra, both run by the national broadcasting service, RTE. It should be pointed our that the adjective 'national' has replaced 'royal' (the latter still retained by a profoundly conservative institution like the Royal Irish Academy of Music) as a tag denoting high respectability; otherwise, it connotes a measure of monopoly, and has little practical significance. These orchestras are manned by first-rate musicians, but have suffered grievously from the inability of RTE to come up with an acceptable resident conductor (a deficiency that one hopes has been rectified once and for all by the appointment of Kasper de Roo), and from a succession of disputes inseparable from the internal politics of an institution that has never come to terms with democracy.

The fact that RTE has its own classical music radio channel – FM3 – is sometimes envied by other music-lovers who find their particular preferences increasingly marginalised by a head of music whose role appears innocent of any dimension of accountability. This envy is based on an optical illusion: FM3, which shares a wavelength with the Irish-language Radio na Gaeltachta and is not infrequently banished from the airwaves when Gaelic affairs take precedence, concentrates predictably on a middle-of-the-road approach to classical music; from October 1992 to September 1993 contemporary Irish music constituted 0.7% of music played,[4] and contemporary music from the outside world fared no better (these two aspects must always be taken in conjunction – the parochialism that excludes the broader horizon is never beneficial to the parish). FM3, therefore, is symptomatic of the discrimination at the heart of our musical life. Nobody need be surprised that RTE has continued with this policy in the teeth of a persistent battering from all quarters, when one considers the blitheness with which the head of music dismantled a number of programmes devoted to traditional music, jazz, blues, and other 'specialist' genres, despite unanimous opposition from inside and outside the station. The word 'specialist' is important, as it is clearly a euphemism for 'minority'; for a cultural manager, however intent on imposing his private limitations of taste on everybody else, to speak disparagingly of minority interests would be a little too close to the bone. However, the linguistic obfuscation should not disguise the contempt for democracy that is implicit in such transactions.

The above sketchy summary should make clear that each and every one of our 'national' musical institutions is geared towards the exclusion of living music (defined as an inclusive and enriching music-making that explores music of the past in tandem with that of the present with a vigilant ear to the future). Fortunately, there are other less hidebound institutions, some of which display a true sense of national responsibility without ostentatious waving of that adjectival banner.

Opera Theatre Company (OTC) has successfully toured the country with a number of risky projects financed on a shoestring, including two batches of short specially commissioned operas; these 'Opera Now' ventures have also been presented to some acclaim in London. Music Network arranges tours of Ireland by international groups that are requested to include at least one contemporary Irish work in their programmes; it is hoped that the group concerned will then include that work in its repertoire, thus potentially ensuring the export of a local product. The fact that Music Network concerts tend to be well attended despite the inclusion of recent Irish works would seem to unmask the fallacy implicit in the received wisdom that such programming inhibits public support.

The Hugh Lane Gallery of Modern Art can boast the longest-running series of free Sunday afternoon concerts in Dublin, and has never shied away from presenting modern programmes to a faithful and enthusiastic audience. Most recently, the Project Theatre has revived its policy of hosting new music concerts; as yet the attendance at these events is a little unpredictable, but there is no reason to believe that things won't pick up as the venue establishes itself, and the Temple Bar area takes on a significance for classical music that it already possesses for the visual arts.

The Republic boasts two contemporary music groups, the small, long-established Concorde Ensemble, and the larger, more recently established and quaintly-named Nua Nós. In the North of Ireland the ensemble Sequenza has tended to concentrate on composers from that part of the island, a species of cultural partitionism reflected in many other aspects of Northern Irish cultural policy. Belfast's 'Sonorities' Festival, the only event of its kind in Ireland since the demise of the Dublin Festival of Twentieth-Century Music in 1984, and the collapse of its successor ('Accents') after its second outing in 1991, has traditionally shown little readiness to accommodate composers from the Republic, a narrow policy that has only recently shown some symptoms of wavering. It remains to be seen whether RTE's February 1994 'Music Now' mini-festival – with, incidentally, a strong Northern Irish dimension – will be a once-off affair, or whether it will annually serve the function of cramming into a ghetto those more recent works that are still excluded from the regular subscription concert series.

As for the various Irish singers and instrumentalists who have gone on to make names for themselves in the outside world, scarcely one of them is willing to 'take the risk' of including new Irish works in their repertoire (one recalls that 'enterprise' and 'risk-taking' are qualities supposedly prized within the universally upheld market ideology – but not when classical music is involved). Thus while we pride ourselves on exporting performers, we make no attempt to disseminate the works of our composers – small wonder, when so many obstacles are placed in the way of their being heard at home. This brings us to another outrageous efficiency in our musical life: the absence of commercial recordings – particularly on CD – of Irish works. Even if huge profits are scarcely to be anticipated from such recordings, they are indispensable as a means of promotion and dissemination. However, since commercial recording companies cannot as a rule be expected to offer themselves as purely promotional agencies, this is clearly an area where the state has to step in, perhaps by setting up a national recording company. As I write, there are rumours afloat that certain British-based companies are considering issuing series of recordings of Irish music. If this is the case, then our own recording companies that have shied away from taking such a step despite recent inducements from the Arts Council will have been embarrassingly wrong-footed. One must also question whether dependence on British notions of what is market-friendly is the healthiest route towards establishing a flourishing and independent musical culture. As it is, however, the absence of CDs effectively excludes most Irish composers from having their works broadcast on either of the British classical music radio stations, and has led to the exclusion of Irish composers from mention in books about contemporary music based on the criterion of the practical accessibility of that music. Significantly, in this country 'accessibility' tends to be related exclusively to the supposed 'difficulty' or (again) 'elitism of less conventional forms of music-making, and is invariably severed from the democratic notion of giving the greatest number of people access to the widest choice of music. In this sense, 'accessibility' is a populist notion rather than a democratic one – a theme to which I shall return.

It would be imprudent to move on without considering in greater depth the role of the Arts Council (an Chomhairle Ealaíon). Like RTE, this body suffers from those problems with democracy and self-definition that seem part and parcel of national institutions in a post-colonial state. In societies dominated by the ruthless market ethos, art-forms that are partly defined by their inherent opposition to that ethos cannot survive without subsidy. To expect such subsidies to emanate from sponsors in the business community should be an absurdity; the fact that this does occasionally happen merely testifies to an assumed impotence of art seriously to challenge dominant ideologies and thought-control. However, big business usually chooses its clients fairly carefully, and the art that receives most sponsorship is normally that which most gracefully tugs the forelock to commercial values, particularly if it can be decked out with a little populist rhetoric to provide an illusion of social responsibility. The role of an Arts Council ideally would be – and in the past sometimes was – that of a buffer, a guarantee that commercially unexploitable art might at least get a chance of seeing the light of day. However, along came the monetarist movement with Margaret Thatcher and her grey-suited followers and successors flying the flags of Free Enterprise and profitability. In the Republic of Ireland we have tended to define ourselves as opponents of this ideology while stealthily, in a piecemeal fashion, adopting many of its most obnoxious facets. The Arts Council that finished its term in 1993 was the most virulently Thatcherite body ever to have been based in 70 Merrion Square, as classical music was subjected pitilessly to the narrow dogma of 'bums on seats'. This was inevitable when individual artistic disciplines were often represented by powerful managerial types whose knowledge of the ropes and mastery of rules of procedure usually succeeded in ensuring massive support for their own vested interests and a pitiful tossing of crumbs in the direction of classical music – or, indeed, a contemptuous withholding of such crumbs. A further problem lay in the manner whereby many Council appointees were selected on the basis of their political affiliations, while their commitment to and knowledge of the arts left much to be desired (the past tense in the last two sentences is of a diplomatic nature).

The new Arts Council, under its new chairman, has come into office crying the slogans, of 'decentralisation' and 'community arts'. These are worthy ideals, but so far as music is concerned they suffer from fundamental defects and ambiguities. What is the advantage in 'decentralising' something that has already fallen apart? What does one mean by 'community'? What music is one to bring to this hypothetical community – living music, or music that is trapped in a time-warp? Without at least provisional answers to these questions and without an explicit acknowledgement that the crisis in our classical musical life is of such magnitude as to demand preferential measures as an urgent priority, then it will be hard to feel optimistic about the Council's chances of achieving anything satisfactory in this field. There is also, of course, the fact that the Council is grotesquely under-funded; it is universally hoped that the new Minister for Arts, Culture and the Gaeltacht will be able to improve this situation – in fact he has already taken steps in this direction – and composers are holding their breath in anticipation of his showing some interest in their dilemmas. In short, we are in a period of transition, and it would be grossly unfair to offer unduly pessimistic predictions regarding the imminent course of events.

To conclude this section, a few remarks concerning Aosdána. This government-sponsored academy was set up in 1981 to honour creative artists, and offer a *cnuas* or basic tax-free living wage to those artists in need of it, for a renewable five-year period. In many ways Aosdána is an anomaly in a modern capitalist state, acknowledging as it does that creative work cannot be assessed adequately by any of the criteria applicable to normal forms of wage-earning. Since the demise of the Soviet Union, the only countries with anything comparable are the Netherlands and the Scandinavian nations – Finland in particular, a country that compares interestingly with Ireland in many respects, having coped in diametrically opposite ways with many of the same problems that beset ourselves. However, even in Aosdána composers occupy a precarious minority position, there being sixteen composer members at the time of writing (February 1994) as against sixty-nine visual artists and sixty-four writers. The criteria for Aosdána membership specify that a prospective member must have an established reputation based on a substantial body of work. The disproportion of composer members to others reflects the difficulties experienced by them in establishing any kind of reputation at all in the teeth of fierce opposition to the dissemination of their work. However substantial their output, its existence is merely virtual until it is given access to a listenership. In a very real sense, composers are being honoured for not existing.

II

The latter analysis of our musical institutions presents a gloomy picture with a few points of light; however, even if ideal institutions existed – and we are led to believe that one or two of the foregoing institutions are on the point of reform – they would be no guarantee of a perfectly satisfying musical life, and the imperfections of such institutions cannot be adduced as the sufficient cause of our musical poverty.

In general, any analysis of the Irish scene that shirks analysis of its imperialist/colonialist dimension must be inadequate: indeed such an omission may itself be seen as a misguided impulse of post-colonial defensiveness. 'In our time,' writes Edward Said, 'direct colonialism has largely ended; imperialism . . . lingers where it has always been, in a kind of general cultural sphere as well as in specific political, ideological, economic, and social practices.'[5] As we have seen, 'direct colonialism' continues to have an overtly deleterious effect on Irish musical life, insofar as partition has created two musical establishments that rarely interact in any mutually enriching fashion. Such a waste of resources on a small island is destructive, and vividly reflects the broader political and social realities.

The baleful effects of colonialism on our musical life have often been recognised, not least by flautist James Galway who in an interview in the USA some years ago lamented that Ireland's (supposed) lack of composers could be blamed on our having been invaded by the British rather than by the Hapsburgs.[6] It is worth pointing our that Mr Galway himself has never shown much interest in performing contemporary Irish classical music, confining his advocacy of modern composers to people like Stephen Dodgson, a product of the mediocre tradition of British musical conservatism that his contention might seem implicitly to denigrate. Indeed this conservatism itself was partly due to the 'colonisation' of British music by Germanic influences attributable to the Hanoverian inheritance. One might also question the assumption that domination by the Austro-Hungarian Empire would necessarily have stimulated the writing of great music, according to which theory people like Smetana, Dvorak and Mahler might never have emerged had Bohemia been independent or been conquered by (say) Japan or Mongolia – an interesting and possible tenable thesis, but one that would require some elaboration! However, the simple fact is that Mr Galway and many musicians like him choose their repertoire on the exclusive basis of perceived profitability, a stance that seemingly precludes the crusading advocacy of lesser-known composers (this even applies to long-dead composers, as in the remarkable case of Alkan). Under such circumstances a blanket assertion of the non-existence of such composers provides a useful alibi; women composers are familiar with these stratagems of exclusion.

The non-existence of Irish classical composers tends to be contrasted vividly with the internationally high profile of our rock musicians. In June 1993 an astonishing feature appeared in the *Irish Times* under the promising if meaningless (and strident) title 'Let our brilliant music be the food of modern nationalism'.[7] This, it soon turned out, was an immoderate and ecstatic eulogy of the rock group U2, and included the confident assertion: 'There are no great modern Irish painters or composers. . . .' That the author of this diatribe had never been seen at an art exhibition or a concert of classical music in no way mitigated the comprehensiveness of his dogmatism, although it is some cold comfort that non-existence is occasionally

predicated of other artists as well. (Incidentally, both visual artists and composers suffer from the popular illusion that Ireland is pre-eminently a literary
country. However little genuinely innovative work is actually produced to
justify this thesis, it continues to be reiterated parrot-like on the basis of a
maimed handful of writers of yesteryear, most of whom sought salvation outside the country.) 'Only in popular music' continues our oracle, 'is the nature
of the modern world being acknowledged or re-imagined. And we are the
best.' (Note in passing that such childish assertions of 'our' supremacy are
among the most tell-tale symptoms of the post-colonial inferiority complex.)
Earlier in the article 'the nature of the modern world' had been succinctly
defined: 'Everything is technology, commodity, including – *especially* –
ourselves' (author's italics). Thus, by becoming an absolute commodity, U2,
and by extension the rest of us, are finally shaking off our shackles and 'the
notion of Irish backwardness is shown for the lie it is'. In the absence of
great composers or painters, U2 proves that 'Ireland can lead the rest of the
world in matters that matter', revealing ourselves as 'joyous, intelligent,
mad, fearful and hip-to-the-groove'. The consistently Americanised language of our scribe is appropriate in evoking the splendours of a rock group
that – I can testify from enquiries made in the course of my own travels – is
regarded throughout the world as an American band. How could they be
anything else, since they sing with American accents and are named after a
CIA espionage aircraft? Nonetheless, since our identity seems to consist in
conformity with the total commodification of the world that – along with
ever more sophisticated and expensive weaponry – is America's supreme contribution to modern civilisation, it is fitting that we should become Americans
since it appears, by a neat twist, that 'Bob Dylan, . . . Ray Charles, . . . and a
legion of other artists . . . are Irish musicians coming home'.

I have devoted much space to this farrago not in order to rebut or refute
its incoherencies, and still less to denigrate U2 (although one might prof-
itably investigate their negative influence on classical music through the
powerful presence of their manager on successive Arts Councils), but in
order to illustrate the process of auto-colonisation that is steadily replacing
the direct colonialism that has for so long bedevilled us. It is only superfi-
cially a digression to point to the mutation of Irish foreign policy in recent
years; not so long ago we struck a relatively independent stance in the UN,
seeing ourselves (perhaps a little portentously) as a kind of mediator between
the first and third worlds; latterly, we have tended to lie low, unwilling to
antagonise possible investors from the one remaining superpower. Worse
still, we have shown ourselves willing to do business with dictatorships
within the American sphere, without opening our mouths concerning viola-
tions of human rights (Mexico springs to mind). Meanwhile, 'A large part of
the (Irish) debt is foreign-owned . . . in 1990 almost four per cent of the

South's economy leaked out of the country to pay interest on foreign debt'.[8] This is a typical third-world pattern.

It is clear that nowadays we have chosen to seek national pride in becoming 'one of the big boys', an achievement that is seen almost exclusively in mercantile terms. Hence the near-mystical veneration of U2, an attitude that rarely involves any consideration of their music but focuses on their astronomical commercial success and the illusion that they constitute some sort of roving quartet of ambassadors. Let me not be misunderstood. I am neither criticising U2 for the total Americanisation of their music – they are, after all, working within a totally American genre – nor espousing some sort of return to a simplistically perceived notion of national identity. What I am suggesting is that the uncritical acceptance of commercial norms and the frantic exclusion of everything that escapes such norms constitutes the embracing of a new sort of mercantile hegemonism, one that is sometimes perceived as offering an escape from the long shadow of British imperialism, but one that we would almost certainly have resisted more successfully had we not so fully internalised the ancient colonial submissiveness.

It is not so long since we repeatedly heard the doleful question 'Where is the Irish Bartok?', a query that grossly oversimplified the historical role of the real Bartok and the nature and provenance of the folk materials with which he occasionally worked. The notion was that Bartok had put his country on the musical map by adapting its peasant music to revolutionary ends, thus proving the compatibility of heroic modernism with a celebration of national identity. It was thought that Sean Ó Riada in particular had sought to do something of the sort with Irish traditional music, although the essence of Ó Riada's personal tragedy, from a public point of view at any rate, was surely that he failed to create any satisfactory linkage between his nationalism and his saturation in mainstream European traditions. It's worth reflecting on Edward Said's admonition: 'In post-colonial national states, the liabilities of such essences as the Celtic spirit . . . are clear: they have much to do not only with the native manipulators, who also use them to cover up contemporary faults, . . . but also with the embattled imperial contexts out of which they came and in which they were felt to be necessary'.[9] Within such a perspective, Ó Riada's failure seems a particularly honourable one. In relation to Irish history, David Lloyd has written tellingly of 'the attempt by an imperial power to produce identity as the cultural counterpart to the material and political homogenisation of its subject peoples.' 'It is the failing of Irish nationalism', he goes on, 'never to have questioned the idealism of identity thinking, which, even in its resistance to imperialism, links it closely to imperialist ideology'. Lloyd's concerns here are specifically with the writer James Clarence Mangan, a 'minor' figure whose proto-modernist strategies of 'use of persona, false translation, patterns of allusion' were subversive both of the imperialist Great Tradition and of nationalist identi-tarianism.[10] Perhaps the musical equivalent of Mangan would be his compa-triot and older contemporary John Field, whose significance consists as much in his anarchic attitude towards established forms (sonata, concerto) as in his supposed invention of the nocturne. Field's 'Irishness' would then be perceived as residing less in the appropriation of national melodies (not a significant aspect of his work in any case) than in (comparative!) formal subversiveness.

However, there is a new school of immensely successful Irish composers whose approach consists in integrating Irish, Gaelic, or 'Celtic' materials and moods into the new multi-national traditionalism known as 'World Music' (in which there is usually to be found a smidgen of 'New Age'). Now let me make myself clear once again: I am not decrying the music of Micheál Ó Súilleabháin, Shaun Davey, Bill Whelan, Patrick Cassidy and the rest, nor am I turning up my nose at those who enjoy such music. The point at issue here is the context within which this music emerges, the populist rhetoric employed by one or two of its practitioners, and the massive media hype with which consent to its premises is manufactured. Ó Súilleabháin in particular, a force-ful and articulate apologist for his cause, has spoken of the 'hegemonism' of high culture (including classical music) in education.[11] This is surely an incon-trovertible point; unfortunately, the reaction has been to replace one hege-monism with another. A textbook like Claire O'Grady's *Tuned In*, approved by the Department of Education, fleetingly mentions a number of living Irish classical composers by name while vehemently and repeatedly urging its readers to listen to and study the scores of Shaun Davey and Micheál Ó Súilleabháin, who are described as continuing 'the mix of classical and traditional' inaccurately described as stemming from Ó Riada.[12] There are disturbing suggestions here of a new indoctrination and exclusiveness.

It sometimes seems that these composers are dogged by an uneasy fusion of inferiority complex and will to power; the label 'classical' is decried until it is bestowed on themselves by the adulatory media, while the supposed belittlement they suffer at the hands of an imaginary classical establishment is largely fictional. While numerous classical composers struggle against mighty odds to have their music recorded, record companies and major British performing artists vie with one another to record Patrick Cassidy's *Children of Lir*, no doubt accurately recognising the continuity of this work with a reactionary English tradition. While Irish classical composers rarely receive more than two-thirds of the internationally accepted minimum commissioning fees for their works, Shaun Davey can expect to command a healthy multiple of that fee.

That these composers should have surgically implanted cosmetic versions of Irish materials into the homogeneous Anglo-American framework of

World Music – itself a cleverly disguised form of cultural imperialism, even when unquestionably well-intentioned (for example, Peter Gabriel) – and that their work should be seen by the media as a triumphant assertion of Irish identity, are potent reflections of the new auto-colonialism. Naturally one wishes them well; but the fact remains that a new elitism has been instituted that has the net result of stultifying the growth and dissemination of classical music (whether or not that music chooses to incorporate elements of cultural crossover), rather than celebrating the diversity of musical possibilities. Record companies, sponsors, cultural managers and apparatchiks, the mass media: all are united in pushing the sovereign and universal claims of the grievously mis-named 'free market' and of music responding primarily to those claims, asserting without adequate proof that this and this alone is synonymous with 'what the public wants'. According to this populist ideology, those composers who pursue an independent path and seek to give access to their works (that are possibly 'difficult' at a first hearing) to the broadest possible spectrum of listeners are 'elitist'; those who so condemn them are the very same people who systematically impede that access. It should by now be evident that such stratagems have little to do with democratic values.

Such, then is the context within which the Irish classical composer must work. If he/she is to perceive such obstacles as those that I have outlined as a spur to enhanced and radicalised creativity, then he/she must be convinced that the resistance to market totalitarianism is aesthetically, morally, and politically worth the effort. This involves paradoxes: the composer must seek to use the market rather than shun it if he/she is not to be crushed by it: the magic formula consists in learning how to do this without capitulating to market values. The composer must avail of whatever token pittances the state tosses in his/her direction in order, if necessary, to produce work that subverts the values of that state, while remaining impervious to accusations of hypocrisy. The important thing is to produce music and to have it performed, recorded, and disseminated. The important thing, in a word, is to *exist*.

NOTES

1. Andrew Ford, *Composer to composer* (Quartet Books, London 1993).
2. Raymond Deane, 'Caterer and Comforter?', *Irish Review*, 8 (1989).
3. The inclusion of Delibes' *Lakme* in a recent festival is only a partial exception to the rule, since it's a nineteenth-century piece containing several bonbons. Nevertheless, its success might tentatively suggest the possibility that the Irish opera-going public is ready for deviations from the norm.
4. Statistics provided by John Kinsella, composer and former head of music at RTE.

5. Edward Said, *Culture and Imperialism* (Vintage, London 1993), 8.
6. I have been unable to recall the source of this interview and neither can Mr Galway. However, through his agent he has kindly confirmed that he made the paraphrased remarks and still stands by them.
7. John Waters, *Irish Times*, 29 June 1993.
8. Ruth Kelly, *The Guardian*, 31 January 1994.
9. Said (as n.5), 17.
10. David Lloyd, *Nationalism and Minor Literature* (University of California Press, 1987), x, 77, xii.
11. Cf. Ó Súilleabháin's interview with Joe Jackson, *Irish Times*, 30 October, 1993.
12. Claire O'Grady, *Tuned in* (Educational Company, Dublin 1992).

Music and the Irish Literary Imagination*

HARRY WHITE

I am mainly interested in this paper in offering a reading of the function of music in Irish cultural history as this applies to modern Irish literature. I should perhaps remark that I am grateful for the opportunity to explore this question because it comprises a kind of epilogue to my study of music in Irish cultural history, a project more honoured in the breach than in the observance for the past eighteen months, but now at last drawing to completion. In this book,[1] I have tried to understand the formation of a recurring problem with regard to music in Ireland by placing it in the context of the history of Irish ideas from the end of the eighteenth century until about 1970, and I have found it useful to think about music in Ireland under the aegis of certain prevailing concepts in that period, notably antiquarianism, romanticism, Irish political history and – inevitably, with regard to music – modernism. I have also been much preoccupied by the language question, by religion (another inevitability) and lastly by the political transformation of certain cultural antagonisms, most especially in terms of romantic nationalism. Throughout my research, the recurring trope of cultural polarisation, particularly between ethnic and colonial ideologies of culture, has intruded like a magisterial *cantus fermus* upon the history of musical ideas in Ireland, and it is this question of polarisation, first and last , which has been the one most difficult to interpret and absorb.

The impact of music upon the Irish literary imagination has seemed to me part of this history of ideas, if only as an epilogue or afterword, because the relationship between music and text has always been so prominent in the cultural history of modern Ireland.

Moreover, the projection of music as an agent of cultural discourse in Irish *literary* history is a phenomenon which bespeaks a significant attitude of mind with regard to the perception of music in Ireland. When literature is so conditioned by implicit or explicit reference to music, the chances are that some consideration of it will prove useful in any exercise in cultural history which has music as its principal focus. In simplest terms, literature can mean 'writing about music', but such writing in Ireland, I would contend, is endemic to the formation of modern Irish literature. One finds again and again that the concept of an independent mode of Irish music is imbued with such strength of extra-musical, and specifically political feeling in the nineteenth century, that the relationship between literature and music is intimate, vexed and formative. I shall want to argue in this essay that the *idea* of music accumulated such a powerful condition of political and cultural significance in Ireland through the nineteenth century that the projection of this idea superseded the will to develop ideologies and infrastructures necessary to the cross-fertilization of ethnic and European musical resources (themselves polarised by the associative properties of music in Ireland). Instead, narrative, poetic and dramatic modes of literary discourse re-animated the idea of 'Irish music' at the turn of the nineteenth century, so that the metaphorical properties of music imaginatively eclipsed any real concern with the cultivation of music *per se*. That music endured as an agent of cultural discourse is naturally not in question here. What I do want to query, however, is the manner in which this discourse was modified and inhibited by strictly non-musical processes and ideologies. The cultural mutation of the ethnic repertory, by which its rehabilitation was transformed to the extent that music became an agent of sectarian civilization, is one such process. The metamorphic consolidation of 'Irish music' as symbol of cultural and then political aspiration and as a function of something other than itself in Irish literature is another. Both of these admittedly complex processes bear upon our understanding of music as a resource in terms of the Irish literary imagination, particularly the second of them. If I can sketch the history of these ideas in this essay, and show the second one to be a demonstrable force in the afterlife of contemporary Irish drama and poetry, it will, I hope be enough. Anything more, and the question of cultural history as the expression of a relationship between literature and music might well be obscured.

Seamus Deane, an Irish cultural historian if ever there was one, has this to say about the proximate condition of music and literature in Ireland during the nineteenth century:

> With the founding of *The Nation* newspaper, and the subsequent separate publication of the volume *The Spirit of the Nation* (1843), comprising what it called 'Political Songs and Ballads', poetry finally achieved popularity by allying itself with music and disengaging itself from any serious attempt to deal with Irish experience outside the conventions imposed by the powerful, if callow, demands of the Young Ireland movement. Thus, three kinds of music influenced the development of poetry through the century, Moore's *Irish Melodies* provided nationalist sentiment with a degree of respectability that was guaranteed by the possession of a drawing room and a pianoforte. When the

sentiment prevailed over the nationalist feeling, these melodies, which were for their audience in Ireland like arias from an extended national operetta, had to compete with songs from three genuine operettas (*sic*) that became such an integral part of Dublin musical life by the turn of the century: *The Bohemian Girl* (1843) by Michael Balfe (1803–70), *The Lily of Killarney* (1862) by Julius Benedict (1804–85) and *Maritana* (1845) by William Vincent Wallace (1814–65). Balfe's 'I dreamt I dwelt in marble halls', Benedict's 'The Moon has raised her lamp above' and Wallace's 'Yes, let me like a soldier fall' and 'There is a flower that bloometh', became, with Moore's songs, part of the standard repertoire of those ubiquitous tenors including James Joyce's Father, Joyce himself and John Mc Cormack. . . .

On the other hand, *The Nation*'s poets used many old Irish airs and some of their own making to further the militant tradition of rebellion against the English, or as they put it 'Saxon rule and oppression'. These songs, often execrable as poetry, had an enormous appeal to all of a national cast of mind, but few of them were deemed to be as 'respectable' as the melodies and arias of Moore and the operettas. Finally, the translators and collectors, from James Hardiman and George Petrie to John O'Daly, D.F. McCarthy, Edward Walsh and Douglas Hyde, were anxious to preserve in English as much as possible of the original spirit of the Irish songs and poems they translated, seeking thereby some ultimate reconciliation between the English language and that essential spirit. . . . This more scholarly tradition,was, oddly, closer to the mass of popular songs that had remained in the common possession of the people at least since the eighteenth century and often from a much earlier period. In all these instances, there was a mobilisation of poetry to the national purpose of reawakening and recovering the sense of Ireland's uniquely tragic and heroic history. As a result, poetry and popular song became an important weapon in the long war against colonialism. . . . It was assumed, therefore, that when the old Irish music was put to new English lyrics, the native spirit would hibernicise the English language rather than be anglicised by it.[2]

This historical overview is useful to our theme because it so purposefully identifies the prevailing condition of music in nineteenth-century Ireland: music as intelligencer of the text.

It is not hard to discover the roots of this condition. They lie within the striking communion of interest between politics and music so powerfully evinced in the period 1792–1848. The attempt to project a sense of music in Ireland as the outgrowth of antiquarian research on the one hand and as the expression of a politically coherent ideology on the other during this (approximate) half-century determined the status of music as the prepotent symbol of renascent culture (notwithstanding the Irish language itself) in the second half of the century. The development of these two complementary ideas in the collections of Edward Bunting and George Petrie, in the songs of Moore and in Thomas Davis' appropriation of the street ballad, together with the publication of James Hardiman's *Irish Minstrelsy* and its review by Samuel Ferguson, signify a degree of cultual self-awareness with regard to music which is unmistakable.[3] In each phase of this development, the origi- nal dialectic between antiquarianism and romanticism which characterised, for example, the tensions between Bunting's impulse to *preserve* Irish music and Moore's explicit intention of re-animating it, informed the understand- ing of 'Irish music' either as a carefully transmitted icon of the past or as an ideologically motivated image of the present. Thus even within the bound- aries of scholarly debate, as in Ferguson's *Dublin University Magazine* review of Hardiman, the inherent aesthetics of Irish music were superseded by Hardiman's own reading of the lyric as an expression of political aggrieve- ment and by Ferguson's counter-reading in which the *textual* quality of Hardiman's translations excluded any concern with the music itself.[4]

I do not mean here to suggest that this preoccupation with text implies an indifference to music but rather an appropriation of music in the service of certain cultural claims and in particular the claim of a coherent celticism. Moore's borrowing from the ethnic repertory of Irish music, for example, is precisely determined by his sense of history and in particular by his sense of outrage, injustice, degradation which explicitly attends so many of his writ- ings on Ireland from the early poem *intolerance (1808)* through *Captain Rock (1824)* and his biography of Lord Edward Fitzgerald. It is not part of my purpose to trace this outrage here, but if Moore has for some writers become a hated darling of the drawing room through the popularity of the *Melodies (1807–1834)*, this reception history cannot be allowed to belie his own conviction that the arrangement of Irish airs, for the purpose of setting a lyric poetry which (however tactfully) removes the oppression of Ireland to the past, was an authentic gesture rather than a fashionable enterprise:

> But we are come, I hope, to a better period both of politics and music; and how much they are connected, in Ireland at least, appears too plainly in the tone of sorrow and depression which characterises most of our early songs.[5]

His preference, moreover, for those 'flattering fictions' of Gaelic Ireland which pervade his verse over the 'sad, degrading truths' of contemporary Ireland is best read, in my opinion, as nothing less than an incipient roman- tic nationalism. It was certainly read thus in Poland, if not in England.[6]

With the advent of Young Ireland, the condition of music as intelligencer of the text, and specifically of nationalism, was such that any consideration of music other than as a force for political change appeared nugatory and insignificant. Davis' famous remark that 'Music is the first faculty of the Irish' derived from just this point of view: 'The use of this faculty and this power, publicly and constantly, to keep up their spirits, refine their tastes, warm their courage, increase their union and renew their zeal is the first duty of every patriot.'[7]

His essays on music in *The Nation* together with the ballads which he contributed to *The Spirit of the Nation* realise this ambition in prescriptive detail. That music should be hospitable to political history, that it should voice the aspirations of the patriot, was a cliché of romantic nationalism, as it was generally of music after the French Revolution. That music should be cultivated *expressly* to foster a climate of political opinion was Davis' utilitarian belief and one which vividly focussed the impact of the ballad tradition of which his own verses were a part. This distinctive note in Davis' musical thought – that cultural history in the making should *influence*, rather than be influenced by, imminent political history – is a significant development in the projection of music in Ireland as the outgrowth of a sectarian culture. In short, the cultural separatism preached by Young Ireland reached its apotheosis in music. 'Davis loved and sang the whole Irish people' was Gavan Duffy's grandiloquent reading of this achievement, even if the postmodern version of this, according to Seamus Deane, is that Davis had 'a good heart but a cloth ear.'[8] It is the latter judgment which earns our sympathy in the face of ballads such as *A Nation Once Again*, but in fact the weight of Davis' influence displaces the merits of any such appraisal. If Davis disavowed the European aesthetic in music (which he did), if he spurned the integration of high art with Irish music ('It is not needful for a writer of our songs to be a musician'),[9] he did so in the ardent wake of a programme of cultural ideology which was nourished and sustained in Ireland long after his short life was over. Davis could not conceive of Irish music except as a purveyor of the text, and his romantic nationalism occluded anything but an intemperate encounter with the notion of music as an independent art. What independence there was existed in the past, as a fact of the past. The native repertory, the songs of Moore, the ballad tradition : these for him were objects of cultural stasis in the strictly musical sense, and were only capable of development not inherently but in the service of new texts, new programmes of political and cultural change.

We might say that under the duress of romantic separatism, music became for Young Ireland a trove of cultural remembrance, a vital resource in the propagation of the nationalist ideal.

The development of cultural nationalism did not belong exclusively to Young Ireland. That Davis should regard music as a means of mobilizing political opinion was remarkable but not absolute. Two other elements were necessary to complete this powerful admixture of cultural consensus as to the growth and perception of music in the later nineteenth century, namely, the regeneration of antiquarian research after the famine and the projection of cultural absolutism associated with the Gaelic League. The ultimate condition of music in Ireland would only become clear with its failure to function within the otherwise abundantly fertile terms of the Celtic Revival except as a symbol of Irish cultural renaissance. In the meantime, that is between the 1840s and the 1890s, the impact of antiquarianism, romantic nationalism and cultural absolutism was such that the growth of the music itself became secondary to the nurturing of these interrelated ideas. The poetry of Ferguson and of James Clarence Mangan, but especially of the latter, fortified in English that seminal association between song and the idea of a distinctly Irish literature which was to enable the poetry of Yeats and the strong tide of the Celtic Renaissance itself. And Mangan's restoration of political allegory to Gaelic song in his version of *Róisín Dhubh* (*My Dark Rosaleen*) would apostrophise for Yeats and his generation the decisive admixture of a fundamentally musical symbolism with the coherence of radical translation which so richly typifies the new Irish literature in English. In this admirable synthesis, by which the arguments for cultural separatism were resolved, music could function not literally but figuratively. It would always retain its symbolic status with regard to the culture of the Gael, but it could also serve as a metaphor of the imaginative process itself.

That it did so in Synge, in Yeats and above all in Joyce is beyond question. But this very prominence entailed a curious disregard for the thing itself in the history of Irish ideas. On one side, there was 'Music', an indiscriminate object of cultural stasis (the folk tradition, the romantic ballad, the handful of well-remembered arias); on the other, there was the burgeoning condition of Irish literature in English at an imaginative rate unprecedented in three centuries. Between these two new polarities, the condition of art music lapsed into mediocrity or silence. New music would remain strictly incidental to the Irish mind (as in the theatre) or as a subject of bewilderment and indifference to those preoccupied by the rich harvest of poetry and drama which was yielded between 1890 and 1920.

When the music itself mattered it did so, as I have already suggested, as an agent of sectarian culture.

The consolidation of the concept of 'Gaelic civilization' as a decisive transformation of Celtic antiquities in the 1880s copperfastened this musical sectarianism. Ideologues of Irish cultural history and of Irish music itself forcefully upheld this cultural stasis. As the literature of Gaelic Ireland fed into the complex of the revival, the music of Gaelic Ireland became ever more distinct and unaccommodating of acculturation and assimilation. As the transmutations of Synge's drama and Yeats' poetry established an original literature in English which was ineluctably Irish, the cultural divide between the ethnic repertory of Irish music and whatever else there was of music in Ireland became impossible to bridge. Music itself had become by the 1890s so closely identified with and symbolic of the culture of Gaelic civilization that it became useless to consider the concept of 'Irish music' in any other meaningful way. To detach part of the repertory in an effort to make it hospitable to the norms of art music (to arrange an Irish folk melody, for instance, or to score a song), would only be to display the shibboleths of a remote culture. Or a ruined one.

The Famine more than any other event in Irish history hastened this sense of ruin. If the concept of Gaelic culture was initially the outgowth of that great tradition of Celtic antiquarianism and then scholarship initiated (as it were) from within the folds of the Ascendancy, then the act of preservation itself became imperilled by the devastations of the potato blight and the massive death and emigration which it brought in its wake. This point is crucial, I think, with regard to music even it has been made over and again in the assessment of Irish literature in the nineteenth century. If the history of music in Ireland is not to be seen as an amorphous and disinterested act of immense preservation, one collection of folk music following upon the other with nothing but sheer accumulation and scholarly acquisition to justify it, then the famine looms as an event which drastically conditions the socio-political significance of the collector in Ireland.

George Petrie is obviously central to this reading. His initially reluctant decision to embark on the collection of music was directly inspired by the famine and by his conviction that the entire corpus of Irish traditional melody lay endangered as a consequence of its devastations.

It is Petrie who remembers the disappearance of the peasantry during and after the famine. It is Petrie who is moved to rationalise his new commitment to the preservation of music after a lifetime's devotion to the survey of a country (now radically changed) by an immediate appeal to the here-and-now of Ireland in the 1850s.[10] It is Petrie, closely abetted by his colleagues in the Royal Irish Academy, who now preserves the cultural artifacts of a civilization at once remote from and curiously subversive of good government in Ireland. If Petrie can be regarded as the centre of an arch which spans the collection of folk music in the nineteenth century, from Edward Bunting to Patrick Weston Joyce, he can also be advanced as the link in the chain of thought which joins the broad conception of 'Celtic' culture, with its attendant connotations of benevolence, to the more narrowly defined issue of a nearly-depleted 'Gaelic' civilization. Unlike Bunting, whose enthusiasm was also inspired by the imminent disappearance of the tradition he sought to record, Petrie belonged to an Ireland in which antiquarianism had become so imbued with political resonance that the recovery of the past could not but signify immediate implications for the present. And in a present determined by the aftermath of famine, by violent struggle and by land reform, the Petrie Collection (an entity which of course endures beyond the partial publication of his materials in 1855) inevitably argued the existence of a cultural discourse radically at odds with the Union and conversely at one with the more recent claims of Gaelic civilization. Despite the history of censure which attaches to his competence as an editor, his significance as a collector lies not only in the sheer volume of music which he amassed but also in the conventional understanding of music in Ireland which he absolutely established.[11] The equivalence which his work established so firmly between Irish music and Gaelic culture was one which would profoundly inhibit the emancipation of music in Ireland when that culture was eclipsed by new forms of artistic consensus, particularly in terms of the literary revival.

This difficulty is at the heart of the matter. As the sheer accumulation of Irish music, i.e., of the ethnic repertory, continued into the 1880s, it was fortified by the wider growth of language revivalism and the alignment of political self-determination with cultural distinctiveness. The founding of the Society for the Preservation of the Irish Language in 1876 and of the Gaelic League in 1893 mark well-known stages in this cultural progression. If the Gaelic League was to prove in some quarters untenable, eclipsed as it was by the literary revival, it nevertheless produced so powerful an identification between political self-determination and cultural integrity that its impact on music was absolute. Whereas the literary revival could bypass, as it were, the language question in its brilliant importation of celticism into English, music had no such easy passage. It remained within the confines of cultural stasis, cherished by Douglas Hyde as 'our most valuable and most characteristic expression' (after the language itself) and incapable of cultural regeneration within the wider terms of the European aesthetic. Music in Hyde's 'The Necessity for De-Anglicising Ireland' would stand *par excellence* as a symbol of sectarian culture.[12] It would also find expression in Hyde's other writings as lyric mode, famously as love song and pervasively as a stimulating adjunct to the text itself. Above all, Hyde's conception of Irish music was circumscribed by its removal to the past. In this respect, his immense influence in the 'philosophy of Irish Ireland' (*pace* D. P. Moran) conjoins with the cult of the collector as 'preserver' in both senses of that word: as one who maintains Irish music of the past, but also as one who safeguards it from any cross-fertilization with the present.

That Irish music should be lodged permanently within the imaginative terms of a Gaelic past was the cultural ideal almost casually evinced from within the literary revival itself (as distinct from the Gaelic revival). It is this assumption which underlies Yeats' virtually constant sense of lyric redress, notwithstanding his own disdain for music *per se*. Music for Yeats is Song, and the notion of verse as texted music appears to permeate his writing, even if his references to Irish music are rarely explicit. His identification, moreover, with Young Ireland and with Davis, Mangan and Ferguson in *To Ireland in the Coming Times* (1893), is voiced in terms of the poet as lyricist, and we may ruefully note that this sense of literary history confirms the reception of music as an idea in Yeats' work which is absolutely contingent upon the communication of textual meaning. Even in the plays, most especially in *The Countess Cathleen* (1899), music enters the text in essentially two ways: (1) as an incidental support for the songs which the old woman recites and (2) as a paradigm for the structure of the play itself.

It is this second mode of musical appropriation which tends to underwrite the appearance of music in Synge's work also. Far more than Yeats, Synge struggled to rationalise what he knew of music with his evolution of a poetic mode answerable to the dramatic vision of Aran and Wicklow. In a remarkable exposition of Synge's musical background, published some years ago in the *Irish University Review*, Ann Saddlemyer established not only the provenance of Synge's musical studies at the Royal Irish Academy of Music but also his determination to compose music, an ambition which was prior to his first efforts as a writer.[13] Saddlemyer indeed imputes to this preoccupation with music a formative influence on Synge's dramatic prose style, and she recounts an amusing letter from his mother to his older brother by way of evidence of this absolute commitment:

> Johnnie is so bewitched with music that I fear he will not give it up. I never knew till lately that he was thinking of making his living by it seriously; he spares no pains or trouble and practises from morning till night, if he can. Harry [her son-in-law] had a talk with him the other day, advising him very strongly not to think of making it a profession. Harry told him that all men who do take to drink. And they are not a nice set of men either, but I don't think his advice has had the least effect . . . the sound of the fiddle makes me quite sad now.[14]

Synge did not repine, and spent a year in Germany as a student of violin and piano. Nevertheless, he did abandon music and his avowed reason for having done so gives one pause for thought: 'I saw that the Germans were so much more innately gifted with the musical faculties than I was that I decided to give up music and take to literature instead.'[15] None of this would be of much moment were it not for the implications it has for our understanding of the place of music in Synge's literary imagination and by extension in the Irish literary imagination as a whole. Synge's plays are shot through with a language that is conventionally described as intensely musical, but the real issue is his awareness of music as a paradigmatic force in the evolution of his own dramatic structures. The *caoine* and ballad poetry, he argued, were 'form without ulterior ideas', music, architecture and painting were 'form with ideas' , higher poetry and drama, 'ideas with form'. He would aspire to the last of these. Ann Saddlemyer argues that Synge's realisation of this aspiration was so closely patterned on his understanding of musical structure and his passionate belief that music and dramatic poetry were close kindred, that the plays are best understood as a species of literature controlled by the technical processes of music. Her comment that his adaptation of Vaughan Williams' *Riders to the Sea* barely adds a single line and takes the text otherwise as it stands testifies to the unique implementation of musical structure and articulation which characterises much (if not all) of Synge's dramatic writing. And in *The Playboy of the Western World* (1907), speeches function as arias and plot is suspended to facilitate the outpouring of feeling, as Katharine Worth (among others) has lucidly demonstrated.[16]

Two issues in Irish cultural history may thus be read from Synge's use of music. One is that his wider musical awareness is an exception which proves the general rule of silence with regard to music in terms of the European art tradition. Synge was attracted to far more than the idea of music, he was imbued rather with the thing itself. His explanation for having turned from music to literature deserves a moment's further speculation. He must have realised in Germany a centrality of musical vision, of musical infrastructure and of musical idea in the German mind that was simply unavailable in Ireland. By transferring his attention to the centrality of language in the Irish context, Synge could harmonise his own creative musical impulses with the linguistic cultural matrix in which he found himself. There is evidence that to the end of his life he preferred music to the theatre, but his will to creative expression overcame this preference, in favour of language.

The second issue leads us from Synge to Joyce, where the preoccupation with music is no less intense. This preoccupation is pervasive in terms of its metaphorical condition and occasional in terms of structural paradigm. I would like to suggest that in Joyce the use of music as an expressive resource is itself expressive of the condition of music in Irish cultural history and in the widest possible terms. The amorphous clutter of Joyce's imagination can overpower the will to think through the processes of his imagination, but the taxonomy of that imagination is contained at least in large part by his obsessively exact interest in the contours of Irish cultural life at the turn of the century. This is especially true of his interest in music. The secondary literature on Joyce is legion, and the extent of his musical allusions forms a considerable part of it. What would appear to emerge from this research is that Joyce drew upon that vast demotic culture of song

which characterised middle class life (in Dublin especially) so that the categories identified by Seamus Deane – balladry, Moore's Melodies, operatic
arias – together with a host of popular songs and theatrical numbers (including Gilbert and Sullivan) are woven into an immense fabric of musical
metaphor by which music is drawn upon as a means of imagining the past
and modifying the present. If Joyce's imagination proves the contingency of
music in Ireland more thoroughly than that of any other writer, it is because
his works convert the raw material of this music into metaphor. This act of
conversion is various: in *The Dead*, for example, the succession of musical
events is an accumulation of distinct types (opera, salon music, musical
anecdotage) which gradually narrows to the prepotent impact of *The Lass of
Aughrim*, a ballad which crucially encodes the central concern of Joyce's
fiction in this instance. In the Sirens episode of *Ulysses*, the attempt to emu-
late the somewhat rarefied structure of a 'fuga per canonem' in language
signifies an experiment with prose which is formally controlled by Joyce's
conception of thematic counterpoint. But Joyce's musical imagination, at
the last, is primarily lyric, and in this respect wholly typical of the cultural
milieu which nourished it. In addition to Moore's Melodies ('Tummy
Moore's Maladies') for example, *Finnegans Wake* contains something in the
order of a thousand songs; in *Ulysses*, there are at least four hundred, many
of which recur at points of structural or emotional significance.

If we do speak here of an essentially lyric imagination, and one moreover
which is biblically comprehensive in its address, it seems reasonable to suggest that Joyce's encounter with music as an imaginative resource tends to
define that sense of music which endures in the Irish mind in the aftermath
of modernism.

Music as a code of remembrance enters a very special claim even in contemporary Irish literature. Sometimes this code reactivates the conventions of
sectarian culture (especially in the theatre) but more frequently it is the second
mode identified in this paper which prevails. In Brian Friel and Seamus
Heaney, this code is constant, and it enters the text not merely as an intelligencer of feeling but as a metaphor for the process of imagination itself.

Friel's plays especially project music in this way. The Mendelssohn violin concerto and the Irish ballads in *Philadelphia, Here I Come!* (1964), the
political balladeering and (fleetingly) the Bach prelude and fugue in *The
Freedom of the City* (1974), the piano music of Chopin in *Aristocrats* (1980)
and the music of Jerome Kern in *Faith Healer* (1980) can in no sense be
regarded as 'incidental': in each of these plays, music functions as a decisive agent in both the dramatic structure and emotional meaning of the play.
This is a point of view sustained by Friel's later work, *Dancing at Lughnasa*
(1990) and *Wonderful Tennessee!* (1993).

This use of music is most easily perceived in *Philadephia, Aristocrats* and *Faith Healer.* (The balladeering in *The Freedom of the City*, which registers the political abuse and sentimental reduction of the central happenings of the play, relates Friel's musical strategies in this work to that of O'Casey and Denis Johnston, in ways that are notably conservative and evocative of the tradition discussed in this essay.) In *Philadelphia*, the Mendelssohn concerto functions both as the sound-embodiment of Gar's imaginative escape from the dreary condition of his surroundings and as the expressive source of his constantly undermined belief that something stable and worthwhile may be redeemed from the apparently barren relationship between himself and his father:

> GAR: (referring to the second movement of the concerto) Listen! Listen! Listen! D'you hear it? D'You know what that music says? . . .
>
> It says that once upon a time a boy and his father sat in a blue boat on a lake on an afternoon in May, and on that afternoon a great beauty happened, a beauty that has haunted the boy ever since, because he wonders now did it really take place or did he imagine it.[17]

Friel offers the hope that this idealized mode of expression, the second movement of the concerto, can be overtaken by the truth of memory and consequently by the recollection of Gar's father singing *All Around My Hat*, a simple love ballad. When this truth is denied, when Gar desperately confronts his father with this single shard of love between them and his uncomprehending father destroys it, music lapses into nervous mockery and silence. The music in retrospect becomes essential, of the core. Throughout the play music absorbs the mental journey which Gar makes as a necessary preparation for his impending exile. The concerto, the ballads, the reworked Jolson number (as in the title of the play) consort as a single force which binds together the vignettes of which *Philadephia* is composed. But this is music as a mode of dramatic discourse, not music as something which might subvert the text, a point borne home by the inclusion of the opening of Burke's *Reflections on the Revolution in France*, a non-musical text which in its mantra-like repetitions is articulated as music. In the same way, the seductive sound of Irish place-names in *Translations* establishes that for Friel, as for any writer, the condition of music, however prominent, must remain at the level of metaphor when it moves beyond its own context.

Douglas Dunn remarks that he can hear a 'disinterested, lyric note' in Seamus Heaney's poetry. Dunn says that it is 'woodnote, chalumeau, reedy and Irish'.[18] It seems to him that it is with that 'frustrated relationship between lyricism and politics' with which much of his poetry is engaged.

And this encounter between lyricism and the idea, between the 'music of what happens' (in Heaney's phrase) and a sense of language which is at perfect pitch would seem to distinguish Heaney's voice in contemporary poetry. His ideas are mediated, conditioned, qualified by a poetic voice which is so self-evidently musical that I am reluctant to comment further on it here. Except in one respect. If there is a conjunction between lyricism and history in Heaney's verse, it echoes that long tradition of verse which passes from Gaelic into English in the nineteenth century via Moore, Ferguson and the later Celtic Revival. Writers establish their own forbears, and in Heaney's case the precedent of bardic impulse to be found in the traditions of High Gaelic civilization and more immediately in the poetry of Yeats, is lyric, musical, even declamatory. When we speak of the music in Heaney's verse we do so more than conventionally: an entirely new register of sound and sensibility informs it. And I am prepared to risk the suggestion that in Heaney one finds intact not merely that long tradition of music as intelligencer of the text but additionally that imaginative emancipation from music which his poetry enacts. To trace in Heaney a line of descent, as it were, from the music and verse of Moore through the reanimated lyric conventions of the Celtic Revival is to trace in effect the dislocated status of music in Ireland. In Heaney, language has so completely absorbed music that music itself becomes redundant. Any one of the ten Glanmore sonnets from *Field Work* (1979), for example, is so intensely musical in its preoccupation with the sound of language that language itself becomes a substitute for music. And in that progression there are implications for the condition of music in Ireland. Throughout Heaney's poetry, music is ostensibly song, in the nominative sense. But it is also those collisions of sound, sense and imagery which his poetry advances. What need of Irish music then?

I think myself that Heaney intuits the sadness of this question in his poem 'In Memoriam Sean Ó Riada', also from *Field Work*. The poem tries to reconcile the condition of Ó Riada's creativity with the wellsprings of the soil ('He conducted the Ulster Orchestra/ like a drover with an ashplant herding them south.'). But Heaney for once does not manage to negotiate terms to sustain this arresting image and the poem instead wavers between reminiscence, inventive natural cameos and the essentially uncoordinated enterprise of Ó Riada's art. In some ways, the poem duplicates precisely that aesthetic dilemma which plagued Ó Riada and at the end it retreats into a suspended lyricism at once intensely beautiful and inconclusive: 'O gannet smacking through scales!/ Minnow of light./ Wader of assonance. 'Just once the poem addresses itself brilliantly to Ó Riada's cruel predicament as the most gifted composer by far in Ireland:

> As he stepped and stooped to the keyboard
> he was our jacobite,
> he was our young pretender
> who marched along the deep
> plumed in slow airs and grace notes.[19]

Heaney is right: the hopes of Irish music lay with Ó Riada, whose character-isation here as the failed redeemer recalls Mangan, the Irish ballad and the doomed promise of political (and hence artistic) emancipation. Our pretender, our Stuart King, our musician versed in the European aesthetic of high art whose heart and musical mind were set on Ireland. Why everything should have gone wrong is another day's work. All I want to suggest here is that Heaney recognises the central problem in Irish music in these lines. There is more than brilliance of intellect in the projection of Ó Riada as the fated pre-tender: there is acute perception into the cultural history of music in Ireland.

George Steiner remarks that in a society made inert by repressive authority, the work of art 'becomes the quintessential deed': an observation that would seem borne out by much of Irish literature.[20] The function of music in this literature, as symbol, as political and cultural signifier and perhaps above all as metaphor of the imagination, has been considerable. The sheer paradig-matic force of the lyric (i.e. of verse made intelligent by music) in Irish lit-erature has unquestionably determined the conventional association between music and cultural separatism in the Gaelic tradition. In the new Irish litera-ture in English, the idea of music, the 'supreme theme of Art and Song' in Yeats' phrase, proved itself so expressively fertile that the *inherent* cultiva-tion of music , to say nothing of its recognition as an art form in its own right, was silently neglected. One might say that the predicaments of lan-guage and history crowded it out. But the relationship between music and Irish cultural history is often at its most intense in that intersection which literature provides. In Irish poetry and drama, the very trace of music as a dislocated presence in Irish affairs is unmistakable.

NOTES

* A version of this paper was delivered at the Royal Musical Association Irish chapter meeting held in University College, Cork, on 7 May 1994.
1. Harry White, *The Keeper's Recital: Music and Cultural History in Ireland, 1770–1970* (forthcoming).
2. Seamus Deane, 'Poetry and Song 1800–1890 [introduction],' *The Field Day Anthology of Irish Writing* (Derry, 1991), Volume II, 4–5.
3. *Irish Minstrelsy* was published in 1831 and Ferguson's review appeared in four issues of the *Dublin University Magazine* (April, August, October and

November, 1834). For a detailed discussion of music as the expression of antiquarian research *versus* the articulation of a political ideology, see chapter III of
my *Keeper's Recital* (as n.1, above)

4. Cf. Seamus Deane, 'The literary myths of the Revival', in *Celtic Revivals*
    (London, 1985), 34: ' . . . James Hardiman's *Irish Minstrelsy* (1831), Samuel
    Ferguson's *Lays of the Western Gael* (1867) and even Douglas Hyde's *Love
    Songs of Connacht* (1894) helped to consign Gaelic poetry to the bookshelf,
    transforming it into one of the curiosities of English literature. They were little
    more than obituary notices in which the poetry of a ruined civilization was
    accorded a sympathy which had been notably absent when it was alive.' One
    would wish to modify this reading by alluding to Ferguson's constant recourse
    to 'song', 'minstrelsy' and the like, (in short to *music*), as a metaphor for Irish
    cultural discourse.

5. Thomas Moore in a letter to (Sir) John Stevenson; see Wilfrid S. Dowden, ed.,
    The Letters of Thomas Moore (Oxford, 1964), vol. I, 116–117.

6. See Charles Gavan Duffy's essay on 'Thomas Moore' published as part of the
    'National Gallery' series in *The Nation* in 1842 and reproduced in *The Field
    Day Anthology of Irish Writing* vol. 1 (as n. 2), 1250–1254. Of Moore's
    melodies Duffy remarks: 'They not only have appeared in every European lan-
    guage, but they supplied the Poles with their most popular revolutionary and
    national songs during the last war – the highest honor ever shown to a lyrist –'
    (*Field Day*, 1251).

    For a detailed analysis of Moore's reception history in Poland, see Eoin
    MacWhite, 'Thomas Moore and Poland', *Proceedings of the Royal Irish
    Academy*, vol. 72 (1972), section C, 49–62.

7. Thomas Davis, preface to *The Spirit of the Nation* (Dublin, 1845), vi. See also
    'Irish Music and Poetry', 'A Ballad History of Ireland', 'Irish songs – I' and
    'Irish songs – II' in *Essays Literary and Historical by Thomas Davis*,
    Centenary edition (Dundalk, 1914).

8. Seamus Deane, *A Short History of Irish Literature* (London, 1986), 78.

9. Davis, 'Irish Songs' (as note 7), 274. 'But constantly listening to the playing of
    Irish airs will enable any man with a tolerable ear, and otherwise qualified [i.e.,
    musically literate] to write words to them' (275). The point here is not merely
    to refer to Davis' disdain for technical expertise, but also to his characteristi-
    cally limited conception of Irish music.

10. See the introduction to Petrie's *Ancient Music of Ireland* (1855), in which
    Petrie refers to the famine as the event which 'more than any other overpow-
    ered all my objections, and influenced me in changing to a determination to
    accept the proposal of the Irish Music Society'.

11. Stanford in particular took Petrie to task for many needless duplications and edi-
    torial impoverishments, but Petrie's collection yet awaits scholarly publication.

12. Douglas Hyde, 'The Necessity for De-Anglicising Ireland' (1892), republished
    in *Douglas Hyde, Language, Love, and Lyrics* edited by Brendan Ó Conaire
    (Dublin, 1986), 153–170. See 167: 'Our music, too, has become Anglicised to
    an alarming extent. . . . If Ireland loses her music, she loses what is, after her
    Gaelic language and literature, her most valuable and most characteristic pos-
    session.'

13. Ann Saddlemyer, 'Synge's Soundscape', *Irish University Review* 22, no. 1 (1992), 55–68.
14. Quoted in Saddlemeyer (as n.13), 62.
15. Quoted in Saddlemeyer (as n. 13), 62.
16. See Kathleen Worth, *The Irish Drama of Europe from Yeats to Beckett* (London, 1978), 125 (with reference to *Riders to the Sea*), and *passim*.
17. Brian Friel, *Philadelphia, Here I come!*, in *Selected Plays* (London, 1984), 89. See Harry White, 'Brian Friel, Thomas Murphy and the Use of Music in Contemporary Irish Drama', *Modern Drama xxxiii* (1990), 553–562.
18. Douglas Dunn, 'Real Presences', *Irish Times*, 1 June 1991, Weekend Supplement, 9.
19. Seamus Heaney, 'In Memoriam Sean Ó Riada', *Fieldwork* (London, 1979) 30.
20. George Steiner, *In Bluebeard's Castle* (London, 1971, repr. 1989), 28.

Index